Wines
in
the Wilderness

Recent Titles in
Contributions in Afro-American and African Studies

Wines
IN THE
Wilderness

*Plays by African American Women
from the Harlem Renaissance
to the Present*

Edited and Compiled by
ELIZABETH BROWN-GUILLORY

Contributions in Afro-American and African Studies, Number 135

Greenwood Press
New York • Westport, Connecticut • London

Library of Congress Cataloging-in-Publication Data

Wines in the wilderness : plays by African American women from the
Harlem Renaissance to the present / edited and compiled by Elizabeth
Brown-Guillory.
 p. cm. — (Contributions in Afro-American and African
studies, ISSN 0069-9624 ; no. 135)
  Includes bibliographical references.
  Contents: The pot maker / Marita Bonner — Blue Blood. Safe. Blue-
eyed Black boy / Georgia Douglas Johnson — Hot stuff. Episode /
Eulalie Spence — Riding the goat / May Miller — It's mornin' / Shirley Graham — Florence.
Wine in the wilderness / Alice Childress — Sister Son/ji / Sonia Sanchez — Get
together / Sybil Kein — Mam Phyllis / Elizabeth Brown-Guillory.
ISBN 0-313-26509-7 (lib. bdg. : alk. paper).
  1. American drama—Afro-American authors. 2. American drama—
Women authors. 3. American drama—20th century. 4. Afro-American
women—Drama. 5. Afro-Americans—Drama. I. Brown-Guillory,
Elizabeth. II. Series.
PS628.N4W56   1990
812'.5080352042—dc20   89-25857

British Library Cataloguing in Publication Data is available.

A paperback edition of *Wines in the Wilderness* is available from Praeger Publishers;
ISBN: 0-275-93567-1.

Library of Congress Catalog Card Number: 89-25857
ISBN: 0-313-26509-7
ISSN: 0069-9624

First published in 1990

Greenwood Press, 88 Post Road West, Westport, CT   06881
An imprint of Greenwood Publishing Group, Inc.

Printed in the United States of America

The paper used in this book complies with the
Permanent Paper Standard issued by the National
Information Standards Organization (Z39.48-1984).

10 9 8 7 6 5 4 3 2 1

Copyright Acknowledgments

The author gratefully acknowledges permission to quote from the following sources:

FLORENCE by Alice Childress. Copyright © 1950 by Alice Childress. Used by permission of Flora Roberts, Inc.

WINE IN THE WILDERNESS by Alice Childress. Copyright © 1969 by Alice Childress. Used by permission of Flora Roberts, Inc.

Every reasonable effort has been made to trace the owners of copyright materials in this book, but in some instances this has proven impossible. The publishers will be glad to receive information leading to more complete acknowledgments in subsequent printings of the book, and in the meantime extend their apologies for any omissions.

TO

Camilla Harmon Savoie, my maternal great grandmother
Elizabeth Domingeaux Savoie, my maternal grandmother
Lelia Duplechian Brown, my paternal grandmother
Viola Duplechian LaDay, my paternal great aunt
Olivia LaDay Duplechian, my paternal great aunt
Camilla Savoie Carter, my maternal aunt
Marjorie Savoie Brown, my mother and friend

These are the sturdy bridges on whose backs I have crossed to become a healthy, whole, African American woman. To them and the memories I go when I feel unsure of myself or when my purpose in life seems distorted. All I need do is close my eyes and their spirit becomes mine. These life-giving mothers have patched together for me an ability coat, one that will last me a lifetime and will be passed on to my offspring. Thank you, Mothers, and stay with me as I continue the tradition you have taught me by your very lives.

CONTENTS

ACKNOWLEDGMENTS

This anthology is the product of an enormous amount of encouragement from relatives and friends. My sincerest thanks go to Marilyn Brownstein, Humanities Editor at Greenwood Press, who understood when I talked to her about needing to go in search of my mothers' gardens and who encouraged me to submit a proposal. Thanks, Marilyn, for helping to make a ten-year dream a reality.

I give a very special thanks to my husband, Lucius M. Guillory, who is a steady ship day and night. He believes in me unconditionally.

A word of thanks goes to my parents, Marjorie and Leo Brown, and my siblings, John, Lelia, Oakley Ann, Theresa, Roy, Leo, and Ronnie. Each has found a way to motivate me in this and in other projects. Their pride in me makes me want to do something great with my life.

I am especially grateful to Ineatha Waters and Naomi Lawrence, Dillard University students, who in the early stages of this anthology assisted me with clerical matters.

I cannot forget L. Marie Guillory, my sister-in-law, a Washington, D.C., attorney, who graciously investigated matters concerning copyright permissions and whose interest in my research gave me encouragement.

The University of Houston deserves a special thanks, particularly the Office of Sponsored Programs, which awarded me a Limited-Grant-in-Aid (LGIA), thus allowing me to secure a research assistant for one semester. A very special thanks goes to my research assistant, Shennette Garrett, who typed the first draft of the plays included in the anthology as well as assisted me in compiling a list of plays produced and published by black women.

Two other sources of encouragement at the University of Houston were Dr. Terrell Dixon, English department chairperson, and Dr. Roberta Weldon, Director of Graduate Studies in English, both of whom shared in my enthusiasm to bring this project to fruition.

Finally, I wish to express sincere thanks to Anne Rowe, Professor of English at Florida State University and director of my dissertation. It was my friend, Anne, who when I complained of a lack of availability of plays by black women in 1979 politely told me that if not me than who and if not now than when. So I took her advice and determined that it would be me and now.

PREFACE

The plays included in this anthology represent seven decades of black female vision, beginning in the 1920s and concluding in the 1980s. There was a real need for an anthology that includes plays by black women that span from the earliest efforts to the present. This collection represents an effort to make available plays written by black women that have not been published or have appeared in now defunct journals or books now out of print. Scholars will now be able to take a close look at these plays and see the contributions that black women dramatists have made not only to African American theater but to American theater.

Wines in the Wilderness: Plays by African American Women from the Harlem Renaissance to the Present pulls together plays by nine black women, including Marita Bonner, Georgia Douglas Johnson, Eulalie Spence, May Miller, Shirley Graham, Alice Childress, Sonia Sanchez, Sybil Kein, and Elizabeth Brown-Guillory. The anthology contains fifteen plays, each with a critical introduction. The selection of these dramatists for inclusion into this anthology was based on two criteria. First, these dramatists are representative and have made considerable contributions to African American theater. Second, the plays of six of these dramatists are the subject of my book *Their Place on the Stage: Black Women Playwrights in America* (Greenwood Press, 1988). With the availability of these plays, scholars may continue mining the riches of African American women's drama.

The title of the anthology was inspired by Alice Childress's play *Wine in the Wilderness*, in which a condescending, middle-class black man is taught by a grass-roots black woman who has been severely abused that what a black man needs is to learn to love his heritage and to learn that he can make it in the jungle if he has a bottle of wine, a loaf of bread, and a good black woman. It seemed fitting that the anthology be given such a title, particularly since the plays by these nine dramatists are about leading African Americans out of the wilderness of self-hatred and into the clearing of self-love and love for each other.

Though the writings of these dramatists span over sixty years, their works are closely linked in terms of themes. Generally speaking, the selected dramatists concerned themselves with women struggling to define their roles in society. The heroines of these plays speak out against intraracial biases, stereotyping, lynchmobs, illiteracy, poverty, promiscuity, self-righteousness, verbally abusive men, rape, and miscegenation.

One important subject that dominates these plays is the theme of women making sacrifices. Marita Bonner's *The Pot Maker* centers around a woman, Lucinda, who remains with her husband in his parents' home, though he subjects her for five years to his insufferably domineering mother. His mother is condescending to Lucinda, largely because she married her son, whom she dominates by making him appear stupid every time he opens his mouth. When Lucinda can sacrifice no longer, she takes a lover and eventually follows him into a well and drowns.

Another example of a woman who makes a sacrifice for her male companion is Ruth in *Riding the Goat* by May Miller, a contemporary of Marita Bonner. Ruth's fiance, a physician not from her community, refuses to participate in a traditional lodge ritual. In order to save his reputation, she rides the goat in his place. She risks offending her community, which holds narrow views about a woman's place.

Georgia Douglas Johnson's *Safe* deals with a mother's sacrifice when she feels that there are no viable alternatives. When Liza, about to deliver her first born, witnesses the lynching of a hardworking, honorable black man, she becomes hysterical. Though she prays hard that the child she is about to bring into the world will be a female, she gives birth to a healthy boy. Without warning the doctor, she chokes the life out of her child in order to keep him safe from white lynchmobs. Rather than see her innocent baby boy grow up in a community where black life has little or no value and where black men, particularly, are at the highest risk of being crushed emotionally and physically, Liza takes his life.

Another violent gesture borne of love and desperation occurs in Shirley Graham's *It's Mornin'*. Cissie is told by the plantation Missie that her daughter, Millie, must be sold to another slave owner in order to prevent the plantation from going bankrupt while the men are off fighting in the Civil War. The slave owner, in Cissie's presence, touches Millie's breasts and insists that she is the one he wants. Cissie is all too painfully aware of what it is like to be sold as well as to become the concubine of a slave master. Her previous master had sworn to break her will, which he did successfully with repeated verbal and sexual assaults. Reliving the misery of her life, she slices her daughter's throat on the morning of the day that she is to be sold to the lecherous master.

Sonia Sanchez's *Sister Son/ji*, a drama about the Black Power Movement, explores the life of a woman who has made numerous sacrifices for the freedom of black people in America. Her sacrifices extend to her very own children. Sister Son/ji does not prevent her thirteen-year-old son from becoming a warrior against whom she calls white devils and beasts who pollute blackness. She allows her son to go out into the revolution, knowing that he will meet certain death.

There are other mothers in these plays who do not make such drastic sacrifices. Mama, in Alice Childress's *Florence*, scrapes up money to send to her daughter who fled to the North to start a new life as an actress after her husband was lynched in the South for trying to vote. Not only does Mama give Florence money, which she can not afford, but she is also raising Florence's little boy.

In some instances, the mothers look to education as a means of empowering their children to cope with and even triumph over the racism in society. The heroine in Elizabeth Brown-Guillory's *Mam Phyllis* works for many years as a nurse/midwife to white and black women in order to pay for her niece's college education. Taking in Helena when she was a baby, Mam Phyllis nurtured her and made every necessary sacrifice to ensure her chances of succeeding against difficult odds.

The selected dramatists are worthy of serious critical attention because their works have for several decades been overshadowed by masculine literature. They

looked at the world with feminine hearts and saw much that disappointed and angered them in the American society. . . . Each of these women speaks to and for African Americans then and now. Becoming increasingly socially aware of the problems facing African Americans, these women move from the concerns of women to the concerns of colored women and their families . . . With feeling hearts, they present a slice of United States history from the unique perspective of women who have been both midwives and pallbearers of African American dreamers. (*Their Place on the Stage*, p. 20)

Wines
in
the Wilderness

MARITA BONNER
(1899–1971)

The Pot Maker (1927)

BIOGRAPHY AND ACHIEVEMENTS

Marita Bonner was born in Boston on June 16, 1899. Bonner excelled in German and musical composition at Boston's Brookline High School. Educated at Radcliffe College, she earned a degree in English and comparative literature. After graduation, she taught English in Bluefield, West Virginia, and in Washington, D.C. In 1930, Bonner married William Almy Occomy and moved to Chicago where she nurtured three children. She died on December 6, 1971.

Marita Bonner published essays, plays, reviews, short stories, and serial fictional narratives regularly between 1922 and 1942 in *Crisis* and *Opportunity*, for which she frequently was awarded first- and second-place literary prizes. Bonner's preoccupation with the destructiveness of the rural South and the urban North in her writings may have had an influence on Richard Wright and other Chicago Renaissance writers of the 1940s and 1950s.

Her ability to create characters who struggle against interracial and intraracial inequities is equally matched by her skill at portraying poor and middle-class black women who defend themselves against gender-based, societal constraints. Her well-known essay, "On Being Young—A Woman—and Colored," published in the December 1925 issue of *Crisis*, is a landmark document because of its powerful indictment of a society that devalues women and blacks. Though the bulk of her literary career was devoted to fiction, Bonner wrote three noteworthy plays: *The Pot Maker* (A play to be read), published in *Opportunity*, 1927; *The Purple Flower*, published in *Crisis*, 1928, and *Exit, an Illusion*, published in *Crisis*, 1929.

Though her plays were never produced in her lifetime, they were read and savored during the Harlem Renaissance by some of its finest artists, including Georgia Douglas Johnson, May Miller, and Langston Hughes, who would go on to see their own plays produced.

SYNOPSIS AND ANALYSIS: *THE POT MAKER*

The Pot Maker centers around a young woman, Lucinda, who is disappointed and disillusioned with her husband, Elias, who has recently heard the call to become a preacher. Bonner says of Elias, "He has recently been called from the cornfields by God. Called to go immediately and preach and not to dally in any theological school. God summoned him on Monday. This is Wednesday. He is going to preach at the meeting-house on Sunday." Equally distasteful to Lucinda is Elias's mother, Nettie Johnson, who, because she allows Lucinda and Elias to live under her roof, forces Lucinda to serve her and to endure constant berating. Lucinda's refuge is to take a lover, Lew Fox, a friend of the family. While rehearsing for his first sermon, Elias tries to tell Lucinda in his parable about the pot maker that he knows of the affair and that she can be forgiven by God and him. He hints that any pot with a crack in it can be fixed and made to be gold, silver, or brass, and does not have to be condemned to the life of a worthless tin can. Later that evening, when Lew Fox comes sneaking around the house for an illicit rendezvous, he falls into a well. Elias does nothing to prevent Fox from drowning, which enrages Lucinda and prompts her to run out to Fox and to her death. Discovering that his own pot has a crack in it, Elias runs out when he hears that Lucinda has fallen into the well. He tries to save her, but he too is sucked into the well.

Bonner is concerned with several issues in this morality play. Refusing to romanticize the rural South, Bonner depicts the poverty, illiteracy, and moral decadence that accompany environmentally stifling conditions. On another level, Bonner addresses women who are devalued in a male-dominated society. Lucinda tries to tell her husband that she has lost respect for him because he refuses to keep a steady job and because he insists that they live with his tyrannical mother. Though not condoning Lucinda's affair, Bonner apparently could sympathize with a woman who felt trapped and helpless in a marriage in which the male seemed oblivious to her emotional and financial needs.

Bonner redeems Elias at the end of the play when she has him to realize that he, as does his wife, has a crack in his pot. He recognizes the truth of his own sermon in which he had said, "If you ever feels weak, tell God: Master I got a crack in me. He'll stoop down and take and heal you. He won't ask how you got cracked." Though Elias joins Lucinda and Lew Fox in the well, he is saved when he reaches out to try to prevent Lucinda from drowning.

Marita Bonner's pen may well have reached and inspired other artists in later decades. Flannery O'Connor's Christocentric fiction of the 1950s, for example, resembles Marita Bonner's *The Pot Maker* with its emphasis on redemption and saving grace.

NOTE

For more information about Bonner's life and works, see Joyce Flynn, "Marita Bonner Occomy," in *Afro-American Writers from the Harlem Renaissance to 1940*, edited by Trudier Harris, *Dictionary of Literary Biography*, (Detroit: Gale, 1987), pp. 222–28, and Joyce Flynn and Joyce Occomy Stricklin, editors, *Frye Street and Environs: The Collected Works of Marita Bonner*, (Boston: Beacon Press, 1987).

The Pot Maker (1927) ―――――――――

Marita Bonner

CHARACTERS

ELIAS JACKSON	The Son, "called of God"
MOTHER	Nettie Jackson, Elias' mother
LUCINDA JACKSON	Elias' wife
FATHER	Luke Jackson, Elias' father
LEW FOX	Lucinda's lover

SETTING

See first the room. A low ceiling; smoked walls; far more length than breadth. There are two windows and a door at the back of the stage. The door is between the windows. At left and right there are two doors leading to inner rooms. They are lighter than the door at back stage. That leads into the garden and is quite heavy.

You know there is a garden because if you listen carefully you can hear a tapping of bushes against the window and a gentle rustling of leaves and grass. The wind comes up against the house so much awash—like waves against the side of a boat—that you know, too, that there must be a large garden, a large space around the house.

But to come back into the room. It is a very neat room. There are white sash curtains at the window and a red plaid cloth on the table. Geraniums in red flower pots are in each window and even on the table beside the kerosene lamp which is lit there. An old-fashioned wooden clock sits on a shelf in the corner behind the stove at the right. Chairs of various types and degrees of ease are scattered around the table at center.

As the curtain is drawn, see first MOTHER; a plump colored woman of indeterminable age and an indeterminate shade of brown, seated at the table. The FATHER, Luke, whose brown face is curled into a million pleasant wrinkles, sits opposite her at left. LEW stands at the stove facing the two at the table. He must be an over-fat, over-facetious, over-fair, over-bearing, over-pleasant, over-confident creature. If he does not make you long to slap him back into a place approaching normal humility, he is the wrong character for the part. You must think as you look at him: "A woman would have to be a base fool to love such a man!"

Then you must relax in your chair as the door at right opens and LU-CINDA walks in. "Exactly the woman," you will decide. For at once you can see she is a woman who must have sat down in the mud. It has crept into her eyes. They are dirty. It has filtered through-filtered through her. Her speech is smudged. Every inch of her body, from the twitch of her eyebrow to the twitch of muscles lower down in her body, is soiled. She is of a lighter brown than MOTHER and wears her coarse hair closely ironed to her head. She picks up each foot as if she were loath to leave the spot it rests on. Thus she crosses the room to the side of ELIAS who is seated at the window, facing the center of the room.

It is hard to describe ELIAS. He is ruggedly ugly, but he is not repulsive. Indeed, you want to stretch out first one hand and then the other to him. Give both hands to him. You want to give both hands to him and he is ruggedly ugly. That is enough.

ARGUMENT

When you see ELIAS, he is about to rehearse his first sermon. He has recently been called from the cornfields by God. Called to go immediately and preach and not to dally in any theological school. God summoned him on Monday. This is Wednesday. He is going to preach at the meeting-house on Sunday.

SCENE 1: *As the curtain draws back, expectation rests heavily on everyone. MOTHER is poised stiffly on the edge of her chair. Her face and her body say, "Do me proud! You're my son! Do me proud!" FATHER on his side rests easily on his chair; "Make all the mistakes you want. Come off top notch. Come off under the pile. You're my son! My son." That sums them up in general, too. Can you see them? Do you know them?*

ELIAS: (*rising and walking toward the table*) You all set back kind er in a row like. (*He draws chairs to the far end of the room right.*) There, there, Ma here! Pa there! Lew—(*He hesitates and LEW goes to LUCINDA's side and sits down at once. This leaves ELIAS a little uncertain but he goes on.*) Now—(*He withdraws a little from them.*) Brothers and sisters.

MOTHER: M-m-m-m, Lias, can't you think of nothin' new to say first? I been hearin' that one since God knows when. Seems like there's somethin' new.

ELIAS: Well, what'll I say then?

MOTHER: Oh—"ladies and gent'mun"; somethin' refined like. (*At this point, LEW and LUCINDA seemed to get involved in an amused crossing of glances.*) But go on then, anything'll be all right. (*The MOTHER stops here and glares at LUCINDA to pay her for forcing her into back water. LUCINDA sees LEW.*)

ELIAS: (*continuing*) Well, Brothers and Sisters! There is a tale I'd like for to tell you all this evening, brothers and sisters; somethin' to cheer your sorrowing hearts in this vale of tears.

LUCINDA: What if their hearts ain't happen to be sorrowing?

FATHER: (*cutting in*) Boun' to be some, chile! Boun' to be! (*The SON flashes thanks to FATHER. He appears to have forgotten the jibe and to be ignorant of the look of approval too. He is a delightful mutual peacemaker.*)

ELIAS: A tale to cheer your sorrowing hearts through this vale of tears.—This here talk is about a pot maker who made pots.

LUCINDA: (*laughing to herself—to LEW*) Huh, huh; Lord, ha' mercy.

MOTHER: (*giving LUCINDA a venomous glance and rising in defense*) Look here, Lias, is that tale in the Bible? You is called of God and He aint asked you to set nothin' down He aint writ Himself.

ELIAS: This is one of them tales like Jesus used to tell the Pharisees when he was goin' round through Galilee with them.

MOTHER: Jesus ain't never tol' no tales to Pharisees nor run with them either! Onliest thing He ever done was to argue with them when He met them. He gave 'em a good example like.

ELIAS: Well this'n is somethin' like—wait you all please! Once there was a man who made pots. He lived in a little house with two rooms and all that was in those rooms was pots. Just pots. Pots all made of earthenware. Earthenware. Each one of them had a bottom and a handle just alike. All of them jes' alike. One day the man was talking to them pots—.

LUCINDA: (*just loud enough to be disagreeable*) What kinder fool was talking to pots?

ELIAS: (*ignoring her*) An he says, "Listen you all. You is all alike. Each one of you is got a bottom to set on and a handle. You all is alike now, but you don' have to stay that a way. Do jes' as I tells you and you can turn to be anything you want. Tin pots, iron pots, brass pots, silver pots. Even gold." Then them pots says—

MOTHER: Lias, who in the name of God ever heard tell of a minister saying pots talked. Them folks aint goin' to let you do it.

ELIAS: Ma! Then the pots said, "What we got to do?" And the man, he told them he was goin' to pour something in them. "Don't you all tip over or spill none of the things I put in you. These here rooms is goin' to get dark. Mighty dark. You all is goin' to set here. Each got to set up by hisself. On his own bottom and hold up his handle. You all is goin' to hear rearin' and tearin'. Just set and don't spill on the ground." "Master I got a crack in me," says one of them pots, "I got a crack in me so's I can't hol' nuthin." Then the man took a little dirt and he spit on it and put in on the crack and he patter it—just as gentle like! He never stopped and asked "How'd you get that crack" and he patted it—just as gentle like! He didn't do like some folks would have done. He stooped right down and fixed the crack 'cause 'twas in his pot. His own pot. Then he goes out. Them rooms got so dark that a million fireflies couldn't have showed a light in there. "What's in the corner?" says one of the pots. Then they gets scared and rolls over on the ground and spilled.

LUCINDA: Uhm. (*She sees only LEW again.*)

ELIAS: (*still ignoring her*) It kept getting darker. Bye 'n bye noises commenced. Sounded like a drove of bees had travelled up long a elephant's trunk and was setting out to sting their way out thoo the thickest part. "Wah, we's afraid," said some more pots and they spilled right over. For a long time them rooms stayed right dark and the time they was dark they was full of noise and pitchin' and tarin'—but pres'n'y the dark began leaving. The gray day come creepin' in under the door. The pot maker he come in; "Mornin' ya'll, how is you?" he asks. Some of the pots said right cheery, "We's still settin' like you tol' us to set!" Then they looked at their selves and they was all gol'. Some of them kinder had hung their heads but was still settin' up. The pot maker he says, "Never min', you all, you all can be silver. You ain't spilled over." Then some of the pots on the groun' snuk up and tried to stand up and hol' up their heads. "Since you all is so bol' as to try to be what you aint, you all kin be brass!" An' then he looked at them pots what was laying on the groun' and they all turned to tin. Now sisters and brothers, them pots is people. Is you all. If you'll keep settin' on the truth what God gave you, you'll go be gol'. If you lay down on Him, He is goin' to turn you to tin. There won't be nothin' to you at all. You be as empty as a tin can . . .

FATHER: Amen, amen.

ELIAS: Taint but just so long that you got to be on this earth in the dark—anyhow. Set up. Set up and hold your head up. Don' lay down on God! Don' lay down on Him! Don' spill on the groun'. No matter how hard the folks wear and tear and worry you. Set up and don' spill the things He give you to keep for Him. They tore Him—but He come into the world Jesus and He went out of it still Jesus. He set hisself up as Jesus and He aint never laid down. (*Here, LUCINDA yawns loudly and gives a prolonged "Ah-h-h-h!"*) Set up to be gol' you all and if you ever feels weak tell God, He won't ask how you got cracked. "Master, I got a crack in me." He'll stoop down and take and heal you. He'll heal you; the pot maker done it and he warn't God. The pot maker he didn't blame the pots for bustin'. He knows that pots can bust and God knows that it wouldn't take but so much anyway to knock any gol' pot over and crack it an' make it tin. . . . That's the reason He's sorry for us and heals us. Ask Him. And set. Set you all. Don't spill on the groun'. Amen. (*There is a silence. The father looks along the floor steadily. ELIAS looks at him. LUCINDA sees LEW. The mother sees her son. Finally ELIAS notes LUCINDA has her hand in LEW's and that they are whispering together. But LEW releases her hand and smiles at ELIAS, rising to his feet at the same time.*)

LEW: (*in a tone too nice, too round, too rich to be satisfactory*) Well, well folks! I'll have to go on now. I am congratulating you, sister Nettie, on such a son! He is surely a leadin' light. Leadin' us all straight into Heaven. (*He stops and mouths a laugh.*) I'll be seein' you all at the meetin'—good night. (*He bobs up and down as if he were really a toy fool on a string.*) Ah—Lucinda—ah—may—I—ask—you—for—a drink of water if—ah—it do not bother you? (*The tone is hollow. There will be no water drunk though they may run the water. LUCINDA smiles and leaves behind him giving a defiant flaunt as she passes ELIAS. This leaves the other three grouped beside the table.*)

FATHER: That is a right smart sermon, 'pears to me. Got some good sense in it.

MOTHER: But them folks aint goin' to sit there and hear him go on to tell them pots kin talk. I know that. (*A door bangs within the room in which LUCINDA and LEW have disappeared. LUCINDA comes out, crosses the stage, goes into the room at right. A faint rustling is heard within.*)

MOTHER: (*calling*) 'Cinda, what you doin' in that trunk? Taint nuthin' you need in there tonight. (*The rustling ceases abruptly—you can almost see LUCINDA's rage pouring in a flood at the door.*)

LUCINDA: (*from within*) I ain't doin' nothing'—(*She appears at the doorway fastening a string of red beads around her throat.*)

MOTHER: Well, if you aint doin' nothin', what you doin' with them beads on?

LUCINDA: (*flaring*) None of your business.

MOTHER: Oh, it aint! Well you jes' walk back in there and rest my best shoes under the side of the bed please, ma'am.

FATHER: Now Nettie, you women all likes to look—

MOTHER: Don't name me with that one there!

ELIAS: Ma, don't carry on with 'Cinda so.

MOTHER: You aint nothin' but a turntable! You aint got sense enough to see that she would jam you down the devil's throat if she got a chance.

LUCINDA: I'm goin' long out of here where folks got some sense. (*She starts off without removing the shoes.*)

MOTHER: Taint whilst to go. I'm goin' callin' myself. Give me my shoes. (*LU-CINDA halts at the door. There are no words that can tell you how she looks at her mother-in-law. Words cannot do but so much.*)

LUCINDA: (*slinging the shoes*) There. (*ELIAS picks them up easily and carries them to his MOTHER. She slips them on, and, catching up a shawl, goes off at back followed by her husband. LUCINDA stamps around the room and digs a pair of old shoes up from somewhere. She slams everything aside that she passes. Finally, she tips one of the geraniums over.*)

ELIAS: (*mildly*) Taint whilst to carry on so, Lucinda.

LUCINDA: Of, for God's sake, shut up! You and your "taint whilst to's" make me sick. (*ELIAS says nothing. He merely looks at her.*)

LUCINDA: That's right! That's right! Stand there and stare at me like some pop-eyed owl. You aint got sense enough to do anything else. (*ELIAS starts to speak. LUCINDA is warmed up to her subject. What can he say? Even more rapidly*) No you aint got sense enough to do anything else! Aint even got sense enough to keep a job! Get a job paying good money! Keep it two weeks and jes' when

I'm hoping you'll get a little money ahead so's I could live decent like other women—in my house—You had to go and get called of God to quit and preach!

ELIAS: (*evenly*) God chose me.

LUCINDA: Yas God chose you. He aint chose you for no preachin'. He chose you for some kinder fool! That's what you are—some kinder fool! Fools can't preach.

ELIAS: Some do.

LUCINDA: Then you must be one of them that does! If you was any kind of man you'd get a decent job and hold it and hold your mouth shut and move me into my own house. Aint no woman so in love with her man's mother she wants to live five years under the same roof with her like I done. (*ELIAS may have thought of a dozen replies. He makes none. LUCINDA stares at him. Then she laughs aloud. It is a bitter laugh that makes you think of rocks and mud and dirt and edgy weather. It is jagged.*) Yes you are some kinder fool. Standing there like a pop-eyed owl—(*there follows the inevitable*). The Lord knows what I ever saw in you!

ELIAS: (*still evenly*) The Lord does know Lucinda. (*At that LUCINDA falls back into her chair and curses aloud in a singsong manner as if she were chanting a prayer. Then she sits still and stares at him.*)

LUCINDA: Elias—ain't you never wanted to hit nobody in your life? (*Before he can answer, a shrill whistle is heard outside the window at left. LUCINDA starts nervously and looks at the window. When she sees ELIAS has heard the sound, she tries to act unconcerned.*) What kinder bird is that whistlin' at the window? (*She starts toward it. ELIAS puts out a hand and stops her.*)

ELIAS: Taint whilst to open the window to look out. Can't see nothin' in the dark.

LUCINDA: That aint the side that old well is on, is it? That aint the window, is it?

ELIAS: You ought to know! Long as you been livin' here! Five years you just said. (*There is a crackle of bushes outside the window close to the house. A crash. Then a sound of muttering that becomes louder and louder. A subdued splashing. LUCINDA starts to the window but ELIAS gets there first. He puts his back to the wall.*)

LUCINDA: Somebody's fallin' into that well! Look out there!

ELIAS: Taint whilst to.

LUCINDA: Taint whilst to! Of God—here um calling! Go out there! Taint whilst to! (*She tries to dart around ELIAS. They struggle. He seizes her wrist, drags her back. She screams and talks all the time they struggle.*) Call yourself a Christian! The devil! That's what you is! The devil! Lettin' folks drown! Might be your own mother!

ELIAS: Taint my mother—You know who it is!

LUCINDA: How I know? Oh, go out there and save him for God's sake. (*The struggles and splashings are ceasing. A long drawn out "Oh my God" that sounds as if it's coming from every portion of the room, sifts over the stage. LUCINDA cries aloud. It is a tearing, shrieking, mad scream. It is as if someone had torn her soul apart from her body. ELIAS wrenches the door open.*) Now Cindy, you was goin' to Lew. Go 'long to him. Go'long to him. (*He repeats.*)

LUCINDA: (*trying to fawn at him*) Oh! No! Elias, Oh Master! Ain you no ways a man? I aint know that was Lew! I aint know that was Lew—Oh, yes I did. Lew, Lew. (*She darts past ELIAS as if she has forgotten him. You hear her outside calling*) Lew, Lew. (*Full of mad agony, the screams search the night. But there is no answer. You hear only the sound of the wind. The sound of the wind in the leaves. ELIAS stands listening. All at once there is the same crackling sound outside and a crash and a splash. Once more LUCINDA raises her voice—frightened and choked. He hears the sound of the water. He starts toward the door.*)

ELIAS: Go 'long to Lew. (*He shouts and then sits down.*) You both is tin. (*But he raises himself at once and runs back to the door*). God, God, I got a crack in me too! (*He cries and goes out into the darkness. You hear splashing and panting. You hear cries.*) Cindy, give me your hand! There now! You is 'most out.

(*But then you hear another crash. A heavier splashing. Something has given away. One hears the sound of wood splitting. One hears something heavy splashing in the water. One hears only the wind in the leaves. Only the wind in the leaves and the door swings vacant. You stare through the door. Waiting. Expecting to see ELIAS stagger in with LUCINDA in his arms perhaps. But the door swings vacant. You stare—but there is only wind in the leaves. That's all there will be. A crack has been healed. A pot has spilled over on the ground. Some wisps have twisted out.*)

CURTAIN

GEORGIA DOUGLAS JOHNSON (1880–1966)

Blue Blood (1926)
Safe (c. 1929)
Blue-Eyed Black Boy (c. 1930)

BIOGRAPHY AND ACHIEVEMENTS

Georgia Douglas Camp was born on September 10, 1880, in Atlanta to George and Laura Jackson Camp. She was educated in Atlanta elementary schools and then attended normal school from 1893–1896 at Atlanta University. Upon completion of the normal course, she studied music in Ohio at the Oberlin Conservatory and at the Cleveland College of Music, specializing in violin, piano, voice, and harmony. While teaching music and serving as an assistant principal in Atlanta, she met and married Henry Lincoln Johnson in 1903. The marriage produced two sons within seven years. She and her husband then moved to Washington, D.C., where Henry Johnson established a law firm and became a very influential politician, and Georgia Douglas Johnson attended Howard University. Like her husband, she was involved in the city's social and political arenas. She was particularly active in most of the groups and organizations in the Washington area that focused on issues surrounding women and minorities.

Her husband's death of a stroke in 1925 left Georgia Douglas Johnson with ample time to write. Between 1926 and 1936, usually on Saturday nights, black authors from across the United States fellowshipped in Johnson's home, which made her almost a household name and made Washington, D.C., another mecca for the "New Negro" artists. Founder of the S Street Salon, she opened her house to a host of black writers, including Langston Hughes, Countee Cullen, Alain Locke, Jessie Fauset, S. Randolph Edmonds, Willis Richardson, Marita Bonner, Alice Dunbar-Nelson, May Miller, Owen Dodson, Sterling Brown, Angelina Weld Grimke, Zora Neale Hurston, James Weldon Johnson, Claude McKay, and W. E. B. Du Bois.

Recognized by many as a bit eccentric, Georgia Douglas Johnson spent the last forty years of her life literally amidst piles of papers and books, always to be found with a pad and pencil attached to a ribbon around her neck so as not to miss an idea for a literary work. She wrote and published until she died on May 28, 1966. Her writing did not go unnoticed as she returned to Atlanta University in 1965 to receive an honorary Doctor of Literature.

Georgia Douglas Johnson has come to be regarded as one of the first black feminist poets and the most prolific black woman playwright of the Harlem Renaissance. Best known as a poet, Johnson published several volumes of poetry, including *The Heart of A Woman and Other Poems* (1918), *Bronze* (1922), *An Autumn Love Cycle* (1928), and *Share My World* (1962). Author of approximately twenty plays, many of which have yet to be published, Georgia Douglas Johnson was instrumental in developing the tradition out of which such notable black women dramatists as Alice Childress, Lorraine Hansberry, and Ntozake Shange have come. Her early poetry, regarded as of the "genteel school' because of its racelessness, concerns itself solely with women's issues. However, as the Harlem Renaissance, with its emphasis on black pride, took on great importance, Johnson's concern for women focused on colored women and their families as was manifest in her one-act plays written in the early to mid–1920s. Her plays encompassed a variety of themes, including lynching, miscegenation, black history, passing, black folk life, and the empowerment or disempowerment of blacks. Georgia Douglas Johnson is best known for her play *Plumes*, which won first prize in the 1927 *Opportunity* play contest and was produced Off-Broadway in the same year by the Harlem Experimental Theater in New York City, and for her play *A Sunday Morning in the South*, published in *Black Theater U.S.A.: Forty-Five Plays by Black Americans, 1847–1974*, edited by James Hatch and Ted Shine. Three other plays that demonstrate Johnson's significant role in the development of African American theater are *Blue Blood*, *Safe*, and *Blue-Eyed Black Boy*. She won an honorable mention in the 1926 *Opportunity* play contest for *Blue Blood*, saw the play produced by the Krigwa Players in New York City, and witnessed its publication in 1927 in *Fifty More Contemporary One-Act Plays*. *Safe* and *Blue-Eyed Black Boy*, written circa 1929 and 1930 respectively, have only recently been recovered. Many of her plays, though unpublished, were produced in church halls, lofts, and schools in the Washington, D.C., area.

SYNOPSIS AND ANALYSIS: *BLUE BLOOD*

The play opens with a discussion about the upcoming marriage plans of two mulattoes, May Bush and John Temple. Mrs. Bush, May's mother, confides to the dark-skinned Randolph Strong that she cannot understand why her daughter did not fall in love with him. Randolph Strong, a kind and gentle doctor, has persisted in sending May white roses and trinkets to win her over. Mrs. Bush tries to comfort Randolph by telling him that she would prefer if her daughter were to marry him because she feels that it just is not good luck for two light-skinned people to marry. Mrs. Bush says, "Dark should marry light. You'd be a perfect match." Mrs. Bush also tells Randolph that she prefers him to John Temple, who is a "high-falutin" nothing who has money and good looks but who can never love her as Randolph loves her.

The plot thickens when Mrs. Temple, John's mother, comes over moments before the wedding and begins to brag that May ought to feel blessed to be marrying a blue blood like John. Mrs. Bush, not wishing to be outdone, boasts that May's blood is bluer than John's because she is the daughter of a very wealthy white banker named Captain Winfield McCallister. Much to the disappointment and horror of both women, Mrs. Temple tells Mrs. Bush that John and May share the same father. Mrs. Temple in tears tells how Captain Winfield McCallister raped her only days before she was to marry a black man. Fearing that Mr. Temple would try to defend her honor and get lynched as a result, she chose to protect her husband by refusing to tell who fathered her child. Both Mrs. Bush and Mrs. Temple commiserate on the sad state of black womanhood and how black men have taken on the responsibility of caring for their women who have been defiled by white men.

Mrs. Bush and Mrs. Temple agree not to tell John for fear that he might kill his white father, but they do tell May and Randolph. They are faced with the dilemma of how to call off the wedding without having to admit the secret to the townspeople. Randolph rises to the occasion by offering to marry May. She accepts. They run off, presumably to live happily ever after.

Blue Blood examines several issues that continue to plague the black community. It is certainly a play about the evils of miscegenation. As is typical with literature dealing with miscegenation, violence is always at the core. Like Langston Hughes's Broadway play *Mulatto* (1931), Johnson's *Blue Blood* deals with a mother who tries to protect her son from killing his abusive white father.

Essentially, it is a play that demonstrates the powerlessness of black men and women. *Blue Blood* portrays black women who are raped by white men but who remain silent in order to keep their black men alive. Lynching is subtly hinted at in this compressed one-act play. On another level, Johnson addresses the issue of the color line, pointing out the ludicrousness of intraracial conflicts among dark- and light-skinned blacks. Johnson satirizes the age-old house servant versus field-hand mentality that has set blacks against each other since slavery. She cleverly makes Mrs. Bush and Mrs. Temple, who both brag of how close to white their children are, see that the very thing that they boast of divides the race. Johnson also mirrors for them their own violation and disempowerment. Such serious subjects are couched in humor in quite a sophisticated, short drama.

SYNOPSIS AND ANALYSIS: *SAFE*

Safe is a moving play about a young black mother, Liza, who, after witnessing the lynching of a black man, murders her own newborn son to prevent his growing up to face a similar fate. Sam Hosea, the man who is lynched, is ruthlessly dragged through the streets for defending himself against his white employer who hit him first over a dispute about wages. Sam is portrayed as a responsible man who worked hard "to take kere of his widder mother, doing the best he kin, trying to be a man and stan up for hisself and what do he git?—a slap in the face." Liza, her mother, Mandy, and a neighbor, Hannah, are traumatized as they witness the murder and helplessness of black males in their society. As Sam is being lynched he screams, "Don't hang me, don't hang me! I don't want to die! Mother! Mother!" Liza, becoming hysterical over the violence, cries, "Oh, that poor boy— poor little nigger boy!" Though Dr. Higgins comes in the nick of time to deliver a healthy baby, Sam Hosea's murder has marred the young heroine. Liza chokes the life out of her baby shortly after he is born to keep him safe.

Safe resembles Angelina Weld Grimke's 1916 play *Rachel* (first play by a black woman to be professionally produced) in that both plays portray women who seek to protect black children from racism. Whereas the heroine of *Rachel* vows never to marry nor to bear any black and brown babies for fear they will be called niggers and be physically abused, Liza takes a drastic step in saving her newborn from oppression by murdering him. *Safe* strongly denounces lynching. The play was very relevant, given that over one thousand blacks were lynched in the United States between 1900 and 1931.

Safe is a significant play because it captures the ordinary lives of black folks of the period. Hannah, for example, epitomizes the town's gossiper who spreads the word as she weaves in and out of homes. Yet, Johnson humanizes Hannah by having her rush out in the middle of a lynching to seek a doctor for Liza. Another example of a strong sense of community togetherness occurs as John goes out to find news about Sam Hosea. Though the black townspeople band together, they remain powerless and at the whim of an angry white mob. Johnson points out that black men are not allowed to be men, and when they do stand up to do the right thing or to defend themselves against racists, they are mutilated.

On another level, *Safe* captures the strong religiosity of the black community. When Sam Hosea is being lynched, Mandy repeatedly calls on God and tells Him that the black community is in His hands. When God does not seem to be enough, women in *Safe* take matters into their own hands. Liza protects her male offspring in the only way she knows how: she suffocates him. Johnson seems to be arguing that perhaps death is better than a life of dehumanization.

Georgia Douglas Johnson poignantly captures the unsafety and uncertainty of life for poor, rural southern blacks of the 1920s.

SYNOPSIS AND ANALYSIS: *BLUE-EYED BLACK BOY*

The play centers around a young black man, Tom, who is accused of brushing up against a white woman who claims that he attacked her. Tom is described as a hardworking, upstanding young man by his mother, Pauline, and his sister, Rebecca. His family goes into shock when Hester, a neighbor, brings the news that Tom has been jailed and that a lynchmob wants to hang him without a trial. When Pauline learns of Tom's certain death, she has to break silence about this blue-eyed boy. She orders Rebecca to run into the bedroom to get a small gold ring that she has hidden away for years. She then instructs Dr. Grey, Rebecca's boyfriend, to take the ring to the governor and to give him a special message. Pauline whispers to Dr. Grey, "Just give him this ring and say, 'Pauline sent this. She says they goin to lynch her son born 21 years ago.' Mind you, say 21 years ago. Then say, listen close. 'Look in his eyes and you'll save him.' " Just as the young man is to be hung, the governor's troops come to save him.

Blue-Eyed Black Boy, like *Safe*, is an antilynching play. Johnson seemed preoccupied with pointing to the atrocities faced by many blacks at the hands of the lynchmob. She mirrors a society that sets double standards. On one hand, Tom faces a lynchmob because he allegedly brushed up against a white woman; on the other hand, Pauline is violated by the governor and gives birth to his son without repercussions. Johnson suggests that black women are devalued in American society and are not accorded the same respect given white women. She also makes the point that black men are unable to defend their women and so must often silently bear the burden of raising mulatto children. When Rebecca questions her mother about her brother's blue eyes and says she wished she had blue eyes, Pauline gives no explanation and quickly tells her daughter to be satisfied. She also does not respond when Rebecca presses her and says, "Pa's was black, and yours and mine are black too. It certainly is strange." Though Pauline is proud of her fair-skinned, handsome son, she does see herself as sinful and sinned against. Johnson captures the religiosity of these poor blacks when Pauline prays, "Lord Jesus, I know I've sinned against your holy law, but you did forgive me and let me hold up my head again." The implication here is that Pauline sees herself as guilty for her own violation, as if somehow her forced submission to the governor was her sin as well as his.

Johnson also suggests in *Blue-Eyed Black Boy* that some white men who fathered black children offered some kind of protection. Pauline knows intuitively that if she informs the governor that it is his son who is being lynched that he will call out the state troops. Again, Johnson hints at the double standards under which black people must live when she describes a white mob who threatens to kill and white troops who come to save a white man's black son. The message is clear: the play is about the powerlessness of black people.

NOTE

For more information about Georgia Douglas Johnson's life and works, see Elizabeth Brown-Guillory, *Their Place on the Stage: Black Women Playwrights in America*

(Westport, Conn.: Greenwood Press, 1988); Gloria T. Hull, *Color, Sex and Poetry: Three Women Writers of the Harlem Renaissance*, (Bloomington: Indiana University Press, 1987); Winona Fletcher, "Georgia Douglas Johnson," in *Afro-American Writers from the Harlem Renaissance to 1940*, edited by Trudier Harris, in *Dictionary of Literary Biography* (Detroit: Gale Research Company, 1987).

Blue Blood (1926) _____

Georgia Douglas Johnson

CHARACTERS

MAY BUSH
MRS. BUSH
JOHN TEMPLE
MRS. TEMPLE
RANDOLPH STRONG

These characters are Negroes.

PLACE

Georgia.

TIME

Shortly after the Civil War.

SCENE: *Large kitchen and dining room combined of frame cottage, showing one door leading into back yard. One other door (right side of the room facing stage) leading into hall. One back window, neatly curtained. Steps on right side of room leading upstairs.*
    Enter RANDOLPH STRONG with large bunch of white roses and a package. He places the package, unnoticed, on the table—still holding the roses.

RANDOLPH STRONG: How is my dear Mother Bush?

MRS. BUSH: Feeling like a sixteen-year old! That's right, you come right on back here with me. (*notices roses*) Oh! What pretty roses! Snow white!

RANDOLPH STRONG: Like um? Thought you would . . . May likes this kind!

MRS. BUSH: She sho'ly do. Pore chile! She's turning her back on the best fellow in town, when she turned you down. I knows a good man when I see one.

RANDOLPH STRONG: You are always kind to me, Mother Bush. I feel like a lost sheep tonight, the one-hundredth one, out in the cold, separated by iron bars from the ninety and nine! Bah! What am I doing? The milk's spilt! (*arranging flowers*) Put these in here?

MRS. BUSH: Sure! My, but they look grand. There ain't many young doctors so handy-like!

RANDOLPH STRONG: (*half to himself*) The first time I saw her she wore a white rose in her hair . . .

MRS. BUSH: Jest listen! May's plum blind! Oh! If she'd a only listened to me, she'd be marrying you tonight, instead of that stuck up John Temple. I never did believe in two "lights" marrying no how—it's onlucky. They're jest exactly the same color . . . hair . . . and eyes alike, too. Now you . . . you is jest right for my May. "Dark should marry light." You'd be a perfect match.

RANDOLPH STRONG: (*groans*) Hold, hold, for goodness sake! Why didn't you lend that little blind girl of yours your two good eyes?

MRS. BUSH: Humph! She wouldn't hear me. (*goes to him, speaking confidentially*) 'Tween you and me, I shorely do wish she'd a said "yes" when you popped the question las' Christmas. I hates to see her tying up with this high-falutin' nothing. She'll re'lize one day that money ain't everything, and that a poor man's love is a whole sight better than a stiff-necked, good-looking dude.

RANDOLPH STRONG: It can't be helped now, Mother Bush. If she's happy, that's the main thing!

MRS. BUSH: But is she going to be happy . . . that's jest it!

RANDOLPH STRONG: Let us hope so! And yet, sometimes I think—do you know, Mother Bush, (*lowering his voice*) sometimes I think May cares for me.

MRS. BUSH: (*confidently*) Do you know, honey, somehow, sometimes I do too!

RANDOLPH STRONG: (*excitedly*) You do, too!! Oh, if I could fully believe that—even now—at the last minute—(*snaps his fingers*) Oh, what's the use? (*constrainedly*) Is everything ready?

MRS. BUSH: You bet! I'm all dressed under this apron. (*Swings it back and discloses a brilliant and much decorated gown. Then with a start*) Lord save us! That Lyddie Smith ain't brought that my'nais dressing yet. Vowed she'd have it here by eight sharp, if she was alive. What time you got?

RANDOLPH STRONG: (*looking at his watch*) Eight thirty!

MRS. BUSH: Eight thirty? Good gracious!

RANDOLPH STRONG: I'll run over and get it for you.

MRS. BUSH: Oh yes, honey! Do hurry. Oh, what a son-in-law you would'a' made!

RANDOLPH STRONG: Good joke . . . but I can't laugh! (*He goes. MRS. BUSH busies herself with the table arrangements and finally notices a package that had been left by STRONG; she opens it and discloses a beautiful vase and reads aloud the card attached.*)

MRS. BUSH: (*reading*) "For May and her husband, with best wishes for your happiness, Randolph." (*She sets it aside without saying a word—only wiping her eyes—thinks awhile; shakes her head; picks up the vase again and calls toward the stairway:*) May! May! Run down here a minute. I've got something to show you. (*MRS. BUSH polishes the vase with her own apron and holds her head to one side looking at it admiringly. Enter MAY in negligee. MRS. BUSH—with the vase behind her*) Not dressed yet? . . . Gracious! There . . . look . . . Randolph brought it!

MAY BUSH: Oh! . . . did he? (*reads card*) Randolph is a dear! (*fondles vase and looks sad*)

MRS. BUSH: He bought these roses, too . . . said you liked this kind. (*MAY BUSH takes roses and buries her face in them, then thoughtfully changes them into RANDOLPH's vase; looks at it with head to one side, then breaks off one rose, fondles it, places it in her hair.*) May—May—are you happy?

MAY BUSH: Why—why— (*dashing something like a tear from her eye*) of course I am.

MRS. BUSH: Maybe you is . . . May . . . but, somehow, I don't feel satisfied.

MAY BUSH: (*kisses her mother*) Oh, Ma, everything is all right! Just wait until you see me dressed. (*noise at door*) Oh, somebody's coming in here! (*MAY retreats partly up the stairway. Enter MRS. TEMPLE, talking. Voices and commotion heard as if coming from front of the house, where heated argument is going on at the front door, MRS. TEMPLE's muffled voice being heard. Hall kitchen door opens suddenly. Enter MRS. TEMPLE excitedly.*)

MRS. TEMPLE: Heavens! They tried to keep me from coming out here! The very idea of her talking that way to me—the groom's own mother! Who is that little upstart that let me in at the front door? I told her I was coming right out here in the kitchen, for even though we have not called on each other in the past, moving around—as you know—in somewhat different social circles, and, of course, not being thrown very closely together, yet *now*, at this particular time, Mrs. Bush, since our children are determined to marry, I feel that my place tonight is right back here with you! (*Glancing upward, MRS. TEMPLE discovers MAY upon the stairway.*) Why, May, are you not dressed yet! You'll have to do better than that when you are Mrs. John Temple!

MRS. BUSH: Don't you worry 'bout May; she'll be ready. Where's John? Is he here?

MRS. TEMPLE: Sure—he brought me in his car, but the fellows captured him and said they were going to keep him out driving until the last minute. (*again glancing up toward MAY*) Better hurry, May; you mustn't keep John waiting.

MAY BUSH: (*slowly walking upstairs*) Oh, John will get used to waiting on me. (*Exit MAY.*)

MRS. TEMPLE: (*to MRS. BUSH.*) What's this . . . chicken salad? Is it finished?

MRS. BUSH: No, it ain't. The my'nase ain't come yet. I sent Randolph for it. I jest got tired waiting on Lyddie Smith to fetch it.

MRS. TEMPLE: My gracious . . . give me the things and I'll make the dressing for you in a jiffy. (*MRS. TEMPLE removes her white gloves and gets ready for her new role in the kitchen. Without waiting for MRS. BUSH's consent, she rapidly walks over to wooden peg on wall, takes down extra gingham apron and removes her hat and lightweight coat, hanging both upon the peg.*)

MRS. BUSH: (*remonstratingly*) I'm 'fraid you'll git yo'self spoiled doing kitchen work. Sich folks as you'd better go 'long in the parlor.

MRS. TEMPLE: Oh, no indeed. This is my son's wedding and I'm here to do a mother's part. Besides—he is a Temple and everything must be right.

MRS. BUSH: (*takes materials for making the mayonnaise from the kitchen safe and reluctantly places them before MRS. TEMPLE*) You needn't worry 'bout this wedding bein' right. It's my daughter's wedding—and I'll see to that!

MRS. TEMPLE: (*breaking and stirring up eggs for the dressing*) You'll have to admit that the girls will envy May marrying my boy John.

MRS. BUSH: (*stopping her work suddenly, and with arms akimbo*) Envy MAY!!! Envy MAY!!! They'd better envy JOHN!!! You don't know who May is; she's got blue blood in her veins.

MRS. TEMPLE: (*laughing sarcastically*) You amuse me. I'll admit May's sweet and pretty, but she's no match for John.

MRS. BUSH: (*irately*) She's not, eh? If I told you something about my May—who she is—you'd be struck dumb.

MRS. TEMPLE: (*nervously stirring the mayonnaise, replies in a falsetto or raised tone, denoting sarcasm*) Remarkable... but I am curious!

MRS. BUSH: (*proudly*) I bet you is—you'd fall flat on your face if I told you who she is.

MRS. TEMPLE: (*suspending the operation of the mayonnaise and curiously assuming a soft, confidential tone*) Pray, Mrs. Bush, tell me then. Who is May?

MRS. BUSH: Who is May? Huh! (*Proudly tossing her head*) Who is May? (*lowering her voice, confidentially*) Why...do you know Cap'n WINFIELD McCALLISTER, the biggest banker in this town, and who's got money 'vested in banks all over Georgia? That 'ristocrat uv 'ristocrats... that Peachtree Street blue blood—CAP'N McCALLISTER—don't you know him?

MRS. TEMPLE: (*starts at the mention of the name but recovers herself in a moment*) Y-e-s, I've heard of him.

MRS. BUSH: (*like a shot out of a gun*) Well, I'll have you know—he's May's daddy!

MRS. TEMPLE: (*agitatedly*) W-h-y...I...I...I can't believe it!

MRS. BUSH: (*flauntingly*) Believe it or not, it's the bounden truth so help me God! Ain't you never seed him strut? Well, look at May. Walks jest like him—throws her head like him—an' she's got eyes, nose and mouth jest like him. She's his living image.

MRS. TEMPLE: (*almost collapsing, speaking softly and excitedly*) You..you terrify me. Mrs. Bush...Captain McCallister can't be May's father!

MRS. BUSH: Can't be May's father! Well, I reckon I ought to know who May's father is! Whut do you know 'bout it anyhow? Whut do you know 'bout Cap'n McCallister?

MRS. TEMPLE: Do you mean to tell—

MRS. BUSH: (*interrupting*) I mean jest whut I said. I'm telling you that my daughter—May Bush—has got the bluest blood in America in her veins. Jest put that in your pipe and smoke it! (*MRS. BUSH here proudly flaunts herself around the kitchen, talking half to MRS. TEMPLE and half to herself.*) Huh! Talkin' 'bout May not being a match fur John. I should say they don't come no finer than May, anywhere.

MRS. TEMPLE: (*again collecting herself and speaking in a soft, strained, pleading voice*) Mrs. Bush, Mrs. Bush, I have something to say to you and it must be said right now! Oh, where can I begin? Let me think—

MRS. BUSH: This ain't no time to think, I'm going to act! (*takes mayonnaise from MRS. TEMPLE's apathetic hands*) My chile's gotter get married and get married right. I...

MRS. TEMPLE: (*breaking in*) Please, please, be still a minute for heaven's sake! You'll drive me mad!

MRS. BUSH: Drive you mad! The devil I will (*abruptly runs and stands in a belligerent attitude in front of MRS. TEMPLE*) Say, look here, Miss High-and-Mighty, what's you up to? Git out of here, you ain't going to start no trouble here. (*tries to force MRS. TEMPLE toward the door.*)

MRS. TEMPLE: (*breaking down in tears and reaching for MRS. BUSH's hands*) Please, please, Mrs. Bush, you don't understand, and how can I tell you—what a day!

MRS. BUSH: (*standing squarely in front of MRS. TEMPLE*) Look here, is you crazy? Or just a fool?

MRS. TEMPLE: Neither, Mrs. Bush. I'm just a broken-hearted mother and you must help me, help me, for May's sake, if not for mine!

MRS. BUSH: For May's sake! 'Splain yourself! This is a pretty come off. For May's sake.

MRS. TEMPLE: (*sarcastically*) It's a long story, but I'll tell you in a few words. Oh, oh, how I've tried to forget it!

MRS. BUSH: Forget what! Look here, what time is it?

MRS. TEMPLE: (*looks at her watch*) A quarter to nine.

MRS. BUSH: (*excitedly*) Lord, woman, we ain't got no time fur story telling. I've got to hustle!

MRS. TEMPLE: (*hysterically*) You must hear me, you must, you must!

MRS. BUSH: Well, of all things, what is the matter with you?

MRS. TEMPLE: Be quiet, just one minute and let me tell you.

MRS. BUSH: You'd better hurry up.

MRS. TEMPLE: Once... I taught a country school in Georgia. I was engaged to Paul Temple... I was only nineteen. I had worked hard to make enough to pay for my wedding things... it was going to be in the early fall—our wedding. I put my money in the bank. One day, in that bank, I met a man. He helped me. And then I see he wanted his pay for it. He kept on—kept writing to me. He didn't sign his letters, though. I wouldn't answer. I tried to keep away.

One night he came to the place where I boarded. The woman where I boarded—
she helped him—he bribed her. He came into my room—

MRS. BUSH: The dirty devil!

MRS. TEMPLE: (*continuing her story*) I cried out. There wasn't anyone there that
cared enough to help me, and you know yourself, Mrs. Bush, what little chance
there is for women like us, in the South, to get justice or redress when these
things happen!

MRS. BUSH: Sure, honey, I do know!

MRS. TEMPLE: Mother knew—there wasn't any use trying to punish him. She
said I'd be the one . . . that would suffer.

MRS. BUSH: You done right . . . and whut your ma told you is the God's truth.

MRS. TEMPLE: I told Paul Temple—the one I was engaged to—the whole story,
only I didn't tell him who. I knew he would have tried to kill him, and then
they'd have killed him.

MRS. BUSH: (*interrupting*) That wuz good sense.

MRS. TEMPLE: He understood the whole thing—and he married me. He knew
why I wouldn't tell him the man's name—not even when—when that man's
son was born to me.

MRS. BUSH: You don't mean John?

MRS. TEMPLE: Yes . . . John. And his father. . . .

MRS. BUSH: Oh no . . . no . . .

MRS. TEMPLE: Yes. (*with a groan*) Winfield McCallister . . . is John's father, too.

MRS. BUSH: (*clasping her hands excitedly*) My God! My God! (*whimpering, between
sobs*) Whut kin we do? Just think of my poor, dear chile, May, upstairs there—
all dressed up jest lak a bride—'spectin' to git married—and all them people
from everywhere—in the parlor—waiting for the seymoaney! Oh, whut kin
we tell her—whut kin we tell them?

MRS. TEMPLE: (*looking at watch. gets up, walks up and down excitedly.*) Yes . . . we've
got to think and act quickly! We can't tell the world why the children didn't
marry . . . and cause a scandal . . . I'd be ruined!

MRS. BUSH: (*getting irate*) So far as you is consarned . . . I ain't bothered 'bout your
being ruined. May'll be ruined if we don't tell. Why—folks'll all be saying John
jilted her, and you can bet your sweet life I won't stand fur that. No siree! I
don't keer who it hurts . . . I'm not agoin' to see May suffer . . . not ef I kin help
it!

MRS. TEMPLE: (*bursting into tears*) Oh! Oh! We must do something!

(*Enter RANDOLPH STRONG, breathlessly, with mayonnaise dressing from Lyddie Smith's—placing large glass of mayonnaise on the kitchen table.*)

RANDOLPH STRONG: Good evening, Mrs. Temple. I'm a little late, Mrs. Bush,
but here's what you sent me for. (*He notices MRS. TEMPLE in tears.*) My,
my, why what's wrong?

MRS. BUSH: Randolph, my dear boy. . . .

RANDOLPH STRONG: What's the matter? What's happened since I left you awhile ago?

MRS. BUSH: (*slowly and feelingly*) Sump'n . . . sump'n turrible!

RANDOLPH STRONG: Has anything happened to May?

MRS. BUSH: Not only to her—to all of us!

RANDOLPH STRONG: All? Heavens!

MRS. BUSH: Listen, Randolph, and help us, for God's sake! May and John can't get married!

RANDOLPH STRONG: (*turning to MRS. TEMPLE*) Can't get married? Why?

MRS. TEMPLE: It's a long story. I've told—I've explained everything to Mrs. Bush. She—she understands.

RANDOLPH STRONG: You can trust me. I'm like one of the family. You both know that I have always cared for May.

MRS. BUSH: (*to MRS. TEMPLE*) Kin I tell him? (*MRS. TEMPLE silently and tearfully nods her assent.*) May mus' know it too—right away. Let's call her down. May! May! Oh, May! My dear chile come down here a minute—quick—right away! My poor chile . . . my poor chile!

MRS. TEMPLE: What a day! What a day!

MAY'S VOICE: Coming, Ma! (*Enter MAY BUSH, coming downstairs in her wedding gown.*) Am I late? (*noting RANDOLPH*) The roses are beautiful. See. (*points to one in her hair*)

MRS. BUSH: Randolph . . . Randolph remembered the kind you like, honey.

MAY BUSH: (*to RANDOLPH*) Just like you!

RANDOLPH STRONG: How sweet of you to wear one!

MAY BUSH: (*proudly walking across room toward MRS. BUSH*) How do I look, Ma?

MRS. BUSH: (*tenderly kissing her daughter several times*) Beautiful, my darlin'. (*adding softly*) Poor chile!

MAY BUSH: (*walking toward and kissing MRS. TEMPLE*) How do you like me—my other mama?

MRS. TEMPLE: Charming—God protect you, my dear!

MAY BUSH: (*noticing the sad expressions on the faces of both mothers*) My, you all look so sad; why so doleful? What is the matter with them, Randolph?

RANDOLPH STRONG: Why . . . I'm wounded, but smiling. The ladies . . .

MRS. BUSH: (*impatiently interrupting*) Oh, children—don't waste this precious time. We've called you together to tell you sump'n . . . (*stuttering*) we've got sump'n to tell you, and we got to tell you right now! (*MRS. BUSH draws MAY aside toward MRS. TEMPLE, hastily and cautiously locking kitchen hall door. Continuing:*) Listen, May. Come here, come here. Randolph, for I feel that both of you are my children. May, you got to be strong—for if ever you needed wits, now's the time to use 'em. May God forgive me—and—and Mrs. Temple there, both of us—I just got to tell you 'bout it quick—for all them folks are in the parlor and if we don't do something quick, right now, this whole town will be rippin' us to pieces—all of us, you and me—Mrs. Temple—and—the las' one of us! There ain't time to tell you the whole story—but—May—my poor chile—I know you kin trus' your own, dear ma that far?

MAY BUSH: (*excitedly*) Yes, Ma, yes, but what is it?

MRS. BUSH: May, you and John can't marry—you jest can't marry!!

MAY BUSH: (*aghast*) Can't marry! Can't marry!

MRS. BUSH: No, never!

MAY BUSH: But why—why!

MRS. BUSH: Your father, and John's father—is—is—

MAY BUSH: You don't mean . . .

MRS. BUSH: Yes, May. John's father is your father.

MAY BUSH: (*wrings her hands*) Oh, I'd rather die—I'd rather die than face this. . . .

MRS. BUSH: (*crooning*) I know, honey . . . I know . . . God forgive me . . . God forgive that man. Oh, no . . . I don't want Him to forgive him.

MAY BUSH: Oh why, why did this have to happen to me—oh!! I wish I were dead!

RANDOLPH STRONG: May—don't say that. You mustn't say that.

MAY BUSH: I do. Oh, God—I've kept out of their clutches myself, but now it's through you, Ma, that they've got me anyway. Oh, what's the use . . .

RANDOLPH STRONG: May!

MAY BUSH: The whole world will be pointing at me . . .

MRS. BUSH: Ah, honey, honey, I'll be loving you . . .

MAY BUSH: I wish I could die right now.

RANDOLPH STRONG: Will you listen to me, now, May?

MAY BUSH: Those people in there—they'll be laughing . . . (*knocking is heard*)

MRS. TEMPLE: It's John. We can't let him come in here now. He mustn't know. . . .

MRS. BUSH: No. We can't let him know or he'll kill his own father. . . .

MRS. TEMPLE: What are you going to do, May?

MRS. BUSH: Yes, May, what are you going to do?

RANDOLPH STRONG: We are going to run away and get married, aren't we, May? Say yes, May—say yes!

MAY BUSH: John . . . (*The knocking is heard again.*)

MRS. BUSH: Keep it from him. It's the black women that have got to protect their men from the white men by not telling on 'em.

MRS. TEMPLE: God knows that's the truth.

RANDOLPH STRONG: May! Come with me *now*!

MAY BUSH: Randolph—do you want me?

RANDOLPH STRONG: I want you like I've always wanted you.

MAY BUSH: (*shyly*) But—I don't love you.

RANDOLPH STRONG: You think you don't. . . .

MAY BUSH: Do you want me now?

RANDOLPH STRONG: I want you now.

MAY BUSH: Ma, oh, ma!

MRS. BUSH: (*in tears*) Quick, darlin'—tell him.

MAY BUSH: My coat.

MRS. BUSH: I'll get your coat, honey.

MRS. TEMPLE: Here, May, take my coat!

MRS. BUSH: What are we going to tell John—and all the people?

MAY BUSH: Tell 'em—Oh God, we can't tell 'em the—truth?

RANDOLPH STRONG: Mother Bush—just tell them the bride was stolen by Randolph Strong! (*STRONG puts the coat around her and they go out the door, leaving the others staring at them.*)

CURTAIN

Safe (c. 1929)

Georgia Douglas Johnson

CHARACTERS

LIZA PETTIGREW	The Wife
JOHN PETTIGREW	The Husband
MANDY GRIMES	Liza's Mother
DR. JENKINS	Physician
HANNAH WIGGINS	Neighbor

SETTING

PLACE:	Southern Town
TIME:	1893
SCENE:	Front room of Pettigrew home

SCENE

Front room of a three room cottage. Back door leading to kitchen. Door to left leading to LIZA's room. A front door and a cot along the wall. A table and oil lamp, three chairs, baby garments, a basket of socks, newspapers, etc.

SCENE OPENS: LIZA is discovered sewing on some small white garments. JOHN is reading the evening paper by an oil lamp on the table.

LIZA: (*lifting her voice*) Ma, come on outer that kitchen—jest stack up them supper dishes and come on and set down and rest, you hear?

MANDY: (*from kitchen*) All right, Liza, I'm coming out in a minute now.

LIZA: (*to JOHN*) Ma's been on her feet all day long. She don't know how to rest herself.

JOHN: (*absently*) Eughhu. She sho don't. (*continues reading*)

LIZA: (*calling again*) Come on, Ma.

MANDY: (*appearing in the kitchen doorway*) I hate to leave them dishes all dirty overnight, but if I must, I must. (*She looks about the room for something to do.*) I reckon I will jest mend John's socks while I'm setting here. (*She brings a basket with socks, needle and thread in it over near the table light with a chair.*)

LIZA: No, Ma, you lay down on your cot and stretch out a while and rest. First thing you know I'll be down and then you got to be up and around waiting on me—so rest while you kin.

MANDY: (*obediently putting up the sewing basket*) All right, honey. I'll stretch out a minute or so if you wants me to. (*She goes over to her cot against the wall and falls down heavily with a sigh upon it.*) My, this feels good to my old bones.

LIZA: Of course, it do—you're plum wore out; you done a sight of washing today.

MANDY: (*yawning*) Yes, I been going pretty steady today. What you making on now?

LIZA: Just hemming some little flannel belly bands. (*She holds up one for her mother to see.*) I got all the night gowns ready now. My time's pretty nigh near.

MANDY: Yes, it's jest about time—nine months I count it.

JOHN: (*lowering the paper*) Well, well, well. I see they done caught Sam Hosea and put him in jail.

MANDY: When they ketch him?

JOHN: Paper says this morning. I reckon his ma is plum crazy if she's heered they got him.

LIZA: I knows her. She's a little skinny brown-skinned woman. Belong to our church. She use to bring Sam along pretty regular all the time. He was a nice motherly sort of boy, not mor'n seventeen I'd say. Lemme see. 'Twant no woman mixed up in it, was it?

JOHN: No, seems like he and his boss had some sort of dispute about wages—the boss slapped him and Sam up and hit him back they says.

MANDY: Eugh eugh—that's mighty unhealthy sounding business for this part of the country. Hittin a white man, he better hadder made tracks far away from here I'm er thinking.

(*Just then there's a soft knock at the door.*)

JOHN: I wonder who that is.

LIZA: Go see!

(*JOHN goes to the door. HANNAH WIGGINS enters.*)

JOHN: Howdy, Miss Wiggins, come in and take a cheer.

HANNAH: (*still standing and excited like*) Howdy! I jest thought I'd drop over here, being as Liza was so near her time and, and—

MANDY: (*sitting up on the cot*) Go on Hannah; what's the matter, you look all flusterated—what's up?

LIZA: Set down, Miss Hannah, there's a cheer.

HANNAH: (*sitting down on the edge of the chair uneasily*) I, I come over here to see how Liza was most special—then I wanted to see if yaw'll knowed about the trouble—

MANDY: Liza's fine. But what trouble is it you're talking 'bout? We ain't heered nothing 'tall!

JOHN: I saw in the papers they done caught Sam Hosea—we all thought he'd got out of town. I jest read 'bout it.

HANNAH: Yes, but that ain't all. (*Shakes her head.*)

LIZA: What else is it? Tell us!

HANNAH: (*looks around the room, again floundering*) You see I heered they done formed a mob downtown and it mout be there'll be hell to pay tonight!

JOHN: (*excitedly*) Who told you that?

HANNAH: Jim Brown told me 'bout it. He dropped in our house jest now and said as how things didn't look good at all downtown. So I thought I better run over and tell yaw'll.

JOHN: Ain't they gointer call out the soldiers, did he say?

HANNAH: No, he jest said the crowds was gathering and it didn't look good in town.

LIZA: (*in awed tones*) You don't reckon they'll take Sam out of the jail, do you, John?

JOHN: I don't know. (*He gets up and goes to the door.*) I think I'll step down the streets and see what they knows by Briggze's store.

MANDY: (*to JOHN*) You think you oughter go out?

LIZA: Be keerful and don't stay long.

JOHN: I'll be right back. Don't yaw'll worry. (*goes out.*)

LIZA: I been setting here thinking 'bout that poor boy Sam—him working hard to take kere of his widder mother, doing the best he kin, trying to be a man and stan up for hissef, and what do he git? A slap in the face.

HANNAH: Chile, that ain't nothing—if he gits off with a slap. These white folks is mad—mad—he done hit a white man back.

MANDY: They ain't gointer stan for it. I done seen it happen before.

LIZA: What's little nigger boys born for anyhow? I sho hopes mine will be a girl. I don't want no boy baby to be hounded down and kicked 'round. No, I don't want to ever have no boy chile!

MANDY: Hush, honey, that's a sin. God sends what he wants us to have—we can't pick and choose.

HANNAH: No, we sho can't. We got to swaller the bitter with the sweet.

(*Just then a shot is heard.*)

MANDY: (*jumping up*) What's that?

HANNAH: Sho sounded like a shot to me. I b'lieve them white folks is up to something this night.

LIZA: Listen, ain't that noise coming this a way?

HANNAH: It sho sounds like it. (*Goes over to the door, cracks it, peeps out and listens.*) They's coming—a big crowd headed this way.

MANDY: (*excitedly*) We better put out the light and pull that curtain way down.

HANNAH: Yes, that's right, you can't tell what them devils might git it in they heads to do.

(*There is an increasing sound.*)

LIZA: (*in awed tones*) They wouldn't come in here? Would they?

MANDY: (*consolingly*) No, they wouldn't, but then we better keep it dark.

(*Another shot rings out. The women jump and look at each other in fear.*)

LIZA: (*plaintively*) I wonder where John is—

MANDY: He oughter been back here before now. (*She goes to the window and peeps cautiously out from behind [the] shade. HANNAH follows and then LIZA.*)

HANNAH: You stay back, Liza. You oughtenter see sich things—not in your delicate state.

LIZA: But what they doing? Where they goin to?

MANDY: Yes, go back, Liza, and set down. Let us watch.

(*a confusion of many footsteps and tramping horses as the roar becomes louder*)

LIZA: (*beginning to walk up and down the room restlessly*) Ma, Ma, do you think they got him—do you think they'll hang him . . . ?

MANDY: (*patting LIZA on the shoulder*) I don't know. You try and kep quiet. You hadn't ought to hear all this screeching hell—God help you! (*goes back to window*)

HANNAH: She sho oughten. It's a sin and a shame! Coming right by here, too
. . .

(*Then a voice rises above the men outside shouting, "Don't hang me, don't hang me! I don't want to die! Mother! Mother!"*)

LIZA: (*jumping up*) That's him! That's Sam! They got him. (*She runs to the door and looks out. HANNAH and MANDY follow her quickly and drag her back, shutting the door quickly.*)

MANDY: They'll shoot you! You can't do that! They're mad—mad!

LIZA: (*crumpling up on the chair shivering, her teeth chattering*) Oh my God, did you hear that poor boy crying for his mother? He's jest a boy—jest a boy—jest a little boy!

(*The roar outside continues*)

HANNAH: (*to MANDY*) This is mighty bad for her, mighty bad—

MANDY: (*looking at LIZA critically*) Yes, it sho is. (*She thinks a minute.*) I hates to ast you, but John ain't got back and we ought to git a doctor. Could you steal out the back and git him?

HANNAH: Yes, I'll go—I kin steal out the back ways.

MANDY: Better hurry, Hannah. I don't like the looks of her.

(*HANNAH goes out through back.*)

LIZA: (*continues to shiver and shake*) Oh, where is John? Where is John? What you reckon has happened? Oh, that poor boy—poor little nigger boy!

MANDY: Try not to worry so, honey. We's in the Lord's hands. (*shaking her head*) My poor, poor chile. I'll heat a kettle of water, then I'm gointer fix your bed so you can lay down when you feel like it.

(*Hoarse laughter is heard outside as the noise grows less and less. MANDY goes into small bedroom adjoining [the] kitchen for a moment, then comes back, looks at LIZA, shakes her head. Then LIZA begins walking up and down the floor all doubled over as if in pain. She goes to the window occasionally and looks out from behind the shade. The noise of the countless passing feet are heard and an occasional curse or laugh. She trembles slightly every time she looks and begins pacing up and down again.*)

MANDY: (*coming over from the bedroom*) Come on and lay down now, chile; the doctor'll be here to reckly. I'll git all your little things together for you. (*goes over and begins to gather up the little white garments LIZA had been sewing on*)

LIZA: (*stands stooped over in the opening of her bedroom door*) Did you hear him cry for his mother? Did you?

MANDY: Yes, honey chile, I heard him, but you musn't think about that now. Fergit it. Remember your own little baby—you got him to think about. You got to born him safe!

LIZA: (*looks at MANDY wild-eyed*) What you say?

MANDY: Born him safe! Born him safe! That's what you got to do.

LIZA: (*turning her head from side to side as she stands half stooped in the doorway. She repeats.*) Born him safe! . . . Safe . . . (*She hysterically disappears into the next room.*)

MANDY: (*sighs and continues picking up the little garments, smoothing them out nervously. Just then the door opens and JOHN enters.*) Oh, where you been, John? Why didn't you come back before now?

JOHN: I tried to but I got headed off—they come right by here too. It was terrible, terrible . . . Where's she?

MANDY: In the room. I done sent fur the Doctor; he'll be here any minute.

JOHN: (*nervously going toward LIZA's bedroom*) I'll go in and see her. Poor little LIZA. (*enters room*)

MANDY: (*goes to the window and peers out and listens as scattering footsteps sound outside on the sidewalk. Then she busies herself about the room, turns down her bed, lights the lamp and turns it down low. Just then there is a knock at the kitchen door. Calling*) John! John! (*JOHN comes to the door.*) See if that ain't Hannah at the back door with the Doctor.

JOHN: (*hurrying*) All right. (*He goes through the kitchen and returns with THE DOCTOR.*)

MANDY: I'm sho glad you come, Doctor; she's right in there. Please hurry.

DR. JENKINS: (*to MANDY*) Get me some hot water.

MANDY: I got it ready for you. John, git the kettle! (*JOHN goes in kitchen.*) She's terrible upset, Doctor, terrible...

DR. JENKINS: I know—Hannah told me all about it; she stopped at her house a minute or two, but said tell you she'd be here to help.

JOHN: (*returning with kettle*) Here 'tis.

MANDY: Set it in the room.

> (*THE DOCTOR goes into the room with his bag and JOHN comes out.*)

MANDY: How is she?

JOHN: Mighty upset.

MANDY: She ain't never seen no lynching not before, and it was terrible—her being so nigh her time too.

JOHN: Do you think she'll git through all right?

MANDY: I pray God she do. But she's shook to pieces.

JOHN: I oughter been here myself, but I didn't know I was gointer be cut off...

MANDY: Course you didn't. We's all in the hands of the Lawd.

JOHN: (*drops his hands helplessly on his knees*) What a terrible night.

MANDY: I wish Hannah would come on back. I'm that nervish.

JOHN: She was right brave to go for the Doctor.

MANDY: Want she?

> (*Just then a baby's cry is heard from the next room and both of them jump up and look toward the closed door. They take a step forward and wait.*)

JOHN: You reckon she's all right?

MANDY: I hope so, but...

JOHN: But what?

MANDY: I don't know zactly; I never did see her look like she looked tonight.

JOHN: (*groaning*) I wish the Lord this night was over.

MANDY: God knows I do too—my poor, poor chile.

> (*They waited for what seemed like an eternity listening to the muffled sounds in the next room. Then THE DOCTOR appears at the door, closing it behind him. His face looks distressed. Nervously*)

MANDY: How is she? Can I go in?

JOHN: (*agitatedly*) How is she, Doc?

DR. JENKINS: (*holding up one hand*) Wait a minute, calm yourselves. I've got something to tell you, and I don't hardly know how...

MANDY: (*bursting into tears*) She ain't dead, is she? Doc, my poor chile ain't dead?

JOHN: (*biting his lips*) Tell us, Doc, tell us! What is it?

DR. JENKINS: She's all right and the baby was born all right—big and fine. You heard him cry...

JOHN: Yes...

MANDY: Yes, we heard.

DR. JENKINS: And she asked me right away, "Is it a girl?"

JOHN, MANDY: (*stretching their necks out further to listen*) Yes, yes, Doc! Go on!

DR. JENKINS: And I said, "No child, it's a fine boy," and then I turned my back a minute to wash my hands in the basin. When I looked around again she had her hands about the baby's throat choking it. I tried to stop her, but its little tongue was already hanging from its mouth. It was dead! Then she began, she kept muttering over and over again: "Now he's safe—safe from the lynchers! Safe!"

(*JOHN falls down on a chair sobbing, his face in his hands, as MANDY, stooped with misery, drags her feet heavily toward the closed door. She opens it, softly and goes in. THE DOCTOR stands, a picture of helplessness as he looks at them in their grief.*)

CURTAIN

Blue-Eyed Black Boy (c. 1930) ____

Georgia Douglas Johnson

CHARACTERS

PAULINE WATERS	The Mother
REBECCA WATERS	Daughter
DR. THOMAS GREY	Fiancee
HESTER GRANT	Pauline's Best Friend

SCENE

A kitchen in Mrs. Water's cottage. A stove with food keeping warm and an iron heating, an ironing board in the corner, a table with a lighted oil lamp and two chairs. Door, slightly ajar, leads to the front room and window opening on to a side street.

SCENE OPENS: PAULINE is discovered seated in a large rocker with her left foot bandaged and resting on a low stool.

PAULINE: (*calling to the other room*) Rebecca, come on. Your iron is hot now, I know.

REBECCA: (*answers from the front room*) I'm coming now, Ma. (*She enters holding a lacy garment in her hands.*) I had to tack these bows on. How you like it now?

PAULINE: (*scanning the long night dress set off with little pink bows that REBECCA is holding up for her inspection*) Eugh-hu, it shore is pretty. I don't believe anybody ever had as fine a wedding gown in this whole town.

REBECCA: Humph! (*She shrugs her shoulders proudly as she tests the iron to see if it is hot and then takes it over to the [ironing] board and begins to press the gown.*) That's to be expected, ain't it? Everybody in the Baptist Church looks up to us, don't they?

PAULINE: Shore they do. I ain't carried myself straight all these years for nothing. Your father was shore one proud man; he put us on a pinnacle!

REBECCA: Well, I sure have tried to walk straight all my life.

PAULINE: Yes, and I'm shore proud. Now here you is getting ready to marry a young doctor. My my! (*then she suddenly says*) Ouch! I wish he would come on over here to change the dressing on my foot. Hope I ain't going to have lock jaw.

REBECCA: You won't. Tom knows his business. (*She tosses her head proudly. She looks over to the stove and goes on.*) Wish Jack would come on home and eat his supper so's I could clean up the dishes.

PAULINE: What time is it?

REBECCA: (*goes to the middle door and peeps in the next room*) The clock in position to exactly five minutes after seven. He oughter been here a whole hour ago.

PAULINE: I wonder what's keeping him?

REBECCA: Well, there's one thing sure and certain: he's not running after girls.

PAULINE: No, he shore don't. Just give him a book and he's happy. Says he's going to quit running that crane and learn engineering soons you get married. He's been mighty tied down since your father died taking care of us.

REBECCA: Everybody says he's the smartest and the finest looking black boy in the whole town.

PAULINE: Yes, he is good looking even if he is mine. Some of 'em lay it to his eyes. (*She looks far off thoughtfully.*)

REBECCA: Yes, they do set him off. It's funny that he's the only one in our family's got blue eyes though. Pa's was black, and yours and mine are black too. It certainly is strange; wish I'd had 'em.

PAULINE: Oh, you be satisfied. You're pretty enough. Sister. Hush, there's the doctor's buggy stopping now. Go let him in. (*Rebecca goes to the door while PAULINE bends over, grunting and touching her foot. DR. GREY enters bag in hand with REBECCA.*)

DR. GREY: Well, how's my patient feeling? Better, I know.

PAULINE: Now don't you be kidding me, Doctor. My foots been paining me terrible, I'm scared to death I'm going to have the lock jaw. For God's sake done let me . . . (*REBECCA places chair for him near her mother.*)

DR. GREY: (*unwinds the bandages, looks at foot and opens his bag*) Fine, it's doing fine. You'll have to keep off it for a week more, and then you'll be all right.

PAULINE: Can't walk on it for a week?

Dr. GREY: Not unless you want to die of blood poisoning—lock jaw, I mean! (*He touches the foot with iodine and puts on new bandage.*) That was an old, rusty nail you stuck in your foot. A pretty close call. (*He looks lovingly at REBECCA.*)

PAULINE: Well, I'm tickled to have such a good doctor for my new son.

DR. GREY: You bet. (*then thoughtfully*) I saw some mighty rough looking hoodlums gathering on the streets as I came in. Looks like there might be some trouble somewhere.

REBECCA: Oh, they're always having a squabble on these streets. You get used to 'em—and you will too after a while.

PAULINE: Yes, there's always something stirring everyday. I just go on and on and don't pay 'em no mind myself.

DR. GREY: (*patting the foot tenderly*) Now that's all right. You keep off of it, hear me? Or I won't vouch for the outcome.

PAULINE: It's so sore; I can't stand up even if I was a kind to. [(*A knock is heard.*)] See who's at the back door, Rebecca. Peeps first.

REBECCA: (*goes to the door and cracks it*) Who there?

HESTER: Me, me, it's Hester—Hester Grant. Lemme in. (*REBECCA opens the door and HESTER comes panting in. She looks around as if hating to speak before the other then blurts out.*) Pauline, it's Jack. You son Jack has been 'rested... 'rested and put in jail.

PAULINE: 'Rested?

REBECCA: Good Lord.

DR. GREY: What for? (*moves about restlessly*)

HESTER: They say he done brushed against a white woman on the street. They had er argument and she hollowed out he's attacking her. A crew of white men come up and started beating on him and the policeman, when he was coming home from work, dragged him to the jailhouse.

PAULINE: My God, my God! It ain't so! He ain't brushed up against no lady. My boy ain't! He's, he's a gentleman, that's what he is.

HESTER: (*She moves about restlessly. She has something else to say.*) And, and Pauline, that ain't the worse, that ain't the worse. They, they say there's gointer to be a lynching tonight. They gointer break open the jail and string him up! (*She finishes desperately.*)

PAULINE: String him up? My son? They can't do that—not to my son, not him!

DR. GREY: (*excitedly*) I'll drive over and see the Judge. He'll do something to stop it.

HESTER: (*sarcastically*) Him? Not him! He's a lyncher his own self. Don't put no trust in him. Ain't he done let 'em lynch six niggers in the last year jes' gone? Him! (*She scoffs again.*)

REBECCA: (*wringing her hands*) We got to do something. (*goes up to DR. GREY*) Do you know anybody else, anybody at all, who could save him?

PAULINE: Wait, wait. I know what I'll do. I don't care what it costs. (*to RE-BECCA*) Fly in yonder (*points to the next room*) and get me that little tin box out of the left hand side of the tray in my trunk. Hurry. Fly! (*REBECCA hurries out while DR. GREY and HESTER look on in bewilderment.*) Lynch my son? My son? (*She yells to REBECCA in the next room.*) Get it? You got it?

REBECCA: (*from next room*) Yes, Ma, I got it. (*She hurries in with a small tin box in her hand and hands it to her mother.*)

PAULINE: (*Feverishly tossing out the odd bits of jewelry in the box, finally coming up with a small ring. She turns to DR. GREY.*) Here, Tom, take this. Run, jump on your horse and buggy and fly over to Governor Tinkham's house and don't you let nobody—nobody—stop you. Just give him this ring and say, "Pauline sent this. She says they goin to lynch her son born 21 years ago." Mind you, say 21 years ago. Then say, listen close. "Look in his eyes and you'll save him."

DR. GREY: (*listens in amazement but grasps the small ring in his hand and hastens toward the door saying*) Don't worry. I'll put in in his hands and tell him what you said just as quick as my horse can make it. (*When he leaves the room, REBECCA and HESTER look at PAULINE in astonishment.*)

HESTER: (*starting as if from a dream*) Well, well, well, I don't git what you mean, but I reckon you knows what you is doing. (*She and REBECCA watch DR. GREY from the front window as he drives away.*)

PAULINE: I shorely do!

REBECCA: (*comes over and throws her arms around her mother's neck*) Mother, what does it all mean? Can you really save him?

PAULINE: (*confidently*) Wait and see. I'll tell you more about it after a while. Don't ask me now.

HESTER: (*going over to the window*) I hope he'll git over to the Governor's in time. (*looking out*) Emp! There goes a bunch of men with guns now and here comes another all slouched over and pushing on the same way.

REBECCA: (*joining her at the window, with bated breath*) And look, look! Here come wagons full. (*The rumble of wagon wheels is heard.*) See 'em, Hester? All piled in with their guns, too.

(*PAULINE's lips move in prayer; her head is turned deliberately away from the window. She sighs deeply now and then.*)

HESTER: Do Lord, do Lord! Help us this night.

REBECCA: (*with trembling voice*) Hussies! Look at them men on horses! (*Horses' hooves are heard in the street outside. REBECCA cries lightly.*)

HESTER: Jesus, Jesus! Please come down and help us this night!

REBECCA: (*running over to her mother and flinging her arms about her neck*) Oh, mother, mother! What will we do? Do you hear 'em? Do you hear all them men on horses and wagons going up to the jail? Poor brother! Poor boy.

PAULINE: Trust in God, daughter. I've got faith in Him, faith in . . . in the Governor. He won't fail. (*She continues to move her lips in prayer.*)

(*REBECCA rushes back to the window as new sounds of wagon wheels are heard.*)

HESTER: (*at window*) Still coming!

REBECCA: Why don't Tom come back? Why don't he hurry?

HESTER: Hush, chile! He ain't had time yet.

PAULINE: (*breaks out in an audible prayer*) Lord Jesus, I know I've sinned against your holy law, but you did forgive me and let me hold up my head again. Help me again, dear Jesus. Help me to save my innocent child, him who never done no wrong. Save him, Lord. Let his father . . . (*She stops and looks around at the two women, then cautiously speaks.*) You understand all I mean, sweet Jesus.

Come down and rise with this wild mob tonight. Pour your love into their wicked hearts. Lord, Lord, hear my prayer.

HESTER: (*at window*) Do Lord, hear.

PAULINE: (*restlessly looking toward the others*) Any sight of Tom yet?

REBECCA: No, Ma. I don't see him no where yet.

HESTER: Give him time.

PAULINE: Time! Time! It'll be too late reckly. Too late . . . (*She sobs, her head lifted, listening.*) What that?

HESTER: (*peers out and listens*) What?

PAULINE: The sound of many feet I hear?

REBECCA: (*looks out interestingly*) I see 'em, I see 'em! Wait! Wait! Ma! Ma! (*hysterically*) It's the state troops! It's the Guards, it's the Guard, Ma! They's coming. Look, Miss Hester!

HESTER: They shore is, Jesus. Shore as I'm born—them military. They's come—come to save him.

REBECCA: And yonders Tom at the gate—he's coming.

DR. GREY: (*rushing in as the others look at him in amazement*) He's saved, Miss Waters! Saved! Did the Governor send the troops?

CURTAIN

EULALIE SPENCE (1894–1981)

Hot Stuff (1927)
Episode (1928)

BIOGRAPHY AND ACHIEVEMENTS

Eulalie Spence was born in Nevis, British West Indies, on June 11, 1894. She moved to New York City via Ellis Island with her seven sisters and her father when she was eight years old. Spence earned a B.S. at New York University in 1937 and an M.A. in speech at Columbia University in 1939. For many years she worked as a teacher and dramatic society coach at the Eastern District High School in Brooklyn. She died in New York City in 1981.

Eulalie Spence, unlike the other dozen or so black women dramatists of the Harlem Renaissance, wrote about everyday life in Harlem. Many of her female contemporaries had attended Howard University and settled in the Washington, D.C., area, but Spence chose to remain in New York City where she had grown up and been educated. Like Langston Hughes, she captured the spirit of Harlemites. Primarily concerned with the down-home folks, her plays are identifiably domestic dramas.

During the 1920s, Spence wrote a number of one-act plays, including *Hot Stuff*, (1927) *Fool's Errand*, (1927), *Foreign Mail* (1927), *Her* (1927), *The Hunch* (1927), *The Starter* (1927), *Episode* (1928), *Help Wanted* (1929), and *Undertow* (1929). Her full-length play, *The Whipping* (1933), was optioned by Paramount Productions but was never produced.

Unlike many of her contemporaries, Spence was deeply interested in not only writing plays but also in getting them produced. Spence was extremely active in community theater, where she directed many of her own plays as well as those of her contemporaries such as Eugene O'Neill. She helped establish the Dunbar Garden Players in the late 1920s and directed the group's plays at St. Mark's Theater on Lower Second Avenue. Spence was also very active with the Krigwa Players, which was founded by W. E. B. Du Bois and originally housed in the basement of the Harlem Branch of the New York Public Library at 135th Street. As Du Bois had instructed in the July 1926 issue of *Crisis*, Spence set out to write plays "about us, by us, for us, and near us" (p. 134).

Eulalie Spence's most important contribution to African American theater rests in her attempts at piecing together the cultural and spiritual fabric of blacks in general and of Harlemites in particular. Her involvement in the business of theater—in writing, directing, and producing—initiated a movement away from the "plays to be read" written by the majority of black women of the period and a trend toward viable theater with a viewing audience.

SYNOPSIS AND ANALYSIS: *HOT STUFF*

The drama is set in a Harlem flat where Fanny King, otherwise known as "Hot Stuff," manipulates her neighbors and friends. She is a numbers runner, a dealer in stolen merchandise, and a prostitute. While her husband is out of town, she entertains men. In fact, she and a friend, Mary Green, chat about their conquests. But, Fanny's main interest seems to be the numbers racket. She boasts to Mary that dealing in the numbers business is easy work because of all the suckers in Harlem who are willing to entrust money to her. She gambles away their money, taking as much as $250 a day for herself from unsuspecting victims. When John Cole comes to collect the money she has stolen from him, she insults him and tells him that she lost his winning ticket. She offers to give him back the cost of the ticket, but he storms out.

Minutes later, his girlfriend, Jennie Barbour, challenges Fanny and demands the stolen money. When Fanny denies her guilt, Jennie threatens to expose Walter King, Fanny's husband, as a supplier of stolen goods. Jennie tells Fanny she will go to Walter's supervisor and give him proof that Walter has been stealing from the clothing warehouse. Not wishing to see her husband jailed, Fannie gives back the money that belongs to John.

Fanny moves from one deal to the next when Isadore Goldstein, a Jew, comes in to peddle a fur. He flatters and entices Fanny, but she refuses to pay his price. Instead, she offers him her body to make up the difference. While Fanny is in the bedroom with Isadore, her husband returns from an out-of-town business trip. Walter literally throws out Isadore and beats up Fanny.

When Walter leaves, Fanny grabs her fur and muses that it was some bargain. She also picks up the phone and cancels the date she had with a lover or, perhaps, a paying customer.

Spence characterizes the Harlem that she lived in during the 1920s. For her, it was a place where everyone was on the hustle. Her portrayal of Fanny is antithetical to the stereotypical religious, stalwart matriarch who gives her life to her family. Fanny is depicted as a self-centered and morally decadent woman with an independent spirit. Spence seems to be mirroring a society in which blacks do what they have to in order to survive and to secure material things. Some of them, like John Cole, place all of their trust in the numbers game, hoping to win enough to make ends meet. Some make a living by stealing from corporate America. Some prostitute their bodies in order to live and to have the finer things in life. What permeates the play is a sense of urban poverty and the con games that are enacted in order to survive in a fast-paced, uncaring world.

SYNOPSIS AND ANALYSIS: *EPISODE*

This is a domestic comedy in which Jim and Mamie Jackson run into conflicts because Jim refuses to stay home, and he does not take her out with him. Though Mamie nags him about staying away with his many friends and accuses him of hanging out with women in Harlem bars, Jim seems unperturbed. Shortly after he leaves for a night out, two of Mamie's friends come to visit. Both Mrs. Jennings and Mrs. Robinson offer advice about how to keep a man home.

Mrs. Jennings suggests that a woman ought to find her own friends and go out as often as her man does. She tells Mamie, "Ah never stays home, lessn' Ah wants ter. Ah sure got friends ter take me where Ah wants ter go." When Mamie tells Mrs. Jennings that Jim is jealous and would kill her if she started running around Harlem, Mrs. Jennings quips, "He would—not! It ain' bein done this year. Lemme tell yuh somethin'. Yuh ain' bin married long an' Ah hates ter see yuh makin' a fool uv yuhself. 'Long's yuh Jim knows yuh hangin' roun' here yearnin', he'll let yuh yearn, an' have a wonderful time watchin' yuh do it."

Mrs. Robinson's advice is a bit more subtle. She tells Mamie that her husband gave up running around when he bought a radio. She urges Mamie to do the same for Jim.

Just as Mamie decides to go out to purchase a radio, Jim and his cornet-playing friend, Walt Gilbert, come home to tell Mamie that he'll be staying home nights to learn to play his newly purchased cornet. Mamie, however, hates the cornet because as a child her mother lived next door to a man who was perpetually learning to play the instrument.

Much to Mamie's disappointment, Jim begins to stay home, but she can not pry him away from his horn. His obsession with the cornet leads him to ignore her totally and to disturb daily the apartment tenants with his untrained music. In an act of desperation, Mamie and Jim's friend Harry Williams plot to make Jim jealous. When Mamie tells Jim that she is going to a cabaret and may not be in until dawn, Jim tells her, "Take yuh key, Mamie." When she leaves, he blows his horn with relief.

Episode, on one level, is about the evils of nagging. Mamie, a recently married woman, seems bent on shaping Jim into the perfect husband instead of allowing him and herself the necessary space to grow into a strong team.

Mamie's notions about molding Jim are apparent when she says, "Ain't like what Ah thought marriage was goin' ter be. Ah pictured you an' me—jes' you an' me—settin' here on this couch, same's we useter—in Mom's parler; or mebbe you smokin' or readin' the paper, or mebbe talkin' ter me." Spence seems to be suggesting that married people must strive for a certain amount of independence as well as dependence in a relationship.

On another level, the play is about the extreme need for communication in a relationship. Both Jim and Mamie talk at each other, neither one giving the other an opportunity to express deep feelings. While Mamie has her two girlfriends as sounding boards, Jim chooses the cornet to articulate the depths of his pain as a black man in America. Spence intimates that the real music should be made between the two people in the relationship with as little outside interference as possible.

NOTE

For more information about Eulalie Spence's life and works, see Bruce Kellner, *The Harlem Renaissance: A Historical Dictionary for the Era*, (Westport, Conn.: Green-wood Press, 1984; repr. New York: Methuen, 1984) and James V. Hatch and Ted Shine, *Black Theater U.S.A.: Forty-Five Plays by Black Americans, 1847–1974*, (New York: Macmillan, 1974).

Hot Stuff (1927) ————————————

Eulalie Spence

CHARACTERS

FANNY KING	The "Red Hot" Mama
MARY GREEN	Fanny's Friend
JOHN COLE	A Numbers Addict
JENNIE BARBOUR	John's Girlfriend
ISADORE GOLDSTEIN	A Jew
WALTER KING	The "Red Hot" Mama's "Daddy" (Husband)

SCENE

The living room in Fanny's flat. The furnishings are simple and in good taste. A full length mirror is at left, and a door opening upon the hallway. At right, two windows overlook the street. Heavy portieres at center back separate the living room from the bedroom.

TIME

The present. About eight o'clock on a winter's night.

AT RISE: FANNY is sitting at a table busily assorting slips of paper. Her friend, MARY GREEN, is sitting close by waiting patiently for FANNY to finish what she is doing. FANNY's beauty is a kind called "striking." Large, flashing black eyes, small mouth, regular features and slick bobbed head. Her skin is a golden brown; her figure sensuous to a fault. MARY GREEN is very good-looking, slender and very fair. Although she is rouged and painted every bit as much as FANNY, she lacks the warmth and vividness of the latter's personality.

FANNY: (*looking at a slip*) Reg'lar Dumb Dora—this one! Plays high everyday, never sticks to a number and raises a helluva noise when they come the day she drops 'em! (*She adds the slip to her little pile.*) Say, there's easy money in this game, Mary. I'm thinkin' uh droppin' the other, pretty soon if my luck keeps up! An' talk 'bout suckers! Believe me, it's here you find them.

MARY: Guess nobuddy can put anything over on you, Fanny.

FANNY: I'd like to see 'em try—just once!

MARY: I ain't got no luck in this game. It gets me how some people make out so well!

FANNY: I don't lose nuthin'; you take it from me. (*She slaps the last slip on the pile.*) Well, that's that! Good day for little Fanny.

MARY: How much?

FANNY: Two hundred fifty!

MARY: My Gawd! Ain't you a lucky kid! Gee! It makes me sick hearing you rattle off hundreds like that! How d'ye do it?

FANNY: Secrets of the trade. You gotta be on the inside! Say . . . who was that six foot sheik you was with at Craig's last night?

MARY: Bill Hogan! Met him in Atlantic City . . . doctor's convention last summer.

FANNY: I know it's the truth! He ain't a doctor, is he?

MARY: He ain't nothing but! Dr. Bill Hogan!

FANNY: Well, what d'ye know! Some looker!

MARY: An' that ain't all!

FANNY: I know he don't hang out round here . . .

MARY: Naw. No such luck. He comes from out West. He's only here for a week on business.

FANNY: Well, I know you're steppin' fast while he's here. I tried to get to your table but I didn't have a ghost of a chance. Walter was along an' you know what that means. A wasted evening! Try an' have some fun with a husband like mine dangling at your elbow.

MARY: Where's Walter tonight?

FANNY: He's gone to Brooklyn to see a feller 'bout a deal. He won't be back till late.

MARY: Well, I got a date myself. Gimme twenty-five pair, Fanny. Ten flesh, five black an' ten nude.

FANNY: Right! Don't know if I got ten flesh, though. (*She opens the drawer of a cabinet in the room and takes out a quantity of silk stockings.*) No, I ain't got but five flesh. You better take five uh these parchment. They're the latest.

MARY: All right. (*She examines the stockings.*) Reg'lar two fifty or I'm a liar.

FANNY: Nothing but! One thing about you, Mary, you sure does know good stuff when you see it!

MARY: An' it don't stop at stockings. I'll tell the world. (*She hands FANNY some bills.*) Twenty-five!

FANNY: Right! (*She tucks the bills in her dress.*) How much you lettin' 'em go at, Mary? I get a dollar sixty-five for the one's I sell.

MARY: That ain't hot enough for my customers. I can't charge more'n a dollar fifty. If I do, they say the price is cold—an' won't buy. Too much competition in this line. (*She puts the stockings in a small black satchel.*)

FANNY: Well, I have a side line, so it's different for me! I don't sell a single dress less'n fifteen.

MARY: An' they're worth forty every one of 'em. Well, kid, I'm off. Dr. Bill ain't got but one more day.

FANNY: What you done with Jack this last week?

MARY: Jack's outa town. Back Sunday!

FANNY: I get you.

MARY: S'long!

FANNY: S'long kid! (*As the door closes on MARY, FANNY picks up the stockings and returns them to the cabinet. The telephone rings. FANNY sits beside the table, takes the phone from beneath the rose tafetta flounces of a tall white-haired doll.*) Hello? Yes, this is Mis' King. What number you say? 429? Yes. 429. Ten cents on the combination. That's sixty cents. All right, Mis' Harris! No, I won't forget! Goodbye! (*She writes the number on a pad and is about to turn away when the phone rings once more.*) Who is it? Oh, that you honey? Not tonight! I'm tired, kid! . . . Well . . . Where we goin'? Half past nine at the usual place! Gone to Brooklyn, won't be back till eleven. I'll leave a note. Oh, Walter won't mind! I'll tell him Mary and me have gone to the theater. Naw . . . Walter don't snoop! If he did I wouldn't live with him five minutes. S'long, kid! (*She hangs up the receiver. There is a knock at the door, and FANNY admits JOHN COLE. COLE is a rather short, dark fellow with a jerky, nervous way of speaking. FANNY freezes instantly at the sight of him and closes the door with a little slam.*) Well? You got my message, didn't you?

COLE: Yes, Mis' King, but I couldn't believe it.

FANNY: Well, it's true. Of course, I'm awful sorry. If I knew any way I could help you out I sure would.

COLE: But . . . (*He swallows convulsively.*) Mis' King, I don't want to make no trouble, but . . .

FANNY: You better not! The idea!

COLE: Two hundred an' fifty dollars! You can't mean it.

FANNY: See here, I'm sorry, darned sorry. If I'd a seen your slip, I'd a played it. Why wouldn't I? I ain't no thief, am I? I dropped that paper. I don't know how I coulda done it! It ain't never happened before. Of course, I'll give you back your fifty cents.

COLE: (*with a gesture of protest*) Fifty cents! Don't talk of fifty cents! I gotta have that money. Mis' King! I gotta have my winnings!

FANNY: (*harshly*) See here! I know you're excited an' all that, but I won't stand fer no funny talk! You gotta have your money! What money! You ain't got no money! You ain't got no winnings!

COLE: (*fiercely*) I believe you took 'em! You ain't honest! You're lyin'! They told me you was like that, but I didn't believe 'em.

FANNY: Now you get outa here! Get right out! The idea! The very idea! (*She opens the door.*) You get right out!

COLE: (*walking to the door*) I'll go, but I ain't done with this. (*He plucks desperately at the band of his hat.*) Nobuddy's gonna rob me an' get away with it. (*FANNY slams the door after him.*)

FANNY: Well, if he ain't got gall! Hm. His two hundred and fifty! Try'n collect, you nut! (*She goes into the adjoining room and returns with an evening gown. She places it over a chair. The doorbell rings. FANNY goes close to the door and calls.*) Who is it?

FEMALE VOICE FROM WITHOUT: Customer, Mis' King.

FANNY: (*opening the door*) Hello! I can't seem to remember you. (*She looks keenly at the newcomer.*)

JENNIE: I ain't bin here before! A friend uh mine told me you had some pretty dresses. Have you got any more left.

FANNY: Sure. Come in. I got some just your size. (*She closes the door and motions toward the bedroom.*) Step right in here, will you?

JENNIE: (*She is a small dark girl with a sharp decisive quality about her voice.*) Just a minute, Mis' King. You're a number agent, ain't you?

FANNY: Yes. You want to play a number?

JENNIE: (*coldly*) Listen, I didn't come here 'bout no dresses . . .

FANNY: (*slowly*) Oh! Well, what the devil did you come fer?

JENNIE: John Cole's a friend uh mine—

FANNY: (*with a slight sneer*) Oh! Very interesting! He sent you to collect for him, did he?

JENNIE: No. I told him I'd come and collect. An' what's more, I'm goin' to keep my promise.

FANNY: (*sharply*) I ain't got no time to waste on you.

JENNIE: You'se got time to hand over that money.

FANNY: Try an' get it! You make me laugh, you do! (*She takes a seat, crosses her legs in a leisurely fashion and surveys the other insolently.*)

JENNIE: Mebbe yuh won't laugh when yuh hears what I gotta say.

FANNY: Say, are you as looney as your boyfriend?

JENNIE: (*angrily*) Yuh can steal all the silk dresses an' stockings yuh wants—I don't care! But when it comes to stealin' cold cash what don't belong to yuh, that's where I take a hand!

FANNY: Well, of all th—

JENNIE: Listen to me! I work in the same building with Walter King. I know the name of the firm he works for. Want to know their name? See yuh don't. Well, yuh shipping clerk daddy ain't pinin' to go up the river, is he?

FANNY: (*springing to her feet*) How dare you! Get outa here, right now, you dirty little . . .

JENNIE: Cut that! I know two people who bought dresses from yuh. They're friends uh mine. Do yuh want 'em to go down to twenty-eighth street with me as witnesses?

FANNY: That kinda bluff won't go here. You got some nerve, I'll tell the world!

JENNIE: Not more'n you'se got.

FANNY: Get outa here! You don't know nothing! Think you're smart, don't you?

JENNIE: Saltzberg and Olinsky. Fifth floor—I work on the sixth. If you don't come across, I'll be there first thing in the mornin'.

FANNY: You can go to hell for all I care—

JENNIE: (*walking over to the door*) All right. I see it suits you if your daddy takes a long rest in the cooler. But lemme tell yuh somethin' kid: he won't go alone. You're his accomplice an' yuh'll get yours same ez him! (*She opens the door, but FANNY, after a moment's hesitation, runs up to her and lays a detaining hand on her arm.*)

FANNY: Close that door.

JENNIE: What fer?

FANNY: I want to tell you somethin'.

JENNIE: (*closing the door*) Well? There's only one thing I'm willin' to hear.

FANNY: I'll give you the money. I can't afford to have you squeal. How do I know you won't tell no how?

JENNIE: Yuh don't know. But you got my word that I won't. I ain't no liar.

FANNY: You might. Just to get even.

JENNIE: I ain't got no love fer Saltzberg and Olinsky, an' I ain't got none fer you. But just the same, I ain't one fer doin' my own people like some folks I know.

FANNY: (*opens the cabinet once more. She takes out a roll of money and hands it to JENNIE.*) Just like it come in.

JENNIE: All right! I'll give it to John. This is a losin' game anyhow, but it could be played on the level. (*She goes out.*)

FANNY: (*closes the cabinet with a slam. She taps impatiently with her neatly slippered foot.*) Dirty little shine! She'd a done it too! (*She snatches up the evening dress and moves toward the bedroom. There is a discreet knock at the door. FANNY throws the dress over the chair once more and opens the street door with an angry jerk. On the threshold stands ISADORE GOLDSTEIN, a Jewish peddlar of questionable reputation. He is good-looking, sleek, possessing an ingratiating smile and a familiar manner. In his hand he carries a briefcase.*)

FANNY: (*shortly*) Well?

GOLDSTEIN: I got something what you should see.

FANNY: Beat it. I don't want nuthin'. (*She makes a movement to slam the door.*)

GOLDSTEIN: (*staying the door with his hand*) Why you should be so mean to me? A good friend of yours, Miss Green, she tells me . . .

FANNY: I ain't got no money to buy nothing.

GOLDSTEIN: I ain't ask you should buy what you don't see.

FANNY: (*stepping aside*) Well, come in an' be quick about it. I gotta go out.

GOLDSTEIN: (*opening his suitcase*) I got something here what is such a bargain you never see. Now, wait! I know you know good stuff. Miss Green she tell me you good picker. Now . . . What you say? (*He shakes out a beautiful ermine wrap.*) I see already you like it. Well, try it on.

FANNY: Gee, it's a beauty! (*She strokes the fur lovingly.*)

GOLDSTEIN: Try it on. It don't cost you nuthin' to try it on. (*He places the wrap about FANNY's shoulders. She glides up to the mirror and preens herself, like a bird. GOLDSTEIN watches her with a gleam of admiration in his eye.*) You look like one queen. Ain't a man wouldn't fall dead fer you in such a coat. Turn round. So. You don't need I should tell you nuthin'. You got eyes in your head. Well, what you say?

FANNY: (*unable to tear her eyes away from her image in the mirror*) How much?

GOLDSTEIN: Cheap. Dirt cheap. If I would sell this coat you couldn't buy it. I give it away, that's all.

FANNY: How much?

GOLDSTEIN: You want to know how much you pay for this coat in Jaeckels? In any big house?

FANNY: I ain't buyin' it from Jaeckels', see?

GOLDSTEIN: I know that. Now that coat—I am givin' it away fer two hundred fifty. I gotta have cash tonight. If I would wait till tomorrow, I could get twice that easy. But I can't wait, see? I gotta get rid of it tonight. Two hundred fifty an' it's a present. What you say?

FANNY: (*derisively*) Know anymore good jokes?

GOLDSTEIN: You think I'm jokin'?

FANNY: I know you're jokin'. (*She takes off the wrap and hands it to GOLDSTEIN.*) Here. I ain't crazy if you is. Say, do I look like two hundred fifty spot cash?

GOLDSTEIN: You look like a million dollar kid to me. Say, would you pass up such a coat like this? It don't suit nobody but you.

FANNY: Then you better give it to me. Make it a present like you said.

GOLDSTEIN: That's just what I'm doin'.

FANNY: Come off!

GOLDSTEIN: Mebbe we can make it a good business. How much you got?

FANNY: A clean hundred an' not another cent.

GOLDSTEIN: (*shaking his head*) Think again, kid.

FANNY: Pack up yuh coat! Reckon we can't do no business.

GOLDSTEIN: (*coming close to her and stroking her arm*) Mebbe you got something what ain't money.

FANNY: What you mean?

GOLDSTEIN: You know what I mean. (*He places his arms about FANNY's waist.*)

FANNY: (*without drawing away*) Get out. I'm a respectable, married woman, an' don't you forget it.

GOLDSTEIN: Who said you ain't? If you wasn't respectable, I wouldn't make no bargain with you. Get me?

FANNY: I got a husband.

GOLDSTEIN: Well, why not? A fine looking girl what you is don't have no trouble getting husbands. Mebbe we make a bargain. What you say? How much you got over a hundred?

FANNY: Not a red cent.

GOLDSTEIN: (*hesitating*) If you could make fifty more. (*FANNY shakes her head.*) Twenty-five? (*FANNY shakes her head.*)

FANNY: You said yourself, I was a million dollar kid. (*She goes up close to him, puts her arms slowly about his neck and kisses him. GOLDSTEIN holds her close, returning her kisses hotly.*) Well?

GOLDSTEIN: (*thickly*) You win, you little brown devil. (*He takes the coat and wraps it around FANNY.*) Well, where's the money? When do I get paid?

FANNY: C.O.D. (*She goes into the bedroom. The portieres close behind her. GOLD-STEIN hesitates and then follows her.*)

THE VOICE OF GOLDSTEIN: You say you got a husband?

THE VOICE OF FANNY: Sure.

THE VOICE OF GOLDSTEIN: He wouldn't come in now an' go for getting excited, would he?

THE VOICE OF FANNY: Naw. He's in Brooklyn. (*The living room door opens slowly. A tall, dark fellow enters. He closes the door and replaces the key in his pocket. He notices the suitcase, frowns in a puzzled fashion and then passes in his same quick manner into the bedroom. There is a loud exclamation, another and another. The sound of a blow and fall. GOLDSTEIN dashes wildly out of the room, WALTER KING in full pursuit. GOLDSTEIN grabs his hat and suitcase, but fumbles at the door. KING yanks him away, opens the door and with a well aimed kick sends the Jew sprawling. The latter scrambles to his feet and plunges out of the room. KING picks up the suitcase and hurls it after the peddlar, slamming the door. Breathing rapidly and heavily, he re-enters the bedroom.*)

VOICE OF FANNY: Lemme alone! I didn't do nuthin'. (*She utters a loud scream. There is the sound of scuffling and other loud screams, sobs and moans. There is never a word from KING.*) Yuh's killin' me! Gawd! Oh! Murder! Murder! (*Shriek after shriek rents the air. There is a loud knocking on the hall door. The shrieks cease. KING comes out. He walks up to the mirror and adjusts his tie and collar. He flicks a bit of thread from his coat and puts it on. He takes up his hat and puts that on. He listens for a moment to the loud sobs and moans in the adjoining room. Then he walks to the hall door, opens it and goes out, banging the door behind him. The moans become noticeably fainter. There is a silence. The portieres are parted and there stands FANNY in a most dishevelled condition. Dangling from one hand is the beloved ermine wrap. She places the wrap close to her face, stroking it with her cheek. She braces up suddenly.*)

She slips the coat about her shoulders. She walks across the floor, painfully, and then as she reaches the mirror, a little sob breaks from her.)

FANNY: The dirty brute! Glad he didn't scratch my face none. (*She smooths her hair. She turns around and around.*) Some bargain! (*She walks to the telephone.*) Bradhurst 2400. Hello! Jim? Jim, this is Fanny. Yes, I'm home. Can't make it tonight, kid. Of course, it's Walter. Tomorrow night, same time. OK. Say, honey, I just bought some coat. It's a peach! You'll see me strut tomorrow night, all right. I don't mean maybe. Goodbye, honey. Goodnight. (*She hangs up the receiver with a sigh.*)

CURTAIN

Episode (1928) ———————————

Eulalie Spence

CHARACTERS

JIM JACKSON
MAMIE JACKSON
MRS. ROBINSON

MRS. JENNINGS
WALT GILBERT
HARRY WILLIAMS

SCENE ONE

The Jackson's apartment about eight o'clock one Saturday night.

SCENE TWO

Another Saturday night in the same apartment, six weeks later.
(*The curtain will be lowered after Scene One for perhaps ten seconds.*)

SCENE I: Let us spend half an hour with the JACKSONS on the second floor of "The Rutherford," an expensive apartment house in Harlem. MAMIE JACKSON's living room is as like every other living room in "The Rutherford" as are the peas in the same pod. MAMIE had seen to that, and felt a glow of satisfaction and content in knowing that in furnishings, at least, all was as it should be. But there were other anxieties. When the curtain rises, we start to inspect the living room, but our attention is immediately attracted by the sound of voices beyond the rose-draped doorway at left.

MALE VOICE: (*exasperated*) Lawd, there yuh go agin'!

FEMALE VOICE: (*tearful*) Kain't yuh even tell the truth? Yuh oughta say there you go agin'. Seems ter me yuh bin out every night for more'n a month.

MALE VOICE: (*placatingly*) Sorry, honey, but Ah's got a date ter-night with some uv the boys.

FEMALE VOICE: (*fiercely*) Seems ter me Ah've heard that before! Well, lemme tell yuh somethin'. Ah's got a date ter-night myself, with one uv the boys! (*The rose portiere is parted angrily and MAMIE enters, throwing herself upon the lounge. Every fiber of her body expresses indignation. What though her skin is somewhat brown? Her sleek, shining head does not own one errant hair. The cut of her bob is flawless. Her eyes, which are snapping now with little flames of wrath, can be soft and gentle, and a more charming figure than MAMIE in her red dress does not dwell within the confines of "The Rutherford."*)

MALE VOICE: Aw, quit yuh kiddin', Mamie.

MAMIE: H'm. See yuh doan believe me.

MALE VOICE: Sure, Ah doan. Say, honey, why'nt yuh ask Mis' Jennings ter the movies ter-night? They's got a mighty fine picture at the Renaissance.

MAMIE: When yuh'd see it?

MALE VOICE: (*guardedly*) Ah didn't say Ah seen it, did Ah?

MAMIE: Well, how'd yuh know it was so good? Bet yuh seen it with some other woman.

MALE VOICE: (*in deep exasperation*) Listen, sister. Let me tell yuh, once fer all— (*JIM, tie in hand, emerges angrily from behind the rose portiere.*)

MAMIE: (*scathingly*) Ah ain' yuh sister, though I might jes' well be for all the 'tenshin Ah gets. (*a pleading note creeping into her voice*) Aw, Jim, kain't yuh take me ter the movies yuhself? Ah'm lonesone, Jim. Seems like yuh out with the boys every night since we been married. Ain't like what Ah thought marriage was goin' ter be. Ah pictured you an' me—jes' you an' me—settin' here on this couch, same's we useter—in Mom's parler; or mebbe you smokin' or readin' the paper, or mebbe talkin' ter me. Yuh ain' never got nuthin' ter say ter me no more.

JIM: (*uneasily*) No, honey—

MAMIE: (*unheeding*) Ah pictured yuh bringin' home yuh friends ter see me. That's what we got a home fer—so's we kin ask friends up an' have some fun. Ah pictured yuh takin' me out places like yuh useter—But now everything's different. Yuh doan love me no more Ah reckon.

JIM: Lawd, there yuh go agin'.

MAMIE: Bet Ah kin tell where *you* goin'.

JIM: 'Tain't no place fer *you*, honey.

MAMIE: (*scornfully*) Low-down prize fights. That's what's takin' yuh out. Yuh'd rather hang around every night with a lot uv tough guys than—

JIM: (*soothingly*) Now, honey, yuh don't listen ter me. Ah bin plannin' a s'prize fer yuh all week. Bin plannin' it all week.

MAMIE: (*doubtfully*) Honest, Jim?

JIM: (*with fine gusto*) Sure, honest! Ah declare ter hear yuh ask a man "honest" everytime he opens his mouth, sure gits mah goat.

MAMIE: Ah doan mean nothin', Jim, only sometimes yuh fergits promises.

JIM: Fergits? Well, any feller kin fergit, kain't he? That ain't sayin' yuh got ter hand him no "honest" everytime he opens his mouth. Ah 'spec you wimmin fergits more'n we men, any ole time.

MAMIE: Mebbe so, Jim. But yuh knows Ah doan fergit nothin'.

JIM: H'm. Wouldn't be so bad ef yuh did fergit once'n a while. Well, keep yuh mind on this s'prize Ah's gettin' yuh. (*He slips hurriedly into his coat. MAMIE jumps up suddenly, her face alight with an idea.*)

MAMIE: (*seizing JIM by his coat lapels as he darts toward the door*) Jim, Ah got ter have somethin' ter keep thinking' 'bout ternight, so tell me what the s'prize is. Please, Jim.

JIM: (*annoyed*) 'Twon't be no s'prize then.

MAMIE: Please, Jim. 'Sides yuh might fergit. If yuh tell me what it is Ah kin remind yuh.

JIM: So, that's it. Yuh kin remind me. What's the matter with me remindin' mahself?

MAMIE: Aw, Jim, tell me. What you bin plannin' ter s'prize me with?

JIM: Ah bin plannin' ter take yuh ter—ter the Cap'tol termorrow night. Now, what do yuh say? Why, what's the matter? Ef yuh doan beat all—

MAMIE: (*drawing back with a bitter laugh*) Oh, yuh bin thinkin' uv me, ain't yuh? Yuh bin plannin' so hard yuh doan remember ter-morrow's Sunday and we got ter spend the evenin' with yer folks in Newark. Oh, yes, yuh bin thinkin' 'bout me hard.

JIM: (*very much annoyed*) Ah knows what yuh thinkin', but Ah did fergit.

MAMIE: (*sneeringly*) But yuh didn' fergit this was Saturday night, did yuh? Yuh never fergits yuh dates with yuh pals and yuh wimmin friends—only dates with me. (*her voice trembling on the verge of tears*) Well, Ah'm goin' ter try my hand at s'prize makin' mahself. Ef yuh thinks Ah needs ter be lonesome one minute longer'n Ah wanters ter—

JIM: (*angrily*) Aw, shut up an' go ter bed. Yuh naggin'd drive any man crazy! (*He goes out, slamming the door. MAMIE throws herself on the couch once more and smothers her sobs in the pillows for a full minute. A discreet knock makes her start up. She dries her eyes hastily. Producing a powder puff from a convenient jar, she dusts her face. Before the caller has knocked for a third time, MAMIE is presentable enough to answer the door. She admits MRS. JENNINGS, her neighbor on the same landing, and MRS. ROBINSON, an acquaintance of MAMIE's. MRS. ROBINSON, plump, plain and homey, wears a coat and a hat. MRS. JENNINGS, tall, lean and shrewd, wears an apron as a badge of her meticulous housekeeping. No sooner are the callers seated than their tongues begin to fly.*)

MRS. JENNINGS: Ah see Jim's out agin'.

MRS. ROBINSON: We seen him rushin' out. He give the door an awful slam. Didn' seem ter see us.

MRS. JENNINGS: He sure looked mad. 'Spose yuh had words agin' about him goin' out. Yuh sure has mah symp'thy. As Ah always tells mah friends, it doan do no harm ter marry a feller what runs on the road. He does his runnin' 'way from home an' stays in of a night when he is home. Joe ain' give me no trouble that way.

MAMIE: But yuh never out tergether. Joe's too tired ter take yuh out when he's home. Seems ter me, it's most as bad as Jim's never takin' me out.

MRS. JENNINGS: (*positively*) It ain' the same at all. Ah has mah own friends, an Joe—he has his. Ah never stays home, lessn' Ah wants ter. Ah sure got friends ter take me where Ah wants ter go.

MAMIE: (*curiously*) But ain't Joe ever mad 'cause yuh go without him? Jim'd be awful mad.

MRS. JENNINGS: Doan yuh fool yuhself, honey. Jim ain't no diff'rent than Joe or any other man.

MAMIE: All men ain't the same, Mis' Jennings. Why, ef Ah had half's many men friends as some women has, he'd kill me.

MRS. JENNINGS: (*derisively*) He would—not! It ain' bein' done this year. Lemme tell yuh somethin'. Yuh ain't bin married long an' Ah hates ter see yuh makin' a fool uv yuhself. 'Long's yuh Jim knows yuh hangin' roun' here yearnin', he'll let yuh yearn, an' have a wonderful time watchin' yuh do it. Yuh wants ter start the way yuh goin' ter keep up. Ain' that so, Mis' Robinson?

MRS. ROBINSON: (*with a reminiscent smile*) Sure, ef yuh kin. We doan all start right, an' that's the truth. Now, take me. Ah bin always fat, or almost fat. When Ah met Charlie, Ah was reducin'. Ah soon found out that he didn' care 'bout no fat girl, so Ah set ter work ter lose fifty pounds. Well, Ah lost thirty-five an' married Charlie. Now Ah'm a homebody, always was, an' always will be, Ah reckon. Charlie likes ter go—but Ah kain't stan' chasin' 'round. Pretty soon, Charlie was goin' without me. Nobody's fault but mine. Well, 'long 'bout the time Ah had put back them thirty-five pounds and twenty more, Ah began ter see lessn' less uv Charlie. Now, guess what happen—Most two years ago, Charlie come one night with a man an' a big bundle. 'Twas a radio set. Well, would yuh believe it, honey, sence that night, Charlie been settin' home reg'lar. Yuh kain't git him out. Ah declare, he hates ter leave it uv a mornin' an' he kain't speak ter no one at night 'till he turns it on. So now we sets home, nights, an Ah ain' bin so happy in the five years we bin married.

MRS. JENNINGS: (*with a faint sniff*) Ah kain't stand the things, mahself, more'n a few minutes. 'Course, ef Ah was dancin'—but jes' settin' still listenin'—not fer me, Ah kin tell you.

MRS. ROBINSON: Ah doan mind. Ah likes it. We has some right wonderful concerts sometimes. Ah reckon Ah likes it most as much as Charlie does.

MAMIE: (*thoughtfully*) Ah think Ah'd like a radio set. Ah wonder—(*She stops, her face radiant with an other Big Idea.*) Oh, Ah wonder ef Jim'd like one, too. Mebbe—Oh, Mis' Robinson, do yuh think he'd stay home ef Ah got a radio?

MRS. JENNINGS: (*in disgust*) Well, Ah never!

MRS. ROBINSON: Well, yuh kain't be sure, but he might. Mis' Taylor was tellin' me last Sunday that her husband bin stayin' in nights sence they got their radio. An' Lawd knows Willie Taylor sure is some gad about. Seems like ef Willie Taylor would stay in ter fool with a radio, an' mah Charlie—

MAMIE: (*trembling with the dawn of a new hope*) Ah tole Jim Ah'd give him a big s'prize, an' Ah'm goin' ter! Ah'm goin' ter buy a radio out'n my own money an' s'prize Jim. Won't he be s'prized though! (*MAMIE laughs in sheer delight.*)

MRS. JENNINGS: Well, uv all the fool ideas, ef that doan beat all! What yuh want ter git a radio ter stay in fer? Thought yuh wanted ter go out?

MAMIE: Oh, yuh doan understan', Mis' Jennings. Ah doan care ef Ah goes or stays, 'slong's Jim's with me. Ah loves him, an' Ah'm terrible lonesome without him.

MRS. ROBINSON: Ah reckon Ah knows jes' how yuh feels.

MAMIE: (*gratefully*) Ah'm so glad yuh gave me that idea. Oh, won't Jim be s'prized?

MRS. JENNINGS: Well, Ah doan think much uv the idea mahself, but then everybody knows his own business best.

MRS. ROBINSON: (*rising*) Well, Ah'll be gettin' 'long. Ah wish yuh all the luck in the world, honey.

MRS. JENNINGS: (*also rising*) Well, Ah 'spose we'll be hearin' plenty music 'cross the hall 'fore long.

MAMIE: (*at the door*) Yuh's cheered me up jes' wonderful. This time next week Jim'n Ah'll be listenin' ter some wonderful music.

MRS. JENNINGS: (*skeptically*) Ah hope so, Ah'm sure.

MRS. ROBINSON: It's worth tryin', honey. Goodbye.

MAMIE: Oh, goodnight. Goodnight. (*MAMIE's friends go out. Happy MAMIE! She rushes into the room beyond the rose portiere, returning immediately with a bankbook. She turns the pages eagerly*). Four hundred dollars! (*MAMIE attempts to express her emotion in the rapid whirl of the Black Bottom. Suddenly she stops short.*) Ah wonder what kind Mis' Robinson got. Ah fergot ter ask her. Mebbe she's still at Mis' Jennings! (*As MAMIE opens the door, she almost collides with JIM, standing at the threshold with a short, pudgy young man.*)

JIM: What's the matter, honey?

MAMIE: Jim! (*She glances in deep surprise from JIM to the stranger.*)

JIM: (*with a chuckle*) Doan say Ah didn' give yuh some s'prize, then. This is Walt Gilbert, a chum Ah ain' seen fer years. Walt—mah wife.

WALT: Delighted ter meet yuh, Ah'm sure. (*Transferring a cornet case from his right hand to his left, he shakes hands solemnly. The party finds seats.*)

JIM: Ain't it a small world though. Here Ah runs into Walt an' Ah ain' seen him in years. Me an' Walt uster be close pals 'fore he moved out Chicago way. An' say, honey, Ah runs into Walt at the club—jes' accident, pure an' simple. Heard a feller playin the cornet an' oh boy! Ah'll tell the world he kin play. An' when Ah takes a good look at the feller, ef it ain't Walt Gilbert! Walt kin sure make that cornet talk!

MAMIE: (*forcing herself to be polite, although she has taken an instinctive dislike to Walt.*) Do yuh play in an orchestra, Mr. Gilbert?

JIM: (*enthusiastically*) Ah'll tell the world, he does. The Jim-Jam-Jem Orchestra. Mamie, that boy sure kin play the cornet.

MAMIE: (*opening her eyes in surprise*) Ah didn't know yuh liked music so much, Jim. Ah'm awful glad though.

JIM: Ah should say Ah was musical! Say, Mamie, yuh won't have to fuss 'bout me stayin' home no more. Guess what?

MAMIE: Oh, Jim dear, tell me. Ah kain't guess.

JIM: Aw guess! Ah jes' bought somethin' sence Ah left here.

MAMIE: Oh, Jim, what? Tell me, quick!

JIM: Well, Ah figgered Ah bin kinder mean, leavin' yuh home so much. So ternight, when Ah left here, Ah thought Ah'd get mebbe a radio.

MAMIE: (*throwing her arms around him with a squeal of delight*) Oh, Jim dear, Ah knew yuh was wonderful!

JIM: (*immensely pleased*) Thought I didn' love yuh no more, didn't yuh? Well, Ah was on my way ter the club ter ask one uv the boys 'bout a good radio, when Ah runs into Walt, here, an' heard him play the sweetest tune yuh ever want ter hear. Gee, but that feller kin play! (*WALT, in a wooden fashion, tries to look modest.*)

MAMIE: Oh, Jim dear, Ah'm so happy yuh goin' ter buy a radio. Yuh couldn't give me nothin' ter make me happier.

JIM: Oh, that was 'fore Ah met Walt. Walt talked me out'n the radio an'—

MAMIE: (*sharply*) No, no—!

JIM: Yuh bet he did, an' he talked me into buyin' a cornet. Jes' think, Mamie! The one he was playin' on ternight. An dirt cheap, too. Ain't it Walt?

WALT: Dirt cheap.

MAMIE: (*faintly*) Not a cornet!

JIM: (*cheerfully*) Yes mam, a cornet. Yuh little Jimmie's goin' ter be the biggest cornet man in this burg 'lessn' a year, 'ceptin' Walt, here. How 'bout it, Walt?

WALT: Give yuh six months ter play real well.

JIM: (*delighted*) Hear that, Mamie? He gimme six months. What's the matter, honey? Ain't yuh glad? Thought yuh was so keen on me stayin' home evenin's. Now, Ah'll be right by yuh side six nights out'n six.

MAMIE: Jim, Jim, yuh doan mean it? Not the cornet. (*shuddering violently*) Ah hate 'em. Lawd, how Ah hate 'em! Once, Mom lived next door to a man who was learnin' the cornet. He never did learn, Jim. Seems Ah kin hear the neighbors now, hollerin' fer him to quit. (*desperately*) Jim, Ah reckon yuh only teasin' me.

JIM: Teasin' yuh? Mah Lawd! Ef you wimmin ain' enuf ter drive a man crazy—

MAMIE: Jim—Yuh didn't buy *that* cornet?

JIM: Ah sure did.

MAMIE: An' yuh goin' ter learn ter play?

JIM: Ah sure am.

MAMIE: (*pleading as if for dear life*) Jim, yuh wouldn't git a radio instead ter please me? Ah'd buy it mahself, Jim. It wouldn't cost yuh a penny. Lemme buy it, Jim. Please!

JIM: (*loftily*) Yuh ain't got no ambition, Mamie. That' what's the matter with yuh. Yuh wants ter listen ter other folks playin' but yuh doan' want yuh own husband ter learn. (*turning coldly away*) Open 'er up, Walt. (*WALT obeys. Relenting, JIM turns once more toward his wife, purposely ignoring the stricken look in her face.*) Now, honey, ef yuh wants ter see how the trick's done, keep yuh bright eyes on Walt Gilbert an' yuh old man. (*JIM raises the instrument to his lips and blows a frightful, gasping note. MAMIE staggers weakly to a chair.*)

WALT: Fine. Now, try agin'. (*JIM obeys in a sort of ecstasy.*) Fine. Now try 'er agin'. (*JIM obeys and at the first choking, wheezing blast, MAMIE begins to laugh, loudly, hysterically, painfully, the tears streaming down her face. The curtain descends while the two astonished men gaze in grave disapproval at the outrageous and unaccountable conduct of MAMIE.*)

SCENE TWO: *Six weeks later. MAMIE is sitting dejectedly upon the couch in the living room, her elbows propped on her knees, her head clasped in her hands. HARRY WILLIAMS, one of JIM's pals, is standing, hat in hand, looking down at MAMIE. He seems anxious to go, yet unwilling to leave MAMIE without some ray of hope.*

HARRY: It sure is tough on yuh, Mamie. Gee! Seems like it kain't be true, Jim gone nuts on a cornet! (*shaking his head sorrowfully*) Well—yuh got ter shake the blues, Mamie. Things got ter brighten up soon.

MAMIE: (*shaking her head slowly*) 'Tain't no use, Harry. Ah useter hope it wouldn't last, but it's gettin' worse. (*sitting up suddenly*) What'd yuh say, Harry, ef Ah tole yuh he blows on that cornet in his sleep.

HARRY: (*horrified*) Good Lawd, Mamie! 'Tain't bad as that?

MAMIE: He doan know Ah'm livin'. Ah 'spec he'll lose his job, soon. He doan think 'bout nothin' but that cornet.

HARRY: We got ter do somethin'. The boys' tired of askin' him out. He's give up everythin'. Gawd, but it's funny—a thing like that happenin' to Jimme Jackson!

MAMIE: Yuh know, Harry, Ah kain't stand it much more. All the folks in the house stop speakin' ter me 'causin' that cornet—

HARRY: Yuh poor kid!

MAMIE: Mis' Jennings slam the door in mah face last week. An' that ain't all, Harry. This mornin' Ah heard her talkin' over the dumbwaiter ter Mis' Simmons. She tole Mis' Simmons that all the tenants had got up a petition ter the landlord ter have us put out. Mis' Simmons said 'twas time we was kicked out.

HARRY: Lawd, but Jim oughter be shot!

MAMIE: Do yuh 'spose they kin get us put out, Harry?

HARRY: Sure not. Leastways, Ah doan think so.

MAMIE: 'Course Ah kain't blame them. Jim plays that cornet after twelve some nights, never stoppin' ter say a word.

HARRY: Well, kid, yuh got ter chase them blues. Yuh lookin' bad, Mamie. Say, 'sposin' Ah takes yuh out ter-night. Aw, come on—

MAMIE: Jim ain't had his supper.

HARRY: Yuh waits on him too much. Quit hangin' 'round here an' mebbe 'fore yuh knows it, Jim'll be follerin' yuh ter see where yuh goin'.

MAMIE: (*shaking her head*) Jim's awful jealous. He'd be sore ef Ah went out with yuh.

HARRY: See here, Mamie. Yuh makin' a big mistake. Now listen, kid. Ah'm goin' ter run along now. When Jim comes in, tell him that some uv the fellers looked Jim up an' ask him ter drop in ter the club ter-night. Ef he says he kain't go, get on yuh coat an' hat an' tell him yuh goin' out with one uv the boys. Yuh needn't mention my name, 'lessen yuh has ter. That'll jolt him some. Make up a string er lies ef yuh has ter. Tell him yuh goin' ter a dance or a cabaret, or somethin' that'll fetch him. See? An' doan yuh wait ter see ef he's follerin'. Jes' put yuh things on an' go out, Jim'll be after yuh 'fore'n yuh kin say Jack Robinson.

MAMIE: Oh, Harry, do yuh think so?

HARRY: Ah sure do.

MAMIE: But where'll Ah meet yuh?

HARRY: Meet me at Hattie Smith's. But, Lawd, Mamie, Jim won't let yuh go— Ah knows Jim—

MAMIE: Ah ain' so sure Ah knows him, Harry. He's 'most a stranger ter me now.

HARRY: Well, kid, buck up. Ef Ah doan see yuh by 'leven o'clock, Ah'll know everything's all right.

MAMIE: (*gratefully*) Yuh awful good ter me, Harry.

HARRY: Aw, save yuh thanks. Ah ain't done nothin' but give yuh some good advice.

MAMIE: An' yuh doan mind takin' me out, 'casin yuh has ter?

HARRY: Gee, Mamie, yuh cert'nly funny. Ah'll be right proud ter take yuh out. Yuh prettier'n most girls, Mamie, an' when it comes ter style—

MAMIE: Yuh awful good, Harry.

HARRY: Aw, fergit it. Well, 'slong, kid. 'Member now ter do like Ah tole yuh. (*Giving MAMIE's hand a firm grip, HARRY hurries out.*)

MAMIE: (*The telephone rings and MAMIE answers it.*) Hello! Yes—This Mis' Jackson. Mr. Cohen, the lanlord? Yes—Ah wish yuh'd speak ter him yuhself, Mr. Cohen. Yes. Ah knows it disturbs the neighbors, but . . . Yes—Yes—all right. Ah'll tell him. Yes. (*The door opens and JIM enters just as MAMIE hangs up the receiver.*)

JIM: Hello, Mamie—(*giving her a hurried kiss on her ear and ducking into the room beyond the rose portieres.*)

MAMIE: Hurry Jim. Ah's kept yuh supper hot.

JIM: (*reappearing, cornet in hand*) Doan need no supper, honey. Run into Walt an' we had a bite tergether. He was 'splain'n ter me—

MAMIE: (*abruptly*) Jim. That was Mr. Cohen Ah was talkin' ter on the phone when yuh come in—

JIM: Mr. Cohen? Who's he? Ah doan know no Cohen.

MAMIE: (*bitterly*) Yuh uster know him, before. Well, seems he knows yuh, all about yuh.

JIM: Yes? How come?

MAMIE: He's yuh landlord, Jim.

JIM: Oh! Well, what'd he want? Yuh paid the rent, didn't yuh?

MAMIE: 'Tain't no rent he wants ter see yuh 'bout. He says the neighbors bin complainin' 'bout yuh cornet an' yuh's got ter stop.

JIM: Ah's got ter stop, has Ah? Well, kin yuh beat that fer nerve?

MAMIE: Stop playin' or move.

JIM: Ah'd like ter see him or anybody else that kin make me stop playin'. Gawd! an' they calls this a free country!

MAMIE: The boys was up ter-night.

JIM: (*surprised*) Here?

MAMIE: Yes. They wants yuh ter come ter the club ter-night. Somethin's on.

JIM: Nothin' doin'. Ah knows that bunch.

MAMIE: (*eagerly*) Ah wish yuh'd go, Jim. Yuh ain't bin out fer more'n a month.

JIM: Not ter-night.

MAMIE: Jim, Ah wants ter go ter a dance ter-night. Won't yuh take me?

JIM: Sorry, kid, but yuh knows how Ah hates dances. 'Sides, Walt's comin' up later ter give me a lesson.

MAMIE: (*She seats herself on the couch. JIM adjusts his music and begins a slow, torturous, nerve-racking rendition of "Old Black Joe." Each note falls just a little short of the true pitch.*) Oh, Ah'm goin' out with one of the boys ter-night, Jim. (*An answering snort is her only answer. bravely*) Goin' to a cabaret after, too. (*Another staggering blast is her only answer. desperately*) Doan wait up for me, Jim.

JIM: (*who has reached a stopping place*) Have a good time, honey. (*The low wail starts once more.*)

MAMIE: Sure yuh doan mind mah goin', Jim?

JIM: (*irritably*) See here, sister! If yuh goin', go on! Yuh keep on interrupting so Ah kain't git no decent practice.

MAMIE: Ah'm goin' with Harry Williams. Harry's *some* feller!

JIM: Sure he is. Have a good time.

MAMIE: Ef Ah has a good time, Ah may not git home 'fore mornin', Jim.

JIM: (*just before he places the cornet to his lips*) Take yuh key, Mamie.

MAMIE: (*who has slipped into her coat and hat*) 'Sposin Ah doan never come back, Jim? What then? (*A hoarse blare of sound is her only answer. Stifling a quick sob,*

Mamie wheels abruptly and rushes out. At the slam of the door, JIM looks up, relieved. He relaxes, sprawling upon the couch, adjusts the cornet at a more convenient angle and blows once more a thundering blast from his beloved instrument.)

CURTAIN

MAY MILLER (1899–)

Riding the Goat (1929)

BIOGRAPHY AND ACHIEVEMENTS

May Miller was born in Washington, D.C., on January 26, 1899, to Annie May Butler and Kelly Miller. May Miller and her four siblings grew up in the John M. Langston house on the Howard University campus where her father served as a sociology professor and scholar. Founder of the Moorland-Spingarn Research Center at Howard University, Professor Miller was sought after by other intellectuals such as W. E. B. Du Bois, Carter G. Woodson, Alain Locke, and Booker T. Washington. The children were encouraged to excel, and May, particularly, was prompted to write poetry and plays by her father who was a poet. May attended Paul Laurence Dunbar High School where she was taught by two notable black women dramatists, Angelina Weld Grimke (*Rachel*, 1916) and Mary Burrill (*Aftermath*, 1919, and *They That Sit in Darkness*, 1919). She enrolled at Howard University in 1916, and studied drama and participated in the Howard University Dramatic Club, organized by Montgomery Gregory and Alain Locke. Upon completing Howard University, she taught speech, dance, and drama at the Frederick Douglass High School and other schools in Baltimore. She married John Lewis Sullivan, who continued to be supportive of her literary pursuits after she retired from the Baltimore schools in 1944. May Miller Sullivan resides in Washington, D.C., where she continues to write and to share with interested scholars the details of nine decades of living.

A close friend of Georgia Douglas Johnson and a host of African American writers in Washington, D.C., and across the United States, May Miller has watched America grow and change through the twentieth century. Her plays and poetry reflect a society in transition but one that recognizes that people of all color want the same things in life: physical, emotional, and financial security. The bulk of Miller's plays were written between 1920 and 1945; thereafter, she began devoting her efforts to writing stories and poetry, which garnered for her numerous literary awards.

Her contribution to black drama is almost inestimable. Her pioneering efforts began as early as 1916 when she involved herself with Montgomery Gregory, Alain Locke, and others to create a black drama movement. Together with a group of artists, Miller struggled to write, direct, perform in, and produce quality shows with a strong degree of professionalism at Howard University. She won several drama prizes during the 1920s and 1930s, beginning with an award presented to her at graduation from Howard University for her play *Within the Shadow*. Her play *Bog Guide* won third place in a 1925 *Opportunity* play competition; this was no small honor given that 65 plays had been submitted to this literary contest. One year later, she won an honorable mention in drama from *Opportunity* for *The Cuss'd Thing*. Her play *Scratches* appeared in 1929 in the *Carolina Magazine* of the University of North Carolina at Chapel Hill. One year later in 1930, two of her plays, *Graven Images* and *Riding the Goat*, were included in Willis Richardson's anthology *Plays and Pageants from the Life of the Negro*.

Miller was catapulted into national prominence when in 1934 she and Willis Richardson published *Negro History in Thirteen Plays*. Her plays in this anthology include *Christophe's Daughters*, *Harriet Tubman*, *Samory*, and *Sojourner Truth*. Many of Miller's plays were produced in Baltimore schools and churches and at such places as Howard University, Morgan State College, Dillard University in New Orleans, and at St. Augustine College in Raleigh, North Carolina. Her one-act plays, like those that were cropping up across the country at the insistence of W. E. B. Du Bois, gave Negroes a sense of pride in their black history.

SYNOPSIS AND ANALYSIS: *RIDING THE GOAT*

The play is set in Baltimore and opens with Carter, a doctor and an outsider to the community, complaining about the heat and his heavy work load to Ant Hetty, the grandmother of the young woman with whom he is in love. Ant Hetty is folksy and humorous as is apparent when she tells Dr. Carter that he should not take a patient like Ike Riles seriously because Ike has "made hisself sick a-thinkin' so. Ain't he been arguin' wid hisself fo' twenty years 'til now even him is convinced he's dyin'?"

Ant Hetty seems to like Dr. Carter, except that she can not understand why he talks negatively about the United Order of Moabites, of which he has been elected the Grand Master. To Ant Hetty, the lodge is one of the most important and prestigious organizations in her community. When Dr. Carter tells her that he thinks it is ridiculous to dress in cumbersome regalia and ride a goat through the streets in scorching heat, Ant Hetty immediately sees the barriers between this educated man and herself and the poor, uneducated community to which he ministers. She warns him to speak softly when he chastises the values and practices of the people he depends on for his very survival.

Ant Hetty later tries to convince her granddaughter, Ruth, to talk to Dr. Carter about supporting the lodge. When Ruth admits that she does not see the importance of the lodge, Ant Hetty reminds her that her grandfather built his life around the United Order of Moabites and that the lodge is what black men join in order to keep their community whole. Ant Hetty brags of how the lodge paraded for her husband's funeral and gave him a going out deserving of a king. When Ruth pretends that she does not see what difference all this makes in the black community, Ant Hetty snaps, "I didn't 'spect you to see. But, child, you'd better hurry an' learn that you gotta see lak some other folks sees if you wanta git alon'! Take Doctor Carter now. He needn't 'spect to get too uppish fo' the lodge an' still come down hopin' to 'tend these folks." She tells Ruth that Dr. Carter must know that he cannot separate himself from the community and yet hope to have them come to him when they are ill. Ant Hetty, and later Chris, intimates that Ruth has allowed her education to alienate her from the poor of their community.

When Ruth tries to convince Dr. Carter to participate in the lodge's annual rituals, he insists that he will not degrade himself. Ruth, though she knows that women are not allowed to join lodges, disguises herself in Carter's costume and rides the goat in his place. Meanwhile, Dr. Carter changes his mind, decides to ride in the parade, and comes back to pick up his robe from Ant Hetty's house. He's too late because Ruth has already gone in his place. The plot thickens, however, when Christopher Columbus Jones, son of a black businessman in the community who is in love with Ruth and who despises Dr. Carter, suspects that Ruth has ridden the goat. He chases her after the parade, trying to prove that Ruth and not Dr. Carter was in the parade. In the nick of time, Ruth throws off the robes and Dr. Carter puts them on before Christopher bursts through Ant Hetty's door to accuse her of being a traitor. Christopher says, "Ruth, you oughta be 'shamed of yourself agoin' back on your own folks fo' some outside nigger." When the robed Dr. Carter greets Christopher, he backs down and salutes his Grand Master. Ruth saves the day by teaching Dr. Carter how to live in their community. The play ends with Dr. Carter's reputation intact and with Ant Hetty approving of their relationship.

Riding the Goat is one of the few early plays by black women that deals with the black middle class. Dr. Carter has to be taught, by two women, Ant Hetty and Ruth, that it is unwise to ridicule those values and practices that are held in high regard in the uneducated black community in which he works. Portrayed as a hardworking, caring physician, his only flaw seems to be a touch of haughtiness. He thinks he has risen too far above the likes of this little illiterate community to share in their rituals. May Miller cleverly emphasizes that the black community traditionally has been steeped in rituals that have enabled them to survive the middle passage, slavery, reconstruction, and beyond. She saturates this one-act comedy with the experiences of blacks that have allowed for Dr. Carter to enter the middle class. With a little help, Dr. Carter comes to understand the value in seeing things as others see them in order to get along with the community, as Ant Hetty remarks. Miller suggests in *Riding the Goat* that education is the key to helping the black race rise above its oppression, but that education must be practical as well as academic. She seems to be arguing that education is of little value if it does not train the person to contribute significantly to his community.

May Miller's plays, in general, depict black men and women in good, sustaining relationships. *Riding the Goat* is a typical Miller play in that Dr. Carter and Ruth work as a team. Ruth, when it appears that Dr. Carter's vision is blurred, serves as a guiding light in their love relationship. Miller's black men and women are not derisive, critical, or insensitive. Instead, they join forces to tear down barriers that threaten to prevent them from giving their best to each other and to their community.

Just as Ruth serves as a beacon of hope for Dr. Carter, so does Ant Hetty function as a guidepost. Miller imbues Ant Hetty with an ancient African ancestral spirit. Ant Hetty is the embodiment of Mother Africa in her wisdom, humor, generosity, strength, endurance, and cultural practices or rituals. She teaches Ruth that no one person can be whole if the community is fragmented. She is the sturdy bridge on whose back Ruth has crossed to become a healthy, whole black woman.

NOTE

For more details about Miller's life and works, see Winifred L. Stoelting, "May Miller," in *Afro-American Poets Since 1955*, edited by Trudier Harris and Thadious M. Davis, *Dictionary of Literary Biography* (Detroit: Gale, 1985), pp. 241–47.

Riding the Goat (1929) ⸺⸺⸺⸺

May Miller

CHARACTERS

WILLIAM CARTER	A Young Physician
RUTH CHAPMAN	
ANT HETTY	Ruth's Grandmother
CHRISTOPHER COLUMBUS JONES	The Lodge Inspector

SCENE

The sitting room of Ant Hetty's home. The action takes place in South Baltimore in a community of draymen.

TIME

Six o'clock of a June evening in the early party of the twentieth century.

SCENE OPENS: The stuffy sitting room of ANT HETTY's home. In the side right wall down stage, a door leading outside. When the door is open, a white stoop and a few white steps can be seen. In the middle of the left wall is a door leading to the kitchen. The room is furnished with the usual three-piece parlor set upholstered in red plush. Diagonally across the corner, an easel supports a portrait of a heavy-set man. Stretched from the table in the middle of the room to the back of a chair is an ironing board before which ANT HETTY stands ironing. She is a stout dark woman of about sixty. Her gingham house dress is open at the throat and a pair of well-worn bedroom slippers are more off her feet than on.

When the curtain rises, she pauses in her ironing of a stiffly starched white dress. She turns the iron upon the board and wetting her finger, tests the heat. She sighs, shakes her head, dries her face on the end of her apron, and then taking the iron, goes into the kitchen humming. She returns with another iron and continues her work singing "Such a Meetin's Goin' Be Here Tonight." When she is half through the second chorus, a knock is heard at the outer door. ANT HETTY calls without stopping at her work.

ANT HETTY: Who's there?

CARTER: It's I, Carter.

ANT HETTY: Why don't cha come on in then? (*CARTER enters with a physician's bag in his hand and a bundle under his arm. He is a slender brown fellow of medium height, neatly dressed in a dark suit. As he enters he takes off his straw hat and mops his brow with a pocket handkerchief.*)

CARTER: Good evening. How're you this time, Ant Hetty? (*He sits on the sofa.*)

ANT HETTY: (*She adjusts the ironing board so that she may see him as she talks.*) Well, son, I guess I can't complain none. Is it hot 'nough fo' you?

CARTER: Too hot with all the work I've had to do.

ANT HETTY: You jest wait, honey, 'til I finishes ironin' this dress an' I'll make you some cool mint water.

CARTER: Thanks.

ANT HETTY: An' the worse is there ain't no change in sight. That wasn't no wet moon that riz las' night. It was there a-shinin' over them rooftops as clear as a whistle—nary a rain ring 'bout it.

CARTER: You can't tell; maybe we'll catch a stray shower.

ANT HETTY: No, I don't b'lieve it. Them stray showers might fool the moon, but they nevah fools Ant Hetty. Sho as it's gonna rain, my feet and limbs begins to trouble me; an' ain't I been standin' on my feet most nigh all day widout ache nor pain? Anyhow who'd want a shower today—the day of the parade?

CARTER: I would.

ANT HETTY: (*turning around abruptly*) Huh?

CARTER: Nothing.

ANT HETTY: (*She takes the dress off the board and drapes it carefully over the back of a chair. She talks to the dress as she smooths its folds.*) Now you'se already spick and span fo' that perade tonight; ain't cha? (*Looking up she remembers CARTER. She takes the ironing board under her left arm and carries the iron in her right hand. She starts toward the kitchen.*) Wait a minute, son, an' your Ant Hetty'll fix you up. (*She goes into the kitchen.*)

(*CARTER stares at the white dress with a frown. He opens the bundle that he brought with him and shakes out his uniform. Holding it at arm's length, he views it with disgust.*)

CARTER: Damn that lodge and all its parades! (*He throws the costume on the floor as ANT HETTY enters carrying a glass of her concoction. He hastily, almost guiltily, replaces the costume on the sofa.*)

ANT HETTY: Now drink that, honey, 'cause you mus' be tir'd chasin' roun' all day in this heat 'tending niggers. Since you been gran' mastah looks lak folks tryin' to outdo one 'nother callin' you.

CARTER: And before I joined the lodge, the same people wouldn't even consider me. (*He takes the proffered glass.*) Thanks.

ANT HETTY: (*sitting in the rocker and watching CARTER as he drinks*) What was you doin' down in Haw Street so lon' befo' perade time?

CARTER: I had a call down the street and I dropped in thinking maybe Ruth would be home early today.

ANT HETTY: Yes, Ruth'll be alon' in a little while now. But Lawd, who's sick in our street now?

CARTER: Mrs. Riles called me to see Mr. Ike.

ANT HETTY: I 'clare ev'ry time that nigger gets tir'd of workin' he gits 'nother spell of rheumatics.

CARTER: Ant Hetty!

ANT HETTY: It's the truf. Lon' time ago I tol' Mary Riles that there wasn't nothin' the mattah wid Ike but laziness, an' she knows it.

CARTER: But he is sick.

ANT HETTY: 'Course he's sick. He's made hisself sick a-thinkin' so. Ain't he been arguin' wid hisself fo' twenty years 'til now even him is convinced he's dyin'?

CARTER: But it's not so easy to convince a doctor.

ANT HETTY: Yes 'tis. Don't I remember ten years ago Mary Riles come runnin' in here. Me an' Mistah Chapman was settin' at the dinner table. She was a-weepin' an' sobbin' out that the doctor said Ike couldn't live 'nother week. I says to her then, "Mary Riles, you dry them tears. Ike'll bury the three of us." There was my Sam a-settin' there as strong as 'n ox; ain't he gone now an' Ike's a-livin' on? Too bad though he can't march in that perade today.

CARTER: It's too hot for parades.

ANT HETTY: That you, the gran' mastah, a-talkin' 'bout it's too hot fo' perades?

CARTER: The heat's enough without having to wear that heavy regalia.

ANT HETTY: But it's only round the block that you has to go. Jest think of all the folks from Fremont to Green Street that'll be standin' on the corners to see the candidates in review!

CARTER: (*bitterly*) How interesting for me!

ANT HETTY: Yes, you know Sara Blake's boy, James, jest turned eighteen an' that reformed scapegoat of a husban' of Rachel Lee's is both 'mong the candidates.

CARTER: Plague the candidates and their parade! I'm getting tired of all this useless thumping over cobblestones. Work all day, and parade all night. I can be just as good a doctor to them outside the lodge as in it.

ANT HETTY: Sh! son, be careful there. Of course, you'se talkin' to your Ant Hetty, but there's them that wouldn't understan'. The gran' 'xalted ruler of the United Order of Moabites can't afford to talk thata away.

CARTER: No, I guess not. All in the line of duty.

ANT HETTY: Now ain't that jest lak a man atalkin' 'bout duty an' there's fifty others wantin' your place. A woman ought to have it; she'd know a good thing.

CARTER: Any woman who'd want it is welcome to the trouble.

ANT HETTY: Oh, there's plenty. I ustah hear my poor dead Sam talk 'bout a woman who hid in a closet at her husban's lodge meeting an' heard an' saw all the 'nitiation. Nobody knew that she was there; but jes' as they was 'bout to leave, she sneezed an' they opens the closet an' there she was.

CARTER: (*laughing*) What did they do to her?

ANT HETTY: They give her a choice—she could jine the lodge or die.

CARTER: Which did she take?

ANT HETTY: She went aridin' the goat, of course.

CARTER: (*rising and taking his bag*) It must have been funny. I wish I could have seen that performance. (*He starts to roll the uniform to make a bundle.*) Ant Hetty, I guess I had better not wait for Ruth. I have a call on Fremont Avenue and I'll be back this way later.

ANT HETTY: All right; but why you gotta tote that uniform up an' down the street to get it all messed up?

CARTER: (*quickly dropping the uniform*) Thanks. I hated to have to bring it with me, but I feared that I could not get uptown again. (*laughing as he pauses in the doorway*) And, Ant Hetty, be sure to take good care of the grand regalia of the grand exalted ruler of the United Order of the Moabites. (*He goes out.*)

ANT HETTY: (*Following CARTER to the door.*) I wonder why he was laffin', the young upstart! (*ANT HETTY goes to the sofa and smooths the rumpled uniform. She straightens the chairs, carefully arranges the much fondled white dress over her arm and starts toward the kitchen.*)

(*RUTH enters. She is a tall, well-developed brown girl of about eighteen. Her smoothly brushed hair and the pretty checked gingham she wears bespeak personal care.*)

RUTH: Hello, grandma!

ANT HETTY: (*pausing at the kitchen door*) How'd you make out this time, child?

RUTH: Very well. I rode down though; I was too tired to walk.

ANT HETTY: Did you meet Doctor Carter?

RUTH: (*a little excited*) No. Was he here?

ANT HETTY: Jes' lef' the minute befo' you come in. He lef' that uniform an' I guess he'll be back.

RUTH: (*talking rapidly as if to change the subject*) Grandma, you should have looked in the sewing room today. You know the Framinghams on Charles Street, don't you?

ANT HETTY: (*coming back into the room to listen*) Now listen, who you'se askin'! 'Course I do; ain't them the folks Mary Riles works fo'?

RUTH: Well, the Framingham girl marries next week.

ANT HETTY: You don't say so?

RUTH: Yes, and we finished her wedding clothes today—every stitch by hand. I'm so tired now that I can't see anything but ruffles, tucks and laces. I think I'll lie down a little. (*She starts toward the door.*)

ANT HETTY: (*shocked*) You ain't got no time to sleep an' eat an' see the parade too.

RUTH: It's too hot for parades.

ANT HETTY: (*looking at RUTH closely*) I've heard that 'nough fo' one day. You young ones gits me. You'se too pert fo' your years. There's Doctor Carter now agettin' too high an' mighty fo' parades, says he's tired of useless marchin'. Did you evah hear the lak of it?

RUTH: I don't blame him.

ANT HETTY: Huh?

RUTH: No, mam, I don't see any sense in all that parading either.

ANT HETTY: O Lawd! An' did I evah think I'd live to hear Sam Chapman's granddaughter talkin' lak that!

RUTH: But, grandma, what sense is there in it?

ANT HETTY: What would your grandpap's funeral've been without his lodges?

RUTH: I don't know; I hardly remember it.

ANT HETTY: The paradin' of his brothers wid their swords ashinin' an' their plumes awavin' was a gran' sight.

RUTH: Yes, mam.

ANT HETTY: But the brightest spot in the whole affair was then they lit them candles 'round the coffin an' the gran' mastah stood at the head ahittin' Sam wid his sword yellin' "Rise, Brother Chapman, an jine the order of departed Moabites." They beat on him so lon' an' I was alookin' so close I thought I seen Sam move under them dim lights.

RUTH: Yes, mam, I am sure that was a grand funeral.

ANT HETTY: 'Course there was them as called him a habitual jiner, but I didn't mind. They was only jealous of that turnout, cause Sam was a member of three lodges an' nary a one failed to show up on his big day.

RUTH: But I can't see that that made any difference to him then.

ANT HETTY: I didn't 'spect you to see. But, child, you'd better hurry an' learn that you gotta see lak some other folks sees if you wanta git alon'! Take Doctor Carter now. He needn't 'spect to get too uppish fo' the lodge an' still come down hopin' to 'tend these folks.

RUTH: But, grandma, they need him so.

ANT HETTY: 'Course they does but they won't have him.

RUTH: What will they do then?

ANT HETTY: Jes' what they done befo' he come. That good ol' white doctor is still livin' an' I guess he's got a few mo' of them pills.

RUTH: Yes, and just a few more of us will die.

ANT HETTY: Well, what difference do that make? Ain't people been dyin' since there was folks?

RUTH: It's all right if it can't be helped, but Doctor Carter can cure them and he wants to.

ANT HETTY: If he's so set on helpin' his folks why don't he act lak it? Instid he laffs at our peradin'—I know.

RUTH: Grandma, why are you so anxious about the parade?

ANT HETTY: Ain't your Ant Sara's Jim marchin' wid the candidates? It seems lak ev'ryone's got somebody an' me widout a frazzlin' soul in the line.

RUTH: I don't understand why you would worry.

ANT HETTY: It was so diff'rent when your grandpap was livin'; I had somethin' to watch fo' then. Since he died I been out of it. Then recently I been thinkin', "Here's Ruthie growed up wid a nice doctor an' he gran' mastah." I could hold my haid higher 'n the res'. Now he's 'bout to spoil it all, an' you aidin' an' abettin' him in it.

RUTH: It's not exactly that, grandma.

ANT HETTY: You know, sometimes I wishes you had liked Chris.

RUTH: Please, grandma, don't start that again.

ANT HETTY: 'Course I thinks Doctor's all right in some ways, but them educated chaps always manage to think a little diff'rent. I guess that's where the trouble comes wid you—them sisters at that convent kinda educated you 'way from me.

RUTH: Grandma, I'm not away from you in any way, but I just can't marry Chris. (*Her voice breaks.*)

ANT HETTY: There now, honey, I didn't mean fo' you to git all riz up 'bout it. You'se tired. Set down a minute an' res' while I fixes you a bite to eat. (*ANT HETTY goes to the kitchen.*)

(*A knock is heard. RUTH walks wearily over and opens the door. JONES enters. He is a very dark, stockily built fellow of about twenty-three. He wears the uniform of the order, the long-tail, double-breasted coat with bright brass buttons. The badges of the order decorate his breast. His helmet-like hat is decorated with a finely curled white ostrich feather. As he enters, he grins broadly.*)

RUTH: Hello, Chris! Coming in?

JONES: I guess mebbe I kin fin' time to tell some of my good friends hello; but 'course this is the busy day an' I ain't got much time—me being made the gran' inspector fo' the lodge.

RUTH: (*with an effort*) Isn't that lovely!

ANT HETTY: (*entering from kitchen*) Christopher Columbus Jones, they ain't gone an' made you lodge inspector, has they?

JONES: (*proudly drawing himself up*) Yes, mam, that's jes what they done.

ANT HETTY: You know I always tol' your ma when she give you that gran' an' mighty name that you was gonna be a great man some day. If your ma had only lived to see this day!

JONES: (*complacently*) Yes, 'tis too bad she can't see me, ain't it? What's the mattah, Ruth, you ain't sayin' nothin'?

RUTH: Your uniform does look nice.

ANT HETTY: It sho does but you wouldn't go doublin' it up an' throwin' it all roun', would you?

(*She looks significantly at CARTER's rumpled suit but JONES is busy surveying himself in the mirror which hangs on the back wall.*)

JONES: No, Ant Hetty, 'course not. When my pa give me this suit, it was such a decent suit that I jest keeps it decent.

ANT HETTY: Your pappy bein' the richest drayman down this way, I bet he could give you many a suit.

JONES: Yes, he is rich; but I does take good care of this suit. 'Course I'm not talkin' 'bout nobody, but there is them that is high in the order what don't look haf so good.

RUTH: Many of them haven't the time you have, Chris, because most of them are working since they have no rich fathers.

JONES: Yes, that's too bad, but they oughta fin' time.

ANT HETTY: We that stands an' watches you pass knows who's keerful an' who ain't. (*sniffing toward the kitchen*) That my baby's dinner burnin'? (*She goes into the kitchen.*)

JONES: I thinks mebbe the lodge oughta stan' an' watch itself in perade sometime, then it might reward them as deserves it.

RUTH: Who is unrewarded now, Chris?

JONES: Nobody particular. 'Course lodge inspector is a mighty good job, but I don't see why I couldn't be gran' mastah same as some nigger from outside. I'm jest as fittin' as that doctor chap.

RUTH: Then you aren't satisfied?

JONES: I'm proud all right of this job, but I'd be prouder of that one. Mebbe if I was gran' mastah you'd like me a little better.

RUTH: Chris, I do like you. Haven't we been friends since we were kids?

JONES: You remember how we ustah race scrubbin' the front stoop? You always made yourn whiter'n mine an' got through sooner.

RUTH: You never did like to work.

JONES: Is that the reason you ain't lovin' me?

RUTH: No, I can't say it's that.

JONES: You'se right, 'taint that. You ustah be my gal 'til you went up on Vine Street to that there place wid the high wall 'roun' it. Since then, you ain't been yourself—wantin' something new all the time.

RUTH: No, Chris, I haven't been the same.

JONES: Turned me down wid all them ol' things, huh?

RUTH: I told you I am still your friend.

JONES: Frien'! I don't want you fo' no frien' when that doctor fella's got you fo' a sweetheart. But don't think I'm givin' you up so easy. Remember how I ustah fight all the gang in Haw Street fo' you? I'm grown a little bit but I ain't changed much. (*He starts toward the door. RUTH starts after him.*)

RUTH: Chris, come back a minute.

JONES: What'cha want?

RUTH: What did you mean by that?

JONES: Nothin'.

RUTH: Oh, yes, you did, too.

JONES: Well, do you think I'm gonna let any fella step in an' take the job that oughta be mine an' my gal to boot an' not raise my hand to stop it?

RUTH: What are you going to do?

JONES: Don't think doctors can't make no mistakes an' just remember Christopher Columbus Jones is watchin' him. (*He goes to the front door. RUTH stands in the doorway looking down the street.*)

ANT HETTY: (*entering from the kitchen*) I 'clare wid all these hindrances nobody kin get a bite. Come now, Ruthie, 'cause I know you're most nigh starved to death.

RUTH: (*standing in the doorway*) No'm, I'm not so hungry now.

ANT HETTY: Chris take your appetite?

RUTH: No'm.

ANT HETTY: But you does lak him a little, don't you, honey?

RUTH: Yes, mam, of course, I do.

ANT HETTY: That's right. Jest remember you'll please your granny. Chris is a right nice boy even if he won't work; but Lawd, he don't have to wid his pappy stablin' five horses an' buggies an' everythin'.

RUTH: Chris is all right.

ANT HETTY: Much better 'n some uppish niggers I knows wid new fangled ideas. Now Doctor Carter—

RUTH: (*turning back into the room*) Sh! here he comes.

ANT HETTY: Talk 'bout the devil!

CARTER: (*standing in the open door*) Here I am, back again, Ant Hetty. Hello, Ruth.

RUTH: Hello, Doctor!

ANT HETTY: Anybody out yit?

CARTER: A few folks dressed in white are sitting on their stoops.

ANT HETTY: I know'd it. I was atellin' Sara this mornin' how them folks 'ud have on everthin' but the kitchen stove. (*She goes toward the kitchen door.*) Ruthie, don't forget your dinner. I'm gonna dress.

RUTH: No'm.

CARTER: What's the matter, Ruth? You haven't much to say today.

RUTH: Nothing.

CARTER: I know better than that.

RUTH: It's nothing much, Doctor Carter—

CARTER: How many more times shall I tell you to drop the "Doctor"!

RUTH: I remember, but you're so different from the rest of the men I know.

CARTER: Tell me about that later. Right now I want to know what is troubling you. (*He pushes the uniform in the corner of the sofa and sits down.*)

RUTH: (*sitting in a chair near the sofa*) Are you—are you going to give up the lodge?

CARTER: Why do you ask?

RUTH: Grandma said you were talking doubtful about it.

CARTER: Oh, Ruth, I am sick of all that foolishness. From the day I put on that little white apron and rode a bony gray mare around the block, I've been hating it, and I'm just about through with all of it.

RUTH: They don't think it's foolishness.

CARTER: They've got to be taught.

RUTH: But not in that way.

CARTER: Why?

RUTH: Because I know them better than you do. If you leave their lodge now, they won't have you attend them; even grandma wouldn't and she's no member.

CARTER: Well, if that's the way they feel, let them cut me. I guess I can manage to get along.

RUTH: But they will suffer for it.

CARTER: Which will be their own fault. They ought to suffer.

RUTH: But aren't they your people?

CARTER: Of course, they are, but not even for my people am I going to don that regalia again. (*He grabs the uniform, looks at it a minute in disgust and drops it in a heap on the floor.*)

RUTH: Don't say that! There are too many waiting for you to take just that attitude.

CARTER: Maybe, but let's forget them. (*He goes over to RUTH's chair and takes her hand to help her rise.*) Come here, I want to say something to you.

RUTH: (*standing beside him and nervously measuring heights with her hand*) In these new shoes, I'm as tall as you are—not quite so big though.

CARTER: Bigger in some ways. I guess that's why I care so much.

RUTH: Do you mean that?

CARTER: Surely. Why?

RUTH: Wouldn't you do almost anything for a person you liked that way?

CARTER: You know I would.

RUTH: (*slipping her hand on his coat, coaxingly*) Well, march today—just today, please.

CARTER: (*looking away*) That's another matter.

RUTH: Then you didn't mean what you said?

CARTER: Certainly I did. I'll always mean that part.

RUTH: But you won't march?

CARTER: Ruth, I'm tired. I've been working all day in this heat and heaven knows when I will collect some of those bills.

RUTH: And if you don't stay in the lodge, they may never pay you.

CARTER: Consider it my contribution to charity.

RUTH: You have definitely decided?

CARTER: Yes, and I wish you wouldn't say anything more about it.

RUTH: I can't help feeling that you're unwise.

CARTER: (*exasperated*) You are so crazy about parading, it's really a pity you can't march yourself.

RUTH: William!

CARTER: Excuse me, Ruth. I'd better be going. I'm talking all kinds of ways. Goodbye, Ruth. (*He takes his bag from the table and goes toward the door hurriedly.*)

RUTH: Goodbye! (*starting after him*) William! (*ANT HETTY appears in the kitchen doorway with her white dress on. She is struggling with the many hooks and eyes. RUTH turns abruptly away from the door.*)

ANT HETTY: Fix this, Ruthie. (*RUTH goes over to her grandmother and fastens the hooks.*) Doctor Carter gone?

RUTH: (*slyly kicking CARTER's uniform under the sofa*) Yes, mam.

ANT HETTY: It's gittin' late, an' me not dressed yit. I leaned out the window upstairs an' heard them callin' the line together. Them folks'll be havin' a monkey an' parrot time, an' I'll be missin' it. Have you ate yit?

RUTH: No'm.

ANT HETTY: (*going back into the kitchen*) Well, hurry.

RUTH: Yes, mam. (*She hears a bugle call, goes to the door and looks out. She comes back into the room, views herself in the mirror a minute. Hastily she goes to the sofa, reaches under it and pulls out the suit. Without taking off her dress she dons the costume which is like JONES' except for a bright golden plume on the hat and a large black mask. She views herself in the mirror and goes out as ANT HETTY calls from the kitchen.*)

ANT HETTY: Ruthie, Ruthie, how many mo' times has I got to call you? (*Entering the room fully dressed.*) I 'clare that gal's gone on. (*She rushes to the door and meets CARTER entering.*) Ain't you gone yit?

CARTER: I had. Where's Ruth?

ANT HETTY: She always sets on the Riles' stoop; the steps is higher an' you can see better. I guess she's there. Why?

CARTER: Nothing particularly. I just wanted to tell her something. (*He looks for his uniform on the sofa.*)

ANT HETTY: Why don't you hurry an' git in line? You'se late already.

CARTER: I want my uniform; I thought I left it here.

ANT HETTY: You taken it wid you when you left befo', didn't you?

CARTER: No, I left it right here. (*He looks nervously under the couch. The strands of "Maryland, My Maryland" are heard.*) Oh, well, it's too late now. I could never fall in in time.

ANT HETTY: (*harshly*) You didn't mean to go in the first place.

CARTER: Yes, I did.

ANT HETTY: But you said as how it was too warm fo' parades.

CARTER: I did, but I have changed my mind about that and a number of other things.

ANT HETTY: You sho'lly had me upset 'cause I was athinkin' you was giving up the lodge an' everythin'. I'm sartinly glad to fin' you'se still got good sense. (*The strains of the music are heard again. ANT HETTY opens the street door wide and sits in the doorway. CARTER looks from the window.*) I won't make the corner now. I guess I kin see jest as well from the stoop mebbe. You'd better set here wid me.

CARTER: No, I don't think it wise to be seen. I'm here not there.

ANT HETTY: You'll have to tell them that you was called on a mattah of life an' death.

CARTER: All right, Ant Hetty, I guess I shall have to depend on you to help me tell it.

(*The strains of music grow louder and there is silence for a minute as both ANT HETTY and CARTER watch intently.*)

ANT HETTY: Doctor, ain't they gran'? In the twilight, they looks jest lak 'n army acomin' on. Look undah that lamppost 'cross the street. See Linda Dodd?

CARTER: Who?

ANT HETTY: Her wid the new silk parasol an' no rain in sight.

CARTER: Uh-huh!

ANT HETTY: Watch her bowin' an' scrapin' to ev'rybody jest ahopin' somebody'll ask fo' Lew.

CARTER: Which one do you call Lew? (*The music is very near.*)

ANT HETTY: That's Lew—the fella what's leadin' the ban'. I 'clare I don't know when that nigger prances mos'—when he's leadin' that ban' in perades or shoutin' in church on Sundays. (*They continue to look intently.*) Doctor, look! Who's leading them candidates?

CARTER: Only my assistant could ride for me, and that isn't him, for he's very fat. (*Pressing closer to the window*) That's my outfit, too—mask and all!

ANT HETTY: If I didn't see you asettin' right there, I'd vow it was you. Even got that sway of yourn. (*The strains of music become fainter.*)

CARTER: Of all odd things! How did anyone get my uniform? I would have sworn that I left it right here. I wonder if I could have taken the bundle out and lost it in my hurry; but who in creation had nerve enough to wear it?

ANT HETTY: Some low-down rascal wid the nerve of Judas.

CARTER: (*Starting toward the table and reaching for his hat*) I'm going to find out.

ANT HETTY: Wait a minute. They're disbandin' at the corner. Well, will you look at Sara Blake! She's gone to cryin' on her James' neck. An' there's Rachel Lee jest makin' a fool of herself over that no-count man. (*In disgust she comes into the room but goes to the window.*) I 'clare Chris jest keeps tryin' to talk to that scapegoat in your outfit. The rascal's sho in a hurry an' he's haided this way.

CARTER: (*grasping his hat*) Well, I'll meet him.

ANT HETTY: (*Suddenly turning away from the window, she grasps CARTER's arm and almost drags him into the kitchen.*) Now we'll fin' out somethin' 'bout this rascal. (*As ANT HETTY closes the kitchen door, RUTH dashes in and locks the outer door. She is panting breathlessly, but without pausing she tears off the mask and helmet and undresses rapidly. A knock is heard at the door. She rolls the regalia together and opening the kitchen door tosses it in without looking. She opens the door for JONES who enters sword in hand.*)

JONES: (*breathlessly*) Where's gran' mastah?

RUTH: (*nervously*) Grand Master! What made you think that he was here?

JONES: You ain't foolin' Christopher Columbus Jones. I seen the one what marched in that perade come in here aracin' an' I believes you was the one.

RUTH: I—the grand master!

JONES: What'cha call yourself adoin'? Tryin' to save him—huh. You ain't bided your time right 'cause all us knowed how that doctor fella's been gitting tir'd of us an' we's been watchin' him. When I goes back an' tells them what you done fo' him he better make hisself scarce in this neighborhood.

RUTH: But, Chris, what can you tell them?

JONES: Tell 'em that I knows the doctor got you to march fo' him in our line.

RUTH: You would tell them that!

JONES: Ruth, you oughta be 'shamed of yourself agoin' back on your own folks fo' some outside nigger. (*The kitchen door opens and CARTER, dressed in the uniform, hat in hand, stands in the doorway almost overshadowing ANT HETTY who is behind him. RUTH and JONES stare at him stupidly.*)

CARTER: Good evening, inspector. Didn't our parade move along smoothly?

JONES: (*with an effort*) Yes, sah, yes, sah, sho did.

CARTER: Ant Hetty said she enjoyed it a great deal. What did your friends think of it?

JONES: I ain't seen my friends, but I guess I got time to speak to 'em an' ax how the new inspector done. Well, folks, I guess I'll be movin' 'lon'.

RUTH: Don't forget to tell them how grand I thought you looked.

JONES: All right. Bye, folks.

ANT HETTY: Goodbye, Chris. (*She follows JONES to the door and closes it after him.*) Ruthie, how'd you evah do it?

RUTH: (*sitting on the couch and sighing with relief*) I don't know.

ANT HETTY: Well, you sartinly saved the doctor's skin 'cause there's mo' lak Chris jest waitin' to give him the devil up Sixth Street.

CARTER: But, Ruth, how did you ever carry it through?

RUTH: I couldn't have if you hadn't put on the suit and come in at just the right moment.

CARTER: I confess that I was a little alarmed when I came back and couldn't find that suit.

RUTH: Then you did change your mind? (*She goes toward CARTER and starts to embrace him.*) Oh, Doctor—William!

ANT HETTY: There, now, ain't you got no respect fo' my presence. (*chuckling*) Go on, Doctor, when a gal does that much fo' a man, he oughta hug her. (*She starts toward the door.*)

RUTH: Where're you going, grandma?

ANT HETTY: Jest keep your shirt on, Miss, I'm goin'. I got to talk to Mary Riles 'bout the perade. (*calling from the doorway*) Lawd, child, I knows you mus' be faint wid hunger. You go right out in that kitchen an' eat 'cause nobody's fixin' to lose you. (*She goes out the front door.*)

RUTH: Yes, mam. (*sinking on sofa exhausted*) I'm so glad that's over.

CARTER: (*standing before her*) Ruth, I don't know what to say.

RUTH: Please don't let's talk about it at all. I tremble every time I think of what I did.

CARTER: (*stooping and placing his helmet on her head*) Very well, grand master, just as you command. (*As the curtain falls he kneels before RUTH in a mock salute.*)

CURTAIN

SHIRLEY GRAHAM
(1896–1977)

It's Mornin' *(1940)*

BIOGRAPHY AND ACHIEVEMENTS

Shirley Lola Graham was born on November 11, 1896, on a farm near Evansville, Indiana, to Reverend David Andrew and Etta Bell Graham. Along with four brothers, Shirley Graham grew up in parsonages across the country. It was her father, an African Methodist Episcopal minister, who became a major influence on her life, particularly because he instilled in her a drive to explore the lives of black heroes and a desire to study African culture and music.

After graduating from Lewis and Clark High School in Spokane, Washington, Graham entered a trade school where she became a certified typist and office clerk. Towards the end of World War I, she moved to Seattle where she worked at the Navy Yard until she married Shadrach T. McCanns in 1921. Two sons were born, Robert and David, before the marriage was dissolved in the mid-twenties.

In 1926, when Shirley Graham's father was appointed administrator of a mission college in Monrovia, Liberia, she and her sons moved to Paris where she studied music at the Sorbonne. Beginning in the late 1920s through 1931, Graham studied and served as a music librarian at Howard University and later headed the music department of Morgan State College in Baltimore, Maryland. Graham earned a B.A. and an M.A. in music from Oberlin College in 1934 and 1935, respectively. After leaving Oberlin College, she served as chair of the department of fine arts at Tennessee A. & I. State College in Nashville.

Wishing to develop further expertise in theater, Graham accepted the position of director at the Chicago unit of the Federal Theater Project (FTP) in 1936, and underwent intensive study of the technical aspects of theater, including acting, directing, dance, and working on full-scale productions at Vassar College. Between 1936 and 1938 Graham wrote, designed, and directed plays and composed and conducted musical scores in addition to her administrative work.

Always in pursuit of professionalism, Graham accepted a fellowship to study at Yale University drama school between 1938 and 1940, when she wrote and had produced five plays. After directing a Y.W.C.A. theater group in Indianapolis from 1940 to 1941, she became director of a Y.W.C.A.–U.S.O. camp at Fort Huachuca in Arizona and developed an interest stronger than her passion for the theater; she became a civil rights activist. She fought hard to end discrimination against black soldiers who were mistreated and jailed on minor charges. Consequently, she was dismissed in 1942 for behavior considered un-American.

Shirley Graham, who had kept in touch frequently with W. E. B. Du Bois since 1936, married in 1951 one of the most influential writers, editors, and educators of the twentieth century. She spent her remaining years writing black biographies and working as an activist first in Ghana where Du Bois died in 1963 and then in Peking, China, where she died on March 27, 1977.

Shirley Graham enjoyed a successful career as a professional writer, composer, conductor, playwright, and director. She was a gifted biographer and published such notable books as *Dr. George Washington Carver: Scientist* (in collaboration with George D. Lipscomb), 1944; *Paul Robeson: Citizen of the World*, 1946; *There Was Once a Slave: The Heroic Story of Frederick Douglass*, 1947; *Your Most Humble Servant*, 1949; *The Story of Phyllis Wheatley*, 1949; *The Story of Pocahontas*, 1953; *Jean Baptiste Pointe du Sable: The Founder of Chicago*, 1953; *Booker T. Washington: Educator of Hand, Head, and Heart*, 1955; *His Day is Marching on: A Memoir of W. E. B. Du Bois*, 1971; *Gamal Abdel Nasser, Son of the Nile: A Biography*, 1972; *Zulu Heart*, 1974; *Julius K. Nyerere: Teacher of Africa*, 1975; *A Pictorial History of W. E. B. Du Bois*, 1976.

Prior to Graham's success as a biographer, she devoted a great deal of time to achieving her goals of becoming an authority on African rhythms and the technical aspects of theater, both of which she managed. Her opera, *Tom-Tom: An Epic of Music and the Negro*, which traces African music through to the United States, premiered on July 8, 1932, to a crowd of over 10,000 people. Its second and final performance drew 15,000 people. *Tom-Tom* was the first all-black opera to be produced on a large scale with a professional cast of approximately 500 actors. It was also the first opera by an African American woman to be produced.

Though Graham, while director of the Chicago unit of the FTP, directed a host of landmark plays, including Theodore Ward's *Big White Fog* in 1938 and Charlotte Chorpenning's *Little Black Sambo* in 1939, playwriting seemed more satisfying to her. While studying at Yale between 1938 and 1940, she wrote five plays: *Dust to Earth*, *I Gotta Home*, *It's Mornin'*, *Track Thirteen*, and *Elijah's Raven*. Her plays were produced by the Yale University Theater, the Gilpin players of Cleveland, Ohio, the Florida A&M Players, and by a number of colleges and schools during the 1940s.

Graham had hoped to see one of her plays on Broadway, particularly since there had been initial negotiations for the appearance of *Tom-Tom* there. She feared, however, that the commercial theater of the 1940s would accept only buffoonery and was not yet ready to see professional black actors portraying the very essence of black life.

Shirley Graham was a black artist who concerned herself with developing her craft among peers. Her full-length plays *Dust to Earth* and *Elijah's Raven* are evidence that she was moving in the direction of the commercial theater. Though she never gave up her love of the theater, Shirley Graham was irrepressibly drawn to the beat of new drums after 1940. She believed that her suffering brothers and sisters could be reached and uplifted more effectively with details about black heroes. It was the tom-tom of an ancient African spirit that guided her back into the jungle of American society where black heroes and heroines are often invisible.

SYNOPSIS AND ANALYSIS: *IT'S MORNIN'*

The play is set on December 31, 1862, on a plantation in the South. It opens in the midst of a celebration containing an enormous amount of eating, drinking, singing, and dancing. The party is in honor of Millie, a young woman about 14 years old. When Millie innocently tries to solicit a kiss under the mistletoe from Sam, a plantation hand, Cissie, Millie's mother, clutches his arm, threatens him with her eyes, and tells him, "Don' you touch mah gal!"

As the night progresses, Millie, who is gifted with a singing voice, delights her friends and relatives with spirituals. During Millie's song, Grannie Lou, the oldest living slave on the plantation and the medicine or voodoo woman, recalls that Millie's mother used to sing as beautifully as Millie does until the white overseer began raping her. She tells of how Cissie was once a proud young woman who pranced around as if she were free. The overseer vowed that he would tame her. Grannie Lou recalls the overseer's cruelty to Cissie, "An' when he'd come along da row, she tremble lak a leaf, an' once she fall down cryin' at his feet. He laf an' kick huh wid his foot, not hard, but lak you kick a bitch what's big wid puppy out o' yo' path."

In the midst of the festivities, Missie or Mrs. Tilden, the plantation mistress, comes down to the slave cabins to find out why Millie is singing and dancing on the night before she is to be sold off to a white plantation owner. Mrs. Tilden begs Cissie to understand that she will one day buy Millie back, but for now selling her is the only way she can keep the plantation afloat until her son returns from the Civil War.

Grannie Lou tells Cissie that Millie does not have to go with the overseer if she follows in the footsteps of an African woman who once killed her three sons rather than have them sold away from her. She tells how the wife used a cane knife to chop off the heads of her sons while they stood looking at the sun rise.

Cissie resolves to take Millie's life rather than allow her to be violated by a white master, particularly since she saw the prospective owner touch Millie's breast and terrorize her with talk of using her for his pleasure. The women of the community cry out against Grannie Lou whom they think has put an evil spell on Cissie and is driving her to plan her daughter's murder. Cissie does not heed their cries; instead she tells them that she wants to make sure that "we'n da saints ob God go marchin' home mah gal will sing! Wid all da pure, bright stars . . . " Though Uncle Dave, the community's minister, tries to sway Cissie, she sharpens her knife and turns a deaf ear.

At dawn, when Cissie hears a horse approaching her cabin, she thinks that it is the white man who has come to take Millie away into concubinage. She slips into Millie's bedroom and emerges with her dead daughter in her arms. She is terrified to learn that the person on the horse was a Union soldier coming to tell them that Abraham Lincoln had freed the slaves.

It's Mornin' is a major breakthrough in African American drama. Shirley Graham's interest in African music and culture is apparent in the structural make up of this tightly compressed one-act play. In this powerful drama, she combines dialogue, music, singing, dancing, and chanting while maintaining the traditional Aristotelian structure.

Graham links the blacks in *It's Mornin'* to their African past in several ways. First, she sets up Grannie Lou, the voodoo woman, as a powerful force in the community. Though Grannie Lou is thought to be both senile and crazy, she is respected. When it is announced that Millie will be sold, the women of the community, functioning like a Greek chorus, look to Grannie Lou, saying, "Let huh talk! We allus call huh crazy but who knows? Maybe da voodoo wo'k dat way. Maybe she bile up sompin' dat kin help. What is it, Grannie? What kin we do?" Grannie Lou represents continuity for blacks in that she is the bridge between the religious beliefs of Africans of old and of the colonized blacks of America.

It is through Grannie Lou that stories of heroism about the first Africans in America are passed on from generation to generation. Grannie Lou's story about the courageous African woman who killed her three sons rather than have them sold away from her is Graham's way of emphasizing that blacks are a proud, defiant, and brave people.

From the anonymous African woman's act of courage, Cissie finds the strength to protect her daughter from violation. However, the ending of the play sends out mixed signals in that it is not the African gods but a Christian God who answers the prayers of Uncle Dave and the other community members. Uncle Dave prays, "Oh! Lawd! Our Lawd! Sittin' on yo' great white throne wid de stars a crown o' beauty fur yo' haid an' de earth a mighty footstool fur yo' feet. Lean down ovah da ramparts of Hebbin dis mawnin', and see us 'umble sinners kneelin' hyear. We been prayin' so long, we been singin' so . . . " The answer to the community's prayers comes in the form of the Union soldier who brings news of freedom for all slaves. The news comes too late as Cissie comes out holding the daughter she has murdered to keep free. The play's ending suggests that Graham, though she believed strongly in African culture, was very much a product of the Christianized western world in which she lived.

In keeping with the Christian tradition, the title of the play takes on significance. *It's Mornin'* alludes to the dawn or rise of a new day, just as Jesus arose from the dead after he died on the cross to save mankind. On another level, *It's Mornin'* refers to the mourning that Cissie and the community will experience as they cope not only with the loss of Millie but with the postwar upheaval.

The helplessness that blacks felt during slavery seems to be the central focus of this play. *It's Mornin'* clearly points out that black women in the south have no protection from the lust of white men, a theme that dominated Georgia Douglas Johnson's play *Blue Blood* and, indeed, the literature of many African Americans.

An interesting twist to this play is the treatment of the Big Missie who is traditionally portrayed as mean, evil, jealous, and vengeful. In *It's Mornin'*, Missie is as powerless as the slaves, maybe more so because she does not have the strength of a community behind her as does Cissie. Missie is alone as her son has gone off to war and left the plantation in a state of demise. She has to sell off slaves in order to keep it from being taken over by the lusty white man who wants Millie for his concubine. Missie is depicted as a caring, pitiful woman who is as much at the mercy of the white patriarchy as is Millie.

It's Mornin' was potent when it was produced by the Yale University Theater in 1940; it is no less powerful and poignant for contemporary readers.

NOTE

For more information about Shirley Graham's life and works, see *Current Biography*, 1946; *Contemporary Authors*, vols. 77–80, and Kathy A. Perkins, "The Unknown Career of Shirley Graham," *Freedomways*, (First Quarter 1985), pp. 6–17.

It's Mornin' (1940) ————————

Shirley Graham

CHARACTERS

CISSIE	A Slave Woman
ROSE	A Slave Woman
MILLIE	Cissie's Fourteen-Year-Old Daughter
PHOEBE	A Slave Woman
JAKE	A Crippled Banjo Player
AUNT SUE	A Slave Woman
FESS	A Field-hand, The One Able-Bodied Man On The Plantation
SALLY	A Young Slave
PETE	A Young Slave
MRS. TILDEN	The Lonely Mistress Of The Plantation
SAM	A Young Slave
UNCLE DAVE	The Old Plantation Preacher
SOLDIER	A White Soldier
GRANNIE LOU	The Oldest Slave On The Plantation, Considered A Little Crazy

SEVERAL OTHER SLAVES

PLACE

A plantation in the Deep South.

TIME

The night of December 31, 1862.

SCENE OPENS: Interior of CISSIE's cabin. Before the curtain lifts, music and laughter may be heard. When the curtain rises a party in full swing is discovered. It is nearly midnight and the dancing of the young people to CRIPPLE JAKE's banjo gives over to the joy of the moment. The bare, unplastered room has been decorated with Spanish moss and bunches of holly stuck among the thick greens. In the fireplace down right burns heaps of pine cones. Around the hearth are pots and pans, evidence of much cooking. Drawn close to the fire, as if to warm her shrunken frame, crouches GRANNIE LOU, her black, wrinkled face screwed up as she watches the dancers. Between her lips is stuck an old corncob pipe. PHOEBE and ROSE are in the background talking together. The door center is pushed back on its loose hinges and through this opening may be seen the glow of a bonfire in the yard. Otherwise, it is very dark outside. Above this door hangs sprays of mistletoe, the tiny white flowers drooping heavily on wilted stems. Another door or opening up left leads to the other room. On the mantle above the fireplace is a lighted lantern. On a table down right are piled heavy, crude dishes.

There are shouts of laughter. In the center doorway appears CISSIE. Her gaunt, black figure seems to fill the frame and even though she claps her hands and her words are joyous, there is something strangely harsh about her voice.

CISSIE: Now den, everybody! C'mon! Da eats is ready!

> (*Shouts of delight as the dancers stop. Only MILLIE, who has been doing a solo dance continues the rhythm as JAKE plays the last chord.*)

SAM: Barbeque! Um-um! Ah can smell it!

PETE: Mah mouf am waterin' down!

SALLY: Hurry, 'fore dat smell blow cross da creek an' da soldiers—

PETE: Ain't no soldier gonna git dis hamhock!

SAM: No, suh! Ah'd butt 'im so hard he done t'ink a cannonball hit 'im! (*laughter*)

MILLIE: (*still poised to dance*) Jus' one mo' chune, Jake. Just one mo' chune!

JAKE: Chile, don' you nevah tiya?

CISSIE: (*who has crossed to hearth*) Sho she do! Hyear, we gotta take des t'ings in da ya'd. Ah got conepone dat'll melt 'fore yo' eyes.

JAKE: (*putting his banjo under his arm*) Lead me to hit!

SALLY: (*in the doorway*) Beat you to da pit! (*At this moment PETE grabs her and sets a resounding smack full on her lips.*)

PETE: (*shouts*) Gotcha under da mistletoe! Oh, you Sally! Ha! Ha! (*They troop out.*)

BOY: Come long, Jake, can' cat widout music!

JAKE: (*hobbling along, banjo under his arm*) Dis sho is some New Year's pahty, Cissie. Sho tis!

MILLIE: (*gayly*) Hit's mah pahty, ain't hit, mammy?

CISSIE: Dat's right. Now, take dis pan o' pone. Dey's gettin' cold. (*hands Millie a pan*)

AUNT SUE: (*bustling over to table*) Ah'll take da plates.

MILLIE: (*posing in doorway, her golden brown body half revealed by the thin dress*) Look, Sam! Ah'm under da mistletoe!

SAM: Glory be! (*He dashes toward MILLIE only to find his arm caught in the iron clasp of a forbidding CISSIE.*)

CISSIE: No! (*quietly to MILLIE*) Go 'long, Millie, gal. (*MILLIE gives her mother a troubled look and disappears.*)

    (*AUNT SUE, glancing over her shoulder at CISSIE, follows MILLIE.*)

CISSIE: (*savagely clutches SAM*) Don' you touch mah gal!

SAM: (*frightened*) No mam! (*CISSIE loosens her grasp and he hurries out.*)

ROSE: Sam didn't mean no hahm. Hit's da pahty!

GRANNIE LOU: (*mouthing her words*) Da jack done call in the moonlight, an' da young gal's love come down.

CISSIE: Millie don't know nothin' bout love! (*She goes out with pain.*)

PHOEBE: Huh, Millie's lak a flower; she watch huh day an' night. (*voices from outside*)

PETE: Cripple Jake's gonna play!

SALLY: An Millie'll sing!

SEVERAL VOICES: C'mon, Millie's gonna sing!

MILLIE: Ready, Cripple Jake? Let's go! (*singing*)

> Oh! Walk togeddar, chillun
> (Group) Don' you get weary,
> Walk togeddar, chillun,
> (Group) Don' you get weary,
> Walk togeddar, chillun,
> (Group) Don' you get weary,
> Dar's a great camp meetin' in da promise lan'.
> Gonna sing an' nevah tiya
> Sing an' nevah tiya
> (All) Sing an' nevah tiya
> Dar's a great camp meetin' in da promise lan'.

GRANNIE LOU: (*shaking her head*) Cissie useter sing lak dat . . . Jes' lak huh gal.

WOMEN: (*astonished*) Cissie! Sing?

GRANNIE LOU: Yes, Cissie! She war beautiful! Black as a berry an' lovely as da night. Slender an' swift as a young colt. She nevah walk, jes' prance an' run about da place. Ah seen da buckra eyein' huh, an' she jes' laf. Den come a day when she war very still, Ah donno why, til one night seen huh slippin' t'rough shadows lak a hounded coon crawls tuh his hole to lick his bleedin' wounds.

ROSE: Ah heared dat she war proud, an' dat da ovahseer swear he break huh will.

GRANNIE: (*bitterly*) He did! An' when he'd come along da row, she tremble lak a leaf, an once she fall down cryin' at his feet. He laf an' kick huh wid his foot, not hard, but lak you kick a bitch what's big wid puppy out o' yo' path.

AUNT SUE: (*entering from yard bearing platter of food*) Cissie say bring our eats inside. Let da chillun play.

ROSE: Ain't she commin'?

AUNT SUE: Yes, but she say don' wait.

> (*AUNT SUE is followed by FESS, a good looking slave who is carrying something in his hand and biting at it.*)

FESS: (*speaking between bites*) Um-um-um! Us ain't had no eatin' laka dis since da stars fall! Mah insides is plum scared.

PHOEBE: Whar Cissie get all des vittuals? How come?

AUNT SUE: (*comfortably*) Hit's New Year's Eve, ain't hit?

ROSE: Yes, but us ain't had no pahties since Massa Frank went off to war.

PHOEBE: Sho ain't. What wid ole Missie up dar all alone—sittin' lookin' at po' young massa Charles picture—an' turnin' white everytime da post come Missie us ain't had no time fur pahties!

AUNT SUE: Well, Cissie say dat—

PHOEBE: Shshshsh!

> (*CISSIE is in the doorway. She is walking very slowly, the life gone out of her movements.*)

AUNT SUE: Cissie, you plum tuck out! Com' sit down. (*CISSIE comes slowly toward the fire.*)

FESS: Dis is gran' eatin'!

PHOEBE: You said someum! But, Cissie, whar you git all dis? Ah ain't seen so much—

FESS: (*proudly*) Ah gits da meat.

ROSE: (*anxiously*) You bes' stay outta dem dar woods, Fess. Iffen any dem soldiers cotch you—

AUNT SUE: Yes. How we ebbar git da wo'k done? You da only man on da place.

FESS: (*shaking his head*) Crops failin' anyhow. Massa Charles say . . . but tain't no use. Well, long as Ah can hunt we uns won't starve.

ROSE: Da soldiers take you off to war.

FESS: Ah ain't scared!

PHOEBE: Dey make you fight.

FESS: Maybe dey takes me, maybe dey don'. (*He draws a long, sharp knife from his side.*) Ah kin fight—when Ah wan's to. (*CISSIE is staring at the knife.*)

CISSIE: Hit's sharp.

FESS: (*boasting*) So sharp dat Ah could draw hit right cross yo' troat—an' you'd not know.

ROSE: You means . . . ?

FESS: Until you saw yo' head come fallin' down! Ha! Ha! Ha!

GRANNIE LOU: (*joining him*) He! He! He! (*Their laughter is cut short by a voice coming from the doorway.*)

MRS. TILDEN: Cissie! (*It is the mistress of the plantation. Four long years have aged her. She has a wrap thrown over a thin dress. She looks at the group with troubled eyes.)*

AUNT SUE: Missie!

FESS: *(jumping up)* You wan' something, Missie?

GRANNIE LOU: *(severely)* How come you runnin' round lak dis at night? You'll cotch yo' death o' cole!

MRS. TILDEN: I . . . couldn't sleep. I heard music. Cissie, I was sure I heard . . . Millie . . . singing . . .

> *(Cissie turns away.)*

ROSE: We's jus' havin' a lil' New Year pahty, Missie.

MRS. TILDEN: A party!

AUNT SUE: Yessum. Fess here wen' huntin' today an' Cissie—

MRS. TILDEN: *(turning to CISSIE)* Cissie . . .

> *(Outside there is a burst of laughter and the banjo sounds again.)*

GRANNIE LOU: Come to da fiah an' warm yo'self.

MRS. TILDEN: *(walks slowly to the window and looks out)* They're dancing. Millie's . . . dancing!

AUNT SUE: Yessum—dat chile sho is a caution!

MRS. TILDEN: *(slowly)* Cissie, do they know?

CISSIE: *(very low)* No, Missie.

MRS. TILDEN: Oh, Cissie! But I don't understand. You . . . a party. They're dancing and singing.

CISSIE: Yassum—dancin' and singin'—so Millie'll be happy one time mo'.

> *(The others look from one to the other not understanding.)*

MRS. TILDEN: *(sinking into a chair)* Oh, dear God, have mercy on us!

ROSE: *(alarmed)* Missie, what is it?

AUNT SUE: What's da mattah, Missie? Tell us!

MRS. TILDEN: *(after a pause)* Millie's going away. She's going away early in the morning.

WOMEN: Away!

MRS. TILDEN: They're coming for her at daybreak.

FESS: *(slowly)* You sole huh?

MRS. TILDEN: I had to. The war's beat us down—our cotton's worthless. There's nothing else.

FESS: *(softly)* You sole huh to dat man. He'll take huh down da ribbah!

> *(A shudder passes over the group. Only CISSIE sits like stone.)*

MRS. TILDEN: I'm an old woman. My heart is breaking with your pain, but I'm helpless. Oh if this war would only end—if our men would only come back! They don't know what it's doing to us. They don't know.

ROSE: No, dey don't know.

MRS. TILDEN: It must end soon. There's nothing to go on. Cissie, I'll buy her back—I promise as God is my judge—we'll get her back.

CISSIE: (*dully*) Yes, Missie.

MRS. TILDEN: (*getting up*) I . . . must go now. I— (*She stops, realizing there's nothing more to say.*)

FESS: (*taking lantern from mantle*) Ah'll light you to da house.

(*CISSIE does not lift her head.*)

MRS. TILDEN: (*MRS. TILDEN lays her hand on CISSIE's shoulder and says softly*) I'm glad she's happy—tonight—Cissie.

(*MRS. TILDEN turns quickly and goes out, followed by FESS. Only the fire now lights the room. The pause is filled by voices outside.*)

MILLIE: Have anodder pone! We dassent leave a scrap.

SALLY: (*regretfully*) Ah can' eat no mo'.

PETE: Give hit tuh me!

SAM: Boy, you gonna fall in da creek an' float! (*laughter*)

AUNT SUE: Ah knows now why ole Missie cry all day. Dat man give huh no peace; he say he will hab Millie gal else tu'n us out tuh starve. An' Missie too.

PHOEBE: He'd do hit, kase he's cruel an' hard. He's lak a beast what's scented fresh, young meat. He's ole . . . he'll suck huh blood lak da swamp t'ing. (*She shudders.*)

AUNT SUE: His jowls hang down lak empty 'tatah sacks, an' bacca juice falls drippin' f'om his mouth leavin' a trail o' slime whar he has passed.

(*CISSIE has sat motionless while the others talked. Now she drops her hand from her face. Her eyes stare straight ahead. She speaks as if from a distance, with difficulty, still looking with horror upon a picture etched on her brain.*)

CISSIE: Ah seed him lick his lips an' smile an' grin. Ole Missie beg him wait till cotton bust an' promise him da best bales in da lot. He say he wait no mo' . . . He wan' da gal. Ah seed his han's . . . dey touch huh golden breas'. She was so scared she couldn't run. An' den she scream . . . an' Missie tell huh go. Ah heared him laf an' spit upon da floah!

PHOEBE: (*rocking her body*) Mussy, Jesus! He'p us, Lawd!

(*The prayer is interrupted by GRANNIE LOU dropping a spoon on the hearth with a loud clatter. The women give a start. GRANNIE LOU breaks into a high pitched, crazy laughter.*)

GRANNIE LOU: He! He! He! He! He!

PHOEBE: Make huh stop! Oh!

ROSE: What's da mattah, Grannie? Why you all laf?

GRANNIE LOU: (*mocking*) Mussy Jesus! Mussy Jesus! (*She snickers while the women gasp.*) She don' hab tuh go, Ah tells you, she don' hab tuh go!

AUNT SUE: Let huh talk! We allus calls huh crazy but who knows? Maybe da voodoo wo'k dat way. Maybe she bile up sompin' dat kin help. (*gently to the old woman*) What is it, Grannie? What kin we do? Might Millie run away?

GRANNIE LOU: (*in a high, sing-song voice*) Da ribbah's high, da rain dat fall las' week make all da ma'shes t'ick wid mud an' deep.

AUNT SUE: Den what? Why you all laf? Hit's Cissie gal been sole!

PHOEBE: Aw, Auntie, why you askin' po' ole Lou?

GRANNIE LOU: (*sharply*) Shut yo' mouf! Ah ain't so ole dat Ah don' membah! (*turning to the others*) Ain't Ah nebbah tole you bout dat 'oman long time gone? Dey say she straight from jungles in da far off Af'ica. She nevah say. Dat war a 'oman—straight lak tree, an' tall, swift as a lion an' strong as any ox. Da sugah cane wen' down fo' huh big knife lak cotton stalks under da fierces' gale. No mahn could walk wid huh . . . An' sing! She ustah sing out in da fields— da niggahs wo'k dem days—when Ah war young. (*Her voice dies away in a mumble of reminiscences. She turns back to her pots, forgetting her audience, lost in the memories of her youth. CISSIE has been staring at her, but she now drops her head again, hopelessly.*)

PHOEBE: Humph! Ah t'ought you gonna tell us sompin' we kin do to help po' Cissie an' huh gal, an' all you all comes talkin' 'bout is some cane-choppin' heathen what kin sing! G'wan! Anybody kin sing!

GRANNIE LOU: (*angrily*) Ain't Ah tol' you shut yo' fat mouf, you? Dat 'oman dar do mo' den sing! Lissen—she hab t'ree sons, dey black an' tall lak she. An' one day come dat dey sole des sons down ribbah . . . dey bring good price. She say dey nebbah go. Da white folk laf, but niggahs dassent laf . . . dey see huh face. She don' say not'in' mo', but go away. An' early in da mawnin' call she boys, an' when dey come, she tell 'em to stan' close an' watch da sun come up out ob da hill. Dey sort ob smile at huh an' look, an' den dat 'oman lift huh big came knife, she cry out sompin' in a wild, strange voice, an' wid one sweep she cut off all dey heads—dey roll down at she feet. All t'ree ob dem!

(*The women gasp, but CISSIE is staring fixedly at the long knife which FESS has tossed on the table. Outside MILLIE is again singing. Slowly CISSIE's hand approaches the knife. The following action happens simultaneously.*)

AUNT SUE: No, Cissie!

ROSE: (*laying her hand on CISSIE's arm*) Cissie!

PHOEBE: Oh, Jesus!

MILLIE: Oh! see dat sun,
  See how he run,
Don' you ebbah let 'im catch you
Wid yo' wo'k undone.
(All) Oh! see dat sun, see how he run
Don' you ebbah let 'im catch you
Wid yo' wo'k undone.
Oh! I'm gonna shine
Lawd, Ah'm a gonna shine.

GRANNIE LOU: (*leaning toward CISSIE*) She—don'—hab—tuh—go!

CISSIE: (*her fingers closing around the knife*) No, she don' hab to go.

AUNT SUE: (*pleading*) Missie say she buy huh back!

CISSIE: Buy huh back? When? Ah'll tell you: aftah huh song is dead, when she can' dance no mo'. (*She looks at the knife, catching its glint in the firelight.*) Dis she'll nevah know. Hit's sharp! (*Putting the knife inside her dress she springs up and rushes to the door calling loudly.*) You all out dar! Da night's mos' gone—just time fur one mo' dance!

VOICES: Some pahty! One mo' dance! Mah feet jus' won' lay down nohow!

CISSIE: (*outside now*) One mo' dance! Now Jake, beat hit down! Make hit a good one! (*The banjo starts.*) Louder! Faster! All togedder now. Dance, Millie, dance! Everybody dance! Dat's hit! Dance! One mo' dance 'fore you go—home! Dance! (*sound of clapping hands, furious dancing and loud music. The women watch from the window.*)

PHOEBE: Oh, God! She's crazy!

ROSE: She's dancin', too! (*The dance comes to an end with much laughter and noise.*)

CISSIE: Now, Millie gal, sing—sing a lil' song!

MILLIE: (*out of breath*) Mammy! You danced. Ah nevah saw you dance before!

CISSIE: Come on, gal—sing! You all gotta get some sleep! Look, da stars is goin' out, da moon am gone . . . mawnin's mos' here.

MILLIE: (*singing gayly*)

> Lil' King David playin' on his harp
> (Group) Some boy! Oh! Some boy!
> Lil' King David playin' on his harp
> (Group) Some boy! Oh! Some boy!
> Lil' King David playin' on his harp
> Laffin' to hisself 'cause his skirt was so short
> Lil' King David playin' on his harp
> (Group) Some boy! Oh! Some boy!

PHOEBE: Ah'll go git Uncle Dave. He'll stop huh. (*She hurries out.*)

ROSE: Dar's Fess. Ah'll tell 'im.

(*ROSE exists*)

(*Singing continued*)

> Ole Goliah comin' right along
> (Group) Some boy! Oh! Some boy!
> Ole Goliah comin' right along
> (Group) Some boy! Oh! Some boy!
> Laffin' at David an' his crazy lil' song
> Ole Goliah comin' right along
> (Group) Some boy! Oh! Some boy!

(*While MILLIE sings, AUNT SUE begins straightening the room. The fire has died down. GRANNIE LOU is nodding in her corner. AUNT SUE shakes her.*)

AUNT SUE: Grannie, da pahty's ovah. Bes' go to bed.

GRANNIE LOU: (*starting*) Eh? Eh? Millie?

AUNT SUE: N'mine, Grannie—git some sleep. (*Tottering, the old woman pulls herself up and stumbles through the doorway up left. She is mumbling to herself. Outside, the song has ended in a burst of final laughter.*)

VOICES: Good night! Sho had a good time. Bye, Millie. T'anks, Cripple Jake. (*et cetera*)

MILLIE: (*in doorway*) Oh! Mammy, Ah don' wanna sleep yet. The air smells so good—and even da da'kness is sweet!

CISSIE: Yes, gal. Da night am sweet . . . but . . . da day am comin'. You gotta sleep now. Come take yo' rest.

MILLIE: (*reluctantly as she crosses room*) Ah reckon Ah is sleepy! 'Night, everybody.

(*CISSIE follows her into other room. MILLIE is heard laughing inside. ROSE, FESS and another woman have come in.*)

ROSE: (*whispering*) She'll nebber do hit. She can't.

AUNT SUE: Ah see hit in huh face. She gotta min' to.

ROSE: You gotta stop huh, Fess, you gotta stop huh.

FESS: Ah donno . . . Ah donno what tuh do. Sometimes when Ah kills wild t'ings in da woods Ah feels bad. Ah has to tell mahself 'bout all us hungry. Ah hates tuh do hit . . . but . . . Millie . . . She ain't free.

AUNT SUE: But Cissie kain't . . .

FESS: (*fiercely*) Why not? Po' Millie's dancin' days am gone. Cissie know 'bout pain dat breaks an' keep on breakin' till dey ain't nothin' left . . . (*sadly*) Ah donno. Right now, Ah'm all mixed up.

CISSIE: (*in doorway of inner room*) Look out, Rose, see if hit's sun-up yet.

(*They hold their breath as ROSE looks out and says.*)

ROSE: No, hit's still dark.

AUNT SUE: (*fervently*) T'ank you, Jesus!

(*CISSIE comes down to the fire, and squatting on the floor draws the knife from her dress. She tests the blade. Her face has no expression.*)

FESS: (*bending over her*) Cissie . . .

CISSIE: (*dully*) You sho hit's sharp?

FESS: Yes, Cissie, hit's sharp, but . . .

CISSIE: (*softly*) She sing an' dance till she kain't dance no mo' . . . Till sleep pull hebby at huh lids, an' she sink down wid belly full o' joy. Happy will be huh dreams—huh long, long dreams.

(*FESS turns away. From the doorway ROSE speaks.*)

ROSE: Hyear come Uncle Dave!

(*In a moment an old man enters, walking slowly. He is followed by an anxious PHOEBE. His hair is white, forming a halo about a gentle, wrinkled face.*)

ROSE: Howdy, Uncle Dave.

AUNT SUE: Praise de Lawd! Maybe she'll listen to you, Uncle Dave.

UNCLE DAVE: Yes, chile, Ah heared da han' ob God lay hebby on you. Whar's Cissie?

(*They draw aside so that he can see CISSIE alone at the fire.*)

PHOEBE: (*loudly*) Hit's all dat black Lou's fault.

VOICES: Shshshshsh! She'll hyear!

PHOEBE: (*lower tone*) She put a spell on Cissie, shuttin' huh eyes an' stoppin' up huh ears tuh evaht'ing dat we kin do an' say. She gotta evil eye, dat's what she got!

UNCLE DAVE: Dar now, daughtah, de Lawd takes care ob His own. Us ain't got no cause tuh fret.

(*Several more slaves slip into the room. They have heard.*)

AUNT SUE: (*shivering*) Shut da door, Fess. Da air's got cold an' damp. Talk to huh, Uncle Dave. We gotta stay wid huh.

(*FESS closes the door. A wavering wail comes softly from the banjo. It hangs suspended in the air a moment and Cripple Jake speaks.*)

JAKE: Ah'm t'inkin' 'bout dis t'ing—Hebben is a high an' holy place. Dat gal ain't done no wrong; dyin' will bring huh joy. Da good book say "Lam's in His Bosm—safe." While Cissie know dat livin's jes' a slow decay wid worms gnawin' lak nits into huh heart an' soul.

FIRST WOMAN: She'll be a murderess!

SECOND WOMAN: She'll bu'n in hell!

JAKE: Yes, Cissie will be lonely—now—an' maybe foh a t'ousand yeahs tuh come.

(*They turn at the unexpected sound of CISSIE's voice. It is low and vibrant.*)

CISSIE: But w'en da saints ob God go marchin' home mah gal will sing! Wid all da pure, bright stars, togedder wid da mawnin' stars . . . She'll sing!

(*CISSIE's head is lifted and for one moment a strange beauty illumines her black, gaunt face. A soft chord sounds from the banjo, gentle as wings brushing across the strings.*)

UNCLE DAVE: (*sternly*) We be forgettin' God! Didn't He bring Daniel out ob da lion's den an' de Hebrew chillun out da fiery furnace? Didn't He open up da Red Sea an' save Jonah from da belly ob da whale?

WOMEN: Yes, mah Lawd! Save us, Jesus! (*They begin to rock back and forth, singing softly.*)

WOMAN: (*humming accompaniment*)

Ah wan' Jesus tuh walk wid me,
Ah wan' Jesus tuh walk wid me,
All along mah hebbenly journey
An wan' Jesus tuh walk wid me.

(*The song sinks to a hum. UNCLE DAVE moves downstage to CISSIE. He places his hand on her shoulder. She starts to rise, but when she sees who it is, sinks back. The light has faded from her face.*)

UNCLE DAVE: Kain't you trus' de Lawd, daughtah? Hit's wid Him. You kain't stain yo' han's wid da blood o' yo' own chile.

CISSIE: Ah t'ought da time is come. Dat man comin' fuh huh at sun-up.

AUNT SUE: Oh! Lawd! Oh! Lawd! Hit's mos' time!

(*Singers are humming.*)

UNCLE DAVE: (*falling on knees*) Oh, Lawd! Our Lawd! Sittin' on yo' great white throne wid da stars a crown o' beauty fur yo' haid an' de earth a mighty footstool fur yo' feet. Lean down ovah da ramparts of Hebbin dis mawnin', an' see us 'umble sinners kneelin' hyear. We been prayin' so long, we been singin' so . . .

(*During the latter half of the prayer, outside is heard the sound of a galloping horse. It draws rapidly nearer. There is the sound of pawing feet. The horse neighs, running footsteps and in a moment a loud knocking at the door.*)

VOICE: Open the door! Open the door!

CISSIE: Da man! He come!

(*CISSIE clutches the knife. The slaves watch her terrified. Two men spring forward to hold the door. PHOEBE cautiously pulls back the cloth which has been drawn over the window. She jerks back and speaks in a whisper. CISSIE does not hear her. She is intent on what she must do. FESS, standing near her, has his eyes only on CISSIE.*)

PHOEBE: Hit's a soldier!

VOICES: Soldiers? (*The pounding on the door comes again. The slaves spring up, per-plexed, crowd to the window. In that moment CISSIE slips out, unnoticed by all except FESS who takes a step as if to stop her and then hesitates, covering his face with his hands. Just as she disappears the outer door gives way, admitting a soldier in a torn and dusty blue uniform. He is hardly more than a boy, his face pale with emotion. Behind him the day is breaking. He gazes around surprised at seeing the room filled.*)

SOLDIER: Up already? You know? (*There is disappointment in his voice, but the slaves only shrink back. His face breaks with smiles.*) Don't be scared of me. You don't have to be scared of nobody no more. You're free! (*They stare at him.*) This is the day! Abe Lincoln said it. You're free! No more slaves!

FESS: (*starting up*) Cissie! (*He rushes into the other room.*)

SOLDIER: Yessir! You been set free! I'm riding ahead of the others, waking folks up telling 'em. Could I get some water here for my horse?

(*He cannot understand the group before him. In the face of such news they turn towards the other way, anxiously straining forward.*)

UNCLE DAVE: (*falling on his knees*) Thank God! Oh, thank . . .

(*His thanksgiving is cut short by a gasping sob. Backing from the room is FESS, his hand before his eyes, his whole body expressing agony. There is a moment of tense waiting. From the distance, borne upon the fresh, morning breeze, comes spirited marching music. Now into the room comes CISSIE, holding in her arms the limp body of MILLIE. She advances slowly, her face a mask of ebony, with set, unseeing eyes.*)

CISSIE: You come too late—mah gal is dead! She how huh red blood falls hyear in da sun. Hit's warm an' pure . . . Come dip yo' han's in hit; she will not shrink away. Huh tears will nevah choke huh song nor will huh limbs grow hebby wid despair . . . Mah gal is dead!

(*Everyone is crouched back except the young soldier, who stands as if paralyzed, his face white. Now he finds his voice.*)

SOLDIER: My God! My God! What? What . . . ?

UNCLE DAVE: (*Reaching up from his knees*) Cissie! Cissie! Dis ain't da man. Dis am a Yankee soldier come tuh tell us dat we's . . .

(*The old man cannot finish. The word chokes in his throat. Outside a chorus of happy, singing voices is swelling, forming a joyous obligato to the music of the band.*)

VOICES: Free, free, free!
    Ah'm free, lil' chillun,
    Free! Free!
    Da sun o' God does sot us free
    Dis mawnin'!

(*Through the door behind CISSIE has come GRANNIE LOU. She stumbles, rubbing her sleep-heavy eyes and shaking her shriveled frame. She sees CISSIE facing the white man and her clouded brain can take in only one meaning.*)

SOLDIER: (*gently to CISSIE*) Do you hear them? It means you're—free! You . . .
(*He is stopped by a burst of wild, loud laughter from GRANNIE LOU who points her skinny finger at the limp body.*)

GRANNIE LOU: He! He! He! Ha! Ha! Ha! Ha! Ah tole you. She don' hab tuh go! He! He! He!

(*Several women rush to her, soothing her as they would a child. Only bewilderment shows in CISSIE's face, but the soldier's poise is completely shattered. Flinging up his hands to shut out the sight, he rushes into the morning sunshine. One of the men follows him. Gradually GRANNIE LOU is quieted. The women have dropped to their knees. They rock their bodies and moan. CISSIE walks to the door, her inert burden clasped to her breast. For a moment she stands in the bright sunshine, gazing out. The music has diminished into the distance. Somewhere in the yard a cock crows. CISSIE looks down into her child's face and speaks quietly.*)

CISSIE: Hit's mawnin'!

(*Then from her throat there comes a cry of anguish as she falls to her knees. Above her, on the door, a single spray of mistletoe sways in the morning breeze and then falls gently on the upturned face of the child.*)

CURTAIN

ALICE CHILDRESS
(1920–   )

Florence (1950)
Wine in the Wilderness (1969)

BIOGRAPHY AND ACHIEVEMENTS

Alice Childress was born on October 12, 1920, in Charleston, South Carolina. At the age of five, Childress boarded a train for New York where she grew up in Harlem under the care of her grandmother, Eliza Campbell. Childress admits that she owes a great debt to her grandmother who empowered her to survive even the harshest conditions. Childress says of her grandmother, "She had seven children and was very poor. There wasn't any time to do anything, except try to keep the children in clothing and someway fed. Always running out of everything. When I came along, all of her children were grown. We were together all of the time. Her name was Eliza . . . I put so much emphasis on my grandmother, Eliza, because my father and mother were separated when I was very little. I vaguely remember him. My mother was always working and on the go. My grandmother was a very fortunate thing that happened to me."

Childress's grandmother inspired her to write, as is evident in her comments, "We used to walk up and down New York City, going to art galleries and private art showings. She used to say to the people in charge, 'Now, this is my granddaughter and we don't have any money, but I want her to know about art' . . . I was storing up things to write about even then . . . My grandmother was a member of Salem Church in Harlem. We went to Wednesday night testimonials. Now that's where I learned to be a writer. I remember how people, mostly women, used to get up and tell their troubles to everybody . . . Everybody rallied round these people. I couldn't wait for person after person to tell her story." Childress recalls that when she and her grandmother returned from their excursions, her grandmother always quizzed her and encouraged her to write about people for whom the act of living is sheer heroism.

Armed with a positive sense of self instilled in her by her grandmother, Childress was able to endure many hardships as she struggled to get an education. She attended Public School 81, the Julia Ward Howe Junior High School, and, for three years, Wadleigh High School, at which time she had to drop out because both her grandmother and mother had died, leaving her to fend for herself. Forced to assume the responsibility of teaching herself, Childress discovered the public library and attempted to read two books a day.

Beginning in the early 1940s, at the conclusion of a first marriage, Childress began establishing herself as an actress and writer, during which time she worked to support herself and her only child, Jean, in a number of odd jobs, including assistant machinist, photo retoucher, domestic worker, salesperson, and insurance agent. She resides in New York City with her musician husband, Nathan Woodard whom she married on July 17, 1957. Childress frequently appears as keynote speaker at international, national, and regional literary conferences. She is at work on a fourth novel and is composing her memoirs.

Alice Childress is the only black woman playwright in America whose plays have been written, produced, and published over a period of four decades. Like a giant in a straitjacket, Childress has remained faithful to the U.S. theater even when it looked upon her with blind eyes and turned to her with deaf ears. Having had plays produced in New York City, across the United States, and in Europe, Childress's legacy to U.S. theater is monumental. In her forty years of writing for the American stage, Childress says she has never compromised her vision. Though she writes mainly about the genteel poor, a diverse audience looks to her for the truth that she gives in numerous small doses and without adulteration.

Alice Childress has written plays that incorporate the liturgy of the black church, traditional music, African mythology, folklore, and fantasy. She has experimented by writing sociopolitical, romantic, biographical, historical, and feminist plays. Striving to find new and dynamic ways of expressing old themes in a historically conservative theater, Childress has opened doors for other black playwrights, particularly Lorraine Hansberry and Ntozake Shange, to make advances in the field of drama.

Childress's contributions to U.S. theater have been varied and consistent. In the early 1940s, Childress help to found the American Negro Theater (ANT), a phenomenal organization that served as a beacon of hope for countless black playwrights, actors, and producers, such as Sidney Poitier, Ossie Davis, Ruby Dee, Frank Silvera, and others. Another major achievement of Childress, a long time Broadway and off-Broadway actress and a member of the Author's League of the Dramatists' Guild, is that she was instrumental in the early 1950s in initiating advanced, guaranteed pay for union off-Broadway contracts in New York City.

Childress became one of the beneficiaries of her efforts to establish equity standards for off-Broadway productions. Her first two plays, *Just a Little Simple* (1950) and *Gold Through the Trees* (1952), were the first plays by a black woman to be professionally produced, i.e., performed by unionized actors. Three years later, Childress became the first black woman to win an Obie Award for the best original off-Broadway play of the year with her production of *Trouble In Mind* (1955), subsequently produced by the BBC in London. Ten years later, Childress's *Wedding Band: A Love/Hate Story in Black and White* (1966) was broadcast nationally on ABC television. *Wine in the Wilderness* (1969) was presented on National Educational Television (NET). Other plays by Childress include *Florence* (1950), *Young Martin Luther King* (1969), *Mojo: A Black Love Story* (1970), *When the Rattlesnake Sounds* (1975), *Let's Hear it for the Queen* (1976), *Gullah* (1984), and *Moms* (1987). A versatile writer, Childress has published four novels: *Like One of the Family: Conversations from a Domestic's Life* (1956), *A Hero Ain't Nothin but a Sandwich* (1973), which was made into a movie, *A Short Walk* (1979), and *Rainbow Jordan* (1981). Additionally, she is editor of *Black Scenes: Collection of Scenes from Plays Written by Black People about Black Experience* (1971), and author of an impressive host of essays on black art and theater history.

Though she demonstrates skill in a variety of literary forms, Childress considers herself principally a playwright telling her stories about poor, dejected heroines who are morally strong, sometimes vulnerable, but resilient. She portrays these women honestly as they fight daily battles not just to survive but to survive whole.

As a result of Childress's innovative achievements and commitment to quality theater, she has received a host of awards and honors, including writer-in-residence at the MacDowell Colony; featured author on a BBC panel discussion on "The Negro in the American Theater"; winner of a Rockefeller grant administered through The New Dramatists and a John Golden Fund for Playwrights; and a Harvard appointment to the Radcliffe Institute for Independent Study (now Mary Ingraham Bunting Institute), from which she received a graduate medal for work completed during her tenure.

SYNOPSIS AND ANALYSIS: *FLORENCE*

This play is set in a railway station in the South where Mama, or Mrs. Whitney, is preparing for a trip to the North. Her daughter, Marge, is eager for her to go to New York City to talk Florence, Mama's other daughter an unemployed actress, into coming home. Marge "knows her place" in the South and thinks Florence is foolish for pursuing a career traditionally opened to whites only. Though Marge has been helping her mother raise Florence's son ever since his father was lynched for voting and his mother moved to New York City, she resents having to take care of her sister's child.

While Mama awaits the train, she meets Mrs. Carter, a white woman who considers herself liberal but who proves to be irrepressibly racist. Mrs.

Carter is pleased to hear that Mama places a great deal of emphasis on family. So comfortable is she with Mama that she confides in her about her brother's troubles. Mrs. Carter's brother is a novelist who writes about black people. She explains that his latest book received poor reviews which led to his depression. She tells Mama that she has come South to nurture him and to boost his ego.

When Mama questions what the book is about, Mrs. Carter tell her it is about a beautiful and talented mulatto woman who commits suicide because she wants to be white. Mama, not at all sympathetic to Mrs. Carter's tears of her brother's failure, quickly tells her that it is a myth that black people kill themselves for wanting to be white. When Mrs. Carter is not convinced, Mama gives her examples of mulattos that she knows who have lived healthy, normal lives without self hatred.

Reality is too stark for Mrs. Carter, so she tries to ease the tension by asking questions about Florence. When she learns that Florence is trying to make it as an actress, Mrs. Carter begs Mama to convince Florence to give up such a ludicrous notion. She essentially tells Mama that if a white woman like herself cannot get any acting jobs, certainly Florence who is black and poor has no chance of success.

Mama is touched by Mrs. Carter's genuine concern for Florence until she offers to help Florence by putting her in touch with an actress who is in need of a maid. Mama is stunned by Mrs. Carter's low expectations for Florence and black people in general.

When Mrs. Carter goes to freshen up her makeup, Mama decides not to go to New York; instead she asks Porter to mail a letter to Florence with money enclosed. Her message to Florence is, "Keep trying."

Florence is fraught with potent symbols and symbolic gestures that serve as signposts to the play's main idea. Childress's symbols point out that blacks must not turn over to white liberals the responsibility of nurturing young, black dreamers but must encourage their children to fight to reach their fullest potential in spite of racial biases.

One very important symbol are the signs that divide the railway waiting room. "Colored" and "White" signs hang over the doorway entrances to each side. The division is further emphasized by the hanging of "Colored women" and "Colored men" and "White ladies" and "White gentlemen" over the restroom doors.

Racial inequity is signaled by the very use of the words "ladies" and "gentlemen" on the restroom doors designated for whites. These titles, which suggest grace, culture, wealth, or royalty, do not appear on the restroom doors for blacks, an implication that Colored men and women are a cut below White ladies and gentlemen. Another example of Childress's orchestration of this sign–symbol occurs when Porter tells Mama that should she need to use the restroom, she must use the Colored men's because the other is out of order. It is illegal for Mama to step into the "White ladies" restroom, so she will have to demean herself and risk having her privacy invaded in the Colored men's restroom.

The out-of-order restroom becomes a symbol of the black woman's historical burden in America, that of struggling to keep together the family that the system of slavery plotted to destroy. This play on words hints that for Colored women, there is no room for rest. Childress implies that the Colored woman, as Zora Neale Hurston once said, is the mule of the world. On another level, Childress's symbol suggests that the American societal structure is out of order, nonfunctioning for African Americans. Childress mirrors a society that is and will remain out of order as long as people are judged by the color of their skin.

In addition to the obtrusive signs that bar whites and blacks from crossing lines, a low railing, dividing the waiting room, serves as a physical and emotional barrier between whites and blacks and is the symbol around which the central idea of the play is developed. Conversations and actions are structured around this dividing line that reminds the audience that there are special limitations placed on blacks and whites. Childress moves both the black and white characters toward or away from this low railing to suggest racial constraints. She ingeniously demonstrates that the railing prevents both blacks and whites from crossing into each other's territory. On one level, the bar symbolizes the need for blacks to fight against the harnesses of racism and to cross the line to secure those privileges in life that belong not just to whites but to all human beings. On another level, the railing suggests that segregation breeds ignorance. Childress illustrates that the Jim Crow laws that were set in place to restrict blacks also kept whites from interacting with blacks. The point is that when whites are barred from firsthand knowledge about blacks, they are forced to imagine, which leads to the creation of stereotypes.

Childress paints a picture of the South as a racist and ignorant place from which to escape. As Marge says her goodbys to her mother in this little railway station, the low railing serves as a constant reminder of existing racial constraints. Marge unconsciously wanders upstage to the railing but stops as she tells her mother to buy coffee when the waiter passes through the Jim Crow cars because she will not be able to go to the segregated diner. In this instance, the audience is reminded that just as Marge cannot cross the railing, blacks are unable to cross lines in other establishments and can only achieve what is prescribed for them by white supremacists. While still at the railing, Marge pleads with her mother to force Florence to come home.

A while later, Marge nears the railing but stops when she tells Mama that Florence must think she is white, pursuing a career in which typically only whites had succeeded. She also reminds Mama of the time Florence went to Strumley's asking to be a salesgirl, knowing that blacks were not hired for such positions. Marge actually crosses over the line and onto the

"White" side of the stage just as she says, "There's things we can't do cause they ain't gonna let us." Once on the forbidden side, Marge sarcastically comments that it does not feel any differently. This crossing over suggests that blacks feel harnessed in their struggle against oppression and, perhaps, envious of the privileges and rights accorded whites. Marge steps back over to the "Colored" side just as she tells her mother that she must not give Florence any money but must, instead, bring her back home. This synchronized movement to the "Colored" side symbolizes Marge's internalization of her designated place in society.

Mama, like Marge, seems to know her place until Mrs. Carter enters and provokes her into realizing that blacks cannot afford to give up the struggle for equality. This struggle is illustrated as Childress catapults both Mama and Mrs. Carter back and forth across the dividing line. Childress seems to be working with a symbol within a symbol, i.e., a trip within a trip. The cross-country trip that the women are going on parallels the cross-cultural trip that they take each time the railing is crossed. These women step in and out of each other's cultures as they try to communicate their limitations. Childress suggests that the railing, representing segregation, has left Mrs. Carter and white liberals like her ignorant and insensitive to blacks. By the same token, the railing serves as a driving force behind black achievement; racial bars must be torn down in order for blacks to be free to succeed.

The cross-cultural trip begins when Mrs. Carter gradually moves near the dividing line to tell Mama about her brother's struggle to capture the lives of black people. Almost on the rail, Mrs. Carter boasts of her brother's novel, "It's profound. Real . . . you know. It's about your people . . . He suffers so with his characters." Leaning on the rail, Mrs. Carter proceeds to tell of the mulatto who, with tears rolling down her cheeks, jumps from a bridge to her death saying, "Almost! Almost white . . . but I'm black! I'm a Negro." Childress's disdain for stereotypes is plain, particularly the tragic mulatto. Mrs. Carter's brother is held up as a white liberal who means well but who knows little about what he writes.

Outraged by the white author's stereotyping of blacks, Mama tells Mrs. Carter, "That ain't so! Not one bit it ain't." At this point, Mrs. Carter backs away from the railing while Mama, citing cases of mulattos who did not kill themselves, works her way around the bar until she crosses about a foot over to the "White" side and is face to face with Mrs. Carter. Crossing the railing in this instance suggests Mama's refusal to accept myths about blacks. Mama moves back to the "Colored" side when she looks up and sees the sign "White ladies." The inference is that only "White ladies" or naive, white liberals would believe that blacks kill themselves for wishing to be white. Also, Childress demonstrates that in 1950 blacks and whites were painfully aware of racial bars. Mama can not exchange ideas with

Mrs. Carter without being reminded that she must remain in her place on the "Colored" side.

Like a skilled checker player, Mrs. Carter hesitantly makes the next move. She approaches the rail to apologize to Mama. This gesture, however, is deflated when Mrs. Carter says, "This whole thing is a completely controversial subject. If it's too much for Jeff... well naturally I shouldn't discuss it with you." Mrs. Carter does not realize that she is condescending in her assumption that Mama is too simple-minded to understand the issues surrounding the poor reviews given the book. The apology, then, becomes a false sign and instead becomes another indicator of Mrs. Carter's racism.

Mrs. Carter crosses over to the "Colored" side as she tells Mama, "You know I try but it's really difficult to understand you people. However... I keep trying." When Mama remains unmoved, Mrs. Carter retreats back to the "White" side and offers another sign of her love and respect for blacks, "I know what's going on in your mind . . . and what you're thinking is wrong. I've . . . I've . . . eaten with Negroes." This gesture is symbolic because it suggests that eating together does not represent equality.

Mrs. Carter insults Mama again during their discussion of Florence's dream of becoming a dramatic actress. Unaware that she is condescending, Mrs. Carter assures Mama that blacks are far better suited to entertainment, such as singing spirituals like "Steal Away" and "Swing Low, Sweet Chariot." Mrs. Carter tells Mama that Florence stands little or no chance in New York, especially since she is without contacts. Mama, genuinely moved by Mrs. Carter's concern for Florence, asks her to help the struggling actress. Knowing that Mama has in mind an acting job, Mrs. Carter instead offers to contact a director friend of hers who will take on Florence as a domestic.

The dividing line takes on significance once more as Mrs. Carter crosses over to the "Colored" side to give Mama the address and phone number of her director friend and to reassure Mama that Florence will be in good hands if she is dependable and trustworthy. Reaching out, Mama clutches Mrs. Carter's arm almost pulling her off balance. It is at this point that Mama understands that white liberals should not be counted on for helping blacks in the struggle because racism in America has blinded and desensitized them. Mrs. Carter cannot empathize, nor can she understand Florence's determination to succeed at acting or at any other career that has been typically open only to whites because she is a product of the railing that has kept her ignorant about blacks. Mama realizes that she, and all blacks, must contribute to the empowerment of her people by offering continued encouragement to their children. Realizing that she is hurting Mrs. Carter, Mama unclutches her and snaps, "You better get on over to the other side of that rail. It's against the law for you to be here with me." Mrs. Carter goes scurrying across the line, rubbing her wrist and not fully understanding why Mama has reacted violently.

Keeping her eyes on the dividing line after Mrs. Carter exits to powder her nose in the "White ladies" room, Mama assures Porter that "Marge can't make her turn back, Mrs. Carter can't make her turn back." She writes a note to Florence telling her to keep trying and that she has a right to be or do anything she wants in this world. Mama's linking Marge to Mrs. Carter is significant because both women believe that Florence does not know her limitations.

One comes away from *Florence* sensing Childress's outrage that blacks are forced to live in a world that prescribes positions or careers for them. Childress uses the railing to show that whites are barred from knowing blacks. She insists that blacks are victimized or oppressed by the dominant race because of this unfamiliarity with black life.

SYNOPSIS AND ANALYSIS: *WINE IN THE WILDERNESS*

The setting is Harlem during a 1964 race riot. The play opens with artist and pseudo-intellectual Bill Jameson chastising Oldtimer, an elderly, uneducated black man, for picking up loot and bringing it into his apartment. Though Oldtimer fears that the policemen might arrest him, he cannot bring himself to throw away the ham, liquor, and a suit that he says he found after the looters left the goods in the streets. Not being able to convince Oldtimer to dispose of the loot, Bill returns to his art project. Oldtimers explains to Bill that he is fortunate to belong to the generation that was given grants and scholarships and explains that in his day he was barred from education and jobs. He questions Bill about his art project, and Bill explains that the triptych will contain three canvases on black womanhood. Bill shows off two of the three paintings, the first of which is "Black girlhood" or innocence and the second is "Wine In The Wilderness" or "Mother Africa" or black womanhood in her noblest form. The third canvas remains blank, but on it he plans to place "the kinda chick that is grass roots, . . . no, not grass roots, . . . I mean she's underneath the grass roots. The lost woman, . . . what the society has made out of our women . . . There's no hope for her." Oldtimer says he knows the type Bill has in mind and says the description sounds like his ex-wife.

Bill and Oldtimer are interrupted by a phone call from two vapid, affected, pompous, middle-class blacks, Sonny-man and Cynthia, telling Bill that they have found Tommy, the perfect model for his "lost black woman," a riot victim whom they've met in a bar. When Sonny-man and Cynthia arrive with Tommy, she sizes Bill up as a possible husband while he examines her and determines that she will do perfectly as "a messed up chick" for his triptych.

Before she will agree to serve as his model, Tommy insists on food. While the men, Oldtimer, Sonny-man, and Bill go out to get her something to eat, Tommy turns to Cynthia demanding to know what she can do to win Bill's affection and make him fall in love with her. Immediately, Cynthia realizes that Tommy has the wrong idea about why they are associating with her and tries subtly to tell Tommy that she is aiming too high. Not wishing to be circumvented, Tommy insists upon concrete suggestions. To appease Tommy, social worker Cynthia glibly enumerates ways to empower black men, i.e., to give them their manhood back. She tells Tommy essentially that she must work to make Bill feel like he is in charge in order to counteract the debilitating effects of the "Matriarchal Society" on black men.

Later, when Tommy is alone with Bill, they argue because she does not feel comfortable that he wants to paint her in the mismatched rags the riot has forced her to wear. He insults her and patronizingly tells her that she is like most black women: too eager to emasculate black men. Bill belittles Tommy at every turn, lording his education over her to humiliate her and remind her that she is grass-roots and he is cultured and refined. They nearly come to blows when he screams at her for not being able to make up her mind about whether she'll model for him. She points to the picture of the white woman on the wall and tells him that she's certain that when he painted that white woman he was grinning and treating her with respect.

Bill and Tommy exchange a few choice words after Tommy spills a soft drink on her lap. While she is changing behind a screen, Bill gets a phone call. He describes for the caller this magnificent woman with whom he claims he is in love. He says that she is "the finest any woman in the world" and "I'm beginnin' to have this deep attachment." Unaware that Bill is describing his painting, Tommy transforms herself into the beautiful woman. Casting off her wig and slipping into an African throw-cloth, Tommy emerges self-assured.

Bill is so taken by Tommy's metamorphosis that he cannot paint, regardless of how hard he tries to recapture in his head that "lost black woman." Tommy feels loved, and Bill finds himself being drawn to her. They talk about each other's past and discover that they are more alike than different. They mutually want each other and morning finds them in bed.

Tommy wakes up singing snatches of spirituals and talking to Bill as he showers. Moments later, Tommy is catapulted into rage when Oldtimer, who comes to retrieve his loot, reveals to her that she is to be "the lost black woman" on Bill's triptych. As Tommy prepares to leave, Sonny-man and Cynthia arrive. Tommy, in the performance of her life, tells Oldtimer he is a fool for letting these middle-class blacks treat him like he is invisible because they perceive that they are better than him. Then she lashes out at the three blacks who have disassociated themselves from grass-roots blacks and tells them that they are "phoney nigger." Tommy tells them that when racist whites say " 'nigger,' just dry-long-so, they mean educated you and uneducated me. They hate you and call you 'nigger,' I called you 'nigger' but I love you." She tells the trio that they think that they are superior to the masses but that they, in fact, are the masses and just don't know it.

Though Sonny-man and Cynthia are first to realize their false sense of pride, Bill eventually has his consciousness raised. With Tommy as a catalyst, Bill comes to understand that his vision was misguided and that his cold, motionless picture of "Mother Africa" does not accurately represent the struggling black woman in America. He says that his "Mother Africa" image is a "dream I drummed up outta the junk room of my mind" and that Tommy is the "Wine in the Wilderness" because she has survived slavery and the race riots while holding her head high and "poppin' her fingers at the world." Bill's new triptych will consist of a revised image of black womanhood, one that has been influenced significantly by a black woman who truly is "Mother Africa."

Wine in the Wilderness explores black Americans' preoccupation with things African and illuminates what it means to be black, female, and poor in America. The play examines this duality by focusing on the spirituality that empowers Childress's heroine to survive. Childress makes the point that sexism, racism, and classism are immutably connected to black women's oppression while making it crystal clear that black women triumph because of a strong spirit of survival inextricably linked to an African heritage. Childress's play suggests that black people continue to keep alive certain aspects of various African religions and culture.

A close examination of *Wine in the Wilderness* reveals that the heroine, in a struggle to become whole in a fragmented community, embraces a tripartite spirituality that is uniquely Afrocentric. This spirituality entails a belief in Mother Africa or God the Mother, Christianity, and ancestral spirits. Childress suggests that African peoples look to Africa not only as homeland but as a deity to whom they can turn for strength. God the Mother and Mother Africa are often synonymous in Childress's plays. Connected with Mother Africa as deity are the African ancestral spirits who bolster African peoples and ensure their resiliency. In Childress's works, in general, African ancestral spirits, usually a deceased mother, grandmother, or great-grandmother, are often conjured up to empower heroines to cope with a difficult life. Childress's heroine, Tommy, survives and succeeds because she finds God the Mother in herself, has a strong faith in Christ, and can summon ancestral spirits to encourage her when her resolve diminishes.

Tommy initially is merely a subaltern female in *Wine in the Wilderness*. Bill Jameson blatantly tells Oldtimer that upon his blank canvas he intends to depict the "ignorant, unfeminine, coarse, rude, vulgar, poor dumb chick that's had her behind kicked until its numb." He falls victim to creating stereotypes of women that depict them as nonentities. Bill's blank canvas or blank page will contain what he considers a "nothing" woman. Childress, as social, cultural, and feminist critic, demonstrates that Bill and other males cannot see the worth of a poor, black female.

When this "nothing" woman, Tomorrow-Marie, alias Tommy, climbs out of the riot of the Harlem streets, she finds herself amidst a cadre of middle-class, pompous blacks who deliberately make her feel stupid. Cynthia, who has donned the robes of male chauvinism, intimates that Tommy is not good enough for Bill or any other middle-class black man. Cynthia proceeds with a plethora of reasons why Tommy is unsuitable for a cultured artist such as Bill: she's too brash, independent, and domineering; she must learn to give back a black male his manhood; allow him to pursue her; stay in the background; ask his opinion; work on sex appeal, and expect more from men. To protect herself from Cynthia's verbal blows, Tommy tries to elicit sympathy. She tells Cynthia about her illiteracy and poverty-stricken background. It is in looking back that Tommy summons a powerful ancestral spirit: the memories of her deceased mother. Tommy painfully comments, "I remember my mother tyin' up her stockin's with strips-a-rag 'cause she didn't have no garters. When I get home from school she'd say, . . . 'Nothing much here to eat.' Nothin' much might be grits and bread and coffee." Later, Tommy tells Cynthia, "My Mama raised me, mostly by herself, God rest the dead." This going back in time does two things for Tommy: first, she remembers her vow that she would find her way out of poverty, and second she is empowered by her mother's suffering. Remembering her mother's burdens only strengthens her resolve to succeed.

While Tommy is in the process of developing and fortifying her self-esteem, Bill assaults her emotionally by telling her that she is like all black women: they always have food on their mind; they want to eat before anything; they all want to be great brains and leave nothing for men to do; they are too opinionated and ought to give in to men sometimes. He boldly tells Tommy, "The Matriarchy gotta go. Y'all throw them suppers together, keep your husband happy, raise the kids." Tommy rebels against Bill's sexist and classist remarks, insisting that he treat her with respect. He responds by screaming and, at one point, shouting an obscenity at her. Wounded, Tommy tells him that if she were a white woman, he would not treat her with apparent disdain. With Tommy's response, Childress hints that black men do not seem to value black women as much as they do white women. Ironically, Tommy wears a cheap, silky wig to try to measure up to beauty standards set by the media. The two argue and Tommy spills a drink on her dress in the excitement. While she is undressing behind a screen, Bill is called away to the phone. He tells the caller that he is looking at his beautiful African queen and that she is "Mother Africa . . . Regal . . . grand . . . magnificent, fantastic . . . She sparkles, man, Harriet Tubman, Queen of the Nile . . . sweetheart, wife, mother, sister, friend . . . The memory of Africa." It is at this moment that Bill unknowingly invokes Mother Africa or God the Mother in Tommy.

Not knowing that Bill is describing his painting, Tommy transforms into a beautiful, desirable, earthy woman as she pulls off her Five and Dime wig to reveal a fluffy Afro, and slips out of dingy, mismatched clothes and into an African wrap. She suddenly awakens to the feeling of being loved and admired. When Tommy equivocates in terms of self esteem, she finds solace in Mother Africa, the embodiment of strength and courage. In fact, she becomes the true representation of Mother Africa. Though it is Bill who serves as a catalyst forth calling forth goddess in Tommy, it is she who instinctively knows that inside lies a power greater than herself, one that can sustain her even in her lowest moment. Tommy looks to Mother Africa for confidence, and she finds it as she steps onto Bill's model stand, relaxed and self confident. She is one with Mother Africa, yearning both for the homeland and the spirit. Tommy's metamorphosis and absorption by the Mother God can be viewed as an African ritual of empowerment.

Tommy, insulated from insecurity by God the Mother, feels free to share with Bill the particulars of her life. In so doing, she reveals another element of her spirituality: her strong belief in Christianity. She tells him about her bond to the African Methodist Episcopal Church and her work as a former Sunday School teacher. She impresses Bill with her knowledge of and belief in her Christian faith.

Tommy's spirituality is again tested when, after spending the night with Bill, she discovers accidentally from Oldtimer that she is to fill up the blank canvas as the lost black woman. Tommy loses her balance temporarily; she cannot seem to comprehend the magnitude of this startling revelation. Tommy is disoriented when she discovers that she is to represent the "nothing" woman in society. One moment she is euphorically singing bits and pieces of spirituals, and the next she is battling her way through an emotional explosion.

At this point in the play, Childress seems to be consciously serving as both playwright and feminist critic. Her treatment of Bill suggests that males often create prescriptive roles for women and that women must begin to name themselves, to express their totality, to fill up the blank page with recognizable images of women. Childress sets up Tommy as creator; she becomes the true artist etching the complexity of what it means to be a poor woman of color. Though the news threatens to weaken Tommy's self-confidence, a very spiritual and spirited woman rises to serve as a healer to her wounded community whose psyche is in need of re-Africanization. She accuses Bill, Cynthia, and Sonny-man of preaching blackness because it is in vogue and castigates them for despising the poor black masses.

In Tommy's finest moment, she reveals to Bill that unlike the pretty lady that he painted, she is a real woman who can talk back, a woman who is "alive and kickin . . . cussin' and fightin' and lookin' out for my damn self 'cause ain' nobody else 'round to do it, dontcha know." The fact that Tommy "talks back" forces Bill to rethink his notion of black womanhood. She tells him that she is the real "Wine in the Wilderness," the closest thing to Mother Africa that he could ever place on his blank page. In essence, she makes him see that she is his salvation. The embodiment of God the Mother, she rescues him from his bourgeoisie vapidness and points him in

the direction of humanity. In the end, Bill changes his plans for the triptych
d decides to make Tommy the true "Wine *in the* Wilderness," the woman
who has labored through psychological and social minefields and has
emerged both whole and holy.

NOTES

Childress's quotes in this section come from Elizabeth Brown-Guillory, "Alice
Childress: A Pioneering Spirit," (an interview) *SAGE: A Scholarly Journal on Black
Women*, Vol. IV, No. 1 (Spring 1987), pp. 66.

For more information about Alice Childress's life and works see Trudier Harris,
"Alice Childress," *DLB*, vol. 38, Afro-American Writers After 1955, pp. 66–79,
and Elizabeth Brown-Guillory, *Their Place on the Stage: Black Women Playwrights in
America*, Westport, Conn.: Greenwood Press, 1988

The analysis of *Florence* is based upon the version that appears in Elizabeth Brown-
Guillory's *Their Place on the Stage: Black Women Playwrights in America*, Westport,
Conn.: Greenwood Press, 1988, pp. 54–58.

Florence (1950) ─────────────

Alice Childress

CHARACTERS

MARGE
MAMA
PORTER
MRS. CARTER

PLACE

A very small town in the South.

TIME

The present.

SCENE: A railway station waiting room. The room is divided in two sections by a low railing. Upstage center is a double door which serves as an entrance to both sides of the room. Over the doorway stage right is a sign "Colored," over the doorway stage left is another sign "White." Stage right are two doors . . . one marked "Colored men" . . . the other "Colored women." Stage left two other doorways are "White ladies" and "White gentlemen." There are two benches, one on each side. The room is drab and empty looking. Through the double doors upstage center can be seen a gray lighting which gives the effect of an early evening and open platform.

At rise of curtain the stage remains empty for about twenty seconds . . . A middle aged Negro woman enters, looks offstage . . . then crosses to the "Colored" side and sits on the bench. A moment later she is followed by a young Negro woman about twenty-one years old. She is carrying a large new cardboard suitcase and a wrapped shoebox. She is wearing a shoulder strap bag and a newspaper protrudes from the flap. She crosses to the "Colored" side and rests the suitcase at her feet as she looks at her mother with mild annoyance.

MARGE: You didn't have to get here so early, mama. Now you got to wait!

MAMA: If I'm goin' someplace . . . I like to get there in plenty time. You don't have to stay.

MARGE: You shouldn't wait 'round here alone.

MAMA: I ain't scared. Ain't a soul going to bother me.

MARGE: I got to get back to Ted. He don't like to be in the house by himself. (*She picks up the bag and places it on the bench by MAMA.*)

MAMA: You'd best go back. (*smiles*) You know I think he misses Florence.

MARGE: He's just a little fellow. He needs his mother. You make her come home! She shouldn't be way up there in Harlem. She ain't got nobody there.

MAMA: You know Florence don't like the South.

MARGE: It ain't what we like in this world! You tell her that.

MAMA: If Mr. Jack ask about the rent, you tell him we gonna be a little late on account of the trip.

MARGE: I'll talk with him. Don't worry so about everything. (*places suitcase on floor*) What you carryin', mama . . . bricks?

MAMA: If Mr. Jack won't wait . . . write to Rudley. He oughta send a little somethin'.

MARGE: Mama . . . Rudley ain't got nothin' fo himself. I hate to ask him to give us.

MAMA: That's your brother! If push come to shove, we got to ask.

MARGE: (*places box on bench*) Don't forget to eat your lunch . . . and try to get a seat near the window so you can lean on your elbow and get a little rest.

MAMA: Hmmmm . . . mmmph. Yes.

MARGE: Buy yourself some coffee when the man comes through. You'll need something hot and you can't go to the diner.

MAMA: I know that. You talk like I'm a northern greenhorn.

MARGE: You got handkerchiefs?

MAMA: I got everything, Marge.

MARGE: (*wanders upstage to the railing division line*) I know Florence is real bad off or she wouldn't call on us for money. Make her come home. She ain't gonna get rich up there and we can't afford to do for her.

MAMA: We talked all of that before.

MARGE: (*touches rail*) Well, you got to be strict on her. She got notions a Negro woman don't need.

MAMA: But she was in a real play. Didn't she send us twenty-five dollars a week?

MARGE: For two weeks.

MAMA: Well the play was over.

MARGE: (*crosses to MAMA and sits beside her*) It's not money, Mama. Sarah wrote us about it. You know what she said Florence was doin'. Sweepin' the stage!

MAMA: She was *in* the play!

MARGE: Sure she was in it! Sweepin'! Them folks ain't gonna let her be no actress. You tell her to wake up.

MAMA: I . . . I . . . think.

MARGE: Listen, Mama . . . She won't wanna come. We know that . . . but she gotta!

MAMA: Maybe we shoulda told her to expect me. It's kind of mean to just walk in like this.

MARGE: I bet she's livin' terrible. What's the matter with her? Don't she know we're keepin' her son?

MAMA: Florence don't feel right 'bout down here since Jim got killed.

MARGE: Who does? I should be the one goin' to get her. You tell her she ain't gonna feel right in no place. Mama, honestly! She must think she's white!

MAMA: Florence is brownskin.

MARGE: I don't mean that. I'm talkin' about her attitude. Didn't she go to Strumley's down here and ask to be a salesgirl? (*rises*) Now ain't that somethin'? They don't hire no Colored folks.

MAMA: Others beside Florence been talkin' about their rights.

MARGE: I know it . . . but there's things we can't do cause they ain't gonna let us. (*She wanders over to the "White" side of the stage.*) Don't feel a damn bit different over here than it does on our side. (*silence*)

MAMA: Maybe we shoulda just sent her the money this time. This one time.

MARGE: (*coming back to the "Colored" side*) Mama! Don't you let her cash that check for nothin' but to bring her back home.

MAMA: I know.

MARGE: (*restless . . . fidgets with her hair . . . patting it in place*) I oughta go now.

MAMA: You best get back to Ted. He might play with the lamp.

MARGE: He better not let me catch him! If you got to go to the ladies' room take your grip.

MAMA: I'll be alright. Make Ted get up on time for school.

MARGE: (*kisses her quickly and gives her the newspaper*) Here's something to read. So long, Mama.

MAMA: G'bye, Margie baby.

MARGE: (*goes to door . . . stops and turns to her mother*) You got your smelling salts?

MAMA: In my pocketbook.

MARGE: (*wistfully*) Tell Florence I love her and miss her too.

PORTER: (*can be heard singing in the distance*)

MAMA: Sure.

MARGE: (*reluctant to leave*) Pin that check in your bosom, Mama. You might fall asleep and somebody'll rob you.

MAMA: I got it pinned to me. (*feels for the check which is in her blouse*)

MARGE: (*almost pathetic*) Bye, Ma.

MAMA: (*sits for a moment looking at her surroundings. She opens the paper and begins to read.*)

PORTER: (*offstage*) Hello, Marge. What you doin' down here?

MARGE: I came to see Mama off.

PORTER: Where's she going?

MARGE: She's in there; she'll tell you. I got to get back to Ted.

PORTER: Bye now . . . Say, wait a minute, Marge.

MARGE: Yes?

PORTER: I told Ted he could have some of my peaches and he brought all them Brandford boys and they picked 'em all. I wouldn't lay a hand on him but I told him I was gonna tell you.

MARGE: I'm gonna give it to him!

PORTER: (*enters and crosses to white side of waiting room. He carries a pail of water and a mop. He is about fifty years old. He is obviously tired but not lazy.*) Every peach off my tree!

MAMA: There wasn't but six peaches on that tree.

PORTER: (*smiles . . . glances at MAMA as he crosses to the "White" side and begins to mop*) How d'ye do, Mrs. Whitney . . . you going on a trip?

MAMA: Fine, I thank you. I'm going to New York.

PORTER: Wish it was me. You gonna stay?

MAMA: No, Mr. Brown. I'm bringing Florence . . . I'm visiting Florence.

PORTER: Tell her I said hello. She's a fine girl.

MAMA: Thank you.

PORTER: My brother Bynum's in Georgia now.

MAMA: Well now, that's nice.

PORTER: Atlanta.

MAMA: He goin' to school?

PORTER: Yes'm. He saw Florence in a Colored picture. A moving picture.

MAMA: Do tell! She didn't say a word about it.

PORTER: They got Colored moving picture theaters in Atlanta.

MAMA: Yes. Your brother going to be a doctor?

PORTER: (*with pride*) No. He writes things.

MAMA: Oh.

PORTER: My son is goin' back to Howard next year.

MAMA: Takes an awful lot of goin' to school to be anything. Lot of money leastways.

PORTER: (*thoughtfully*) Yes'm, it sure do.

MAMA: That sure was a nice church sociable the other night.

PORTER: Yes'm. We raised 87 dollars.

MAMA: That's real nice.

PORTER: I won your cake at the bazaar.

MAMA: The chocolate one?

PORTER: (*as he wrings mop*) Yes'm . . . was light as a feather. That old train is gonna be late this evenin'. It's number 42.

MAMA: I don't mind waitin'.

PORTER: (*lifts pail, tucks mop handle under his arm. He looks about in order to make certain no one is around and leans over and addresses MAMA in a confidential tone.*) Did you buy your ticket from that Mr. Daly?

MAMA: (*in a low tone*) No. Marge bought it yesterday.

PORTER: (*leaning against railing*) That's good. That man is real mean. Especially if he thinks you're goin' north. (*He starts to leave . . . then turns back to MAMA*) If you go to the rest room, use the Colored men's . . . the other one is out of order.

MAMA: Thank you, sir.

MRS. CARTER: (*A white woman . . . well dressed, wearing furs and carrying a small, expensive overnight bag breezes in . . . breathless . . . flustered and smiling. She addresses the PORTER as she almost collides with him*) Boy! My bags are out there. The taxi driver just dropped them. Will they be safe?

PORTER: Yes, mam. I'll see after them.

MRS. CARTER: I thought I'd missed the train.

PORTER: It's late, mam.

MRS. CARTER: (*crosses to bench on the "White" side and rests her bag*) Fine! You come back here and get me when it comes. There'll be a tip in it for you.

PORTER: Thank you, mam. I'll be here. (*as he leaves*) Miss Whitney, I'll take care of your bag too.

MAMA: Thank you, sir.

MRS. CARTER: (*wheels around . . . notices MAMA*) Oh . . . Hello there . . .

MAMA: Howdy, mam. (*She opens her newspaper and begins to read.*)

MRS. CARTER: (*paces up and down rather nervously. She takes a cigarette from her purse, lights it and takes a deep draw. She looks at her watch and then speaks to MAMA across the railing.*) Have you any idea how late the train will be?

MAMA: No, mam. (*starts to read again*)

MRS. CARTER: I can't leave this place fast enough. Two days of it and I'm bored to tears. Do you live here?

MAMA: (*rests paper on her lap*) Yes, mam.

MRS. CARTER: Where are you going?

MAMA: New York City, mam.

MRS. CARTER: Good for you! You can stop "maming" me. My name is Mrs. Carter. I'm not a southerner really. (*takes handkerchief from her purse and covers her nose for a moment)* My God! Disinfectant! This is a frightful place. My brother's here writing a book. Wants atmosphere. Well, he's got it. I'll never come back here ever.

MAMA: That's too bad, mam . . . Mrs. Carter.

MRS. CARTER: That's good. I'd die in this place. Really die. Jeff . . . Mr. Wiley . . . my brother . . . He's tied in knots, a bundle of problems . . . positively in knots.

MAMA: *(amazed)* That so, mam?

MRS. CARTER: You don't have to call me mam. It's so southern. Mrs. Carter! These people are still fighting the Civil War. I'm really a New Yorker now. Of course, I was born here . . . in the South I mean. Memphis. Listen . . . am I annoying you? I've simply got to talk to someone.

MAMA: *(places her newspaper on the bench)* No, Mrs. Carter. It's perfectly alright.

MRS. CARTER: Fine! You see Jeff has ceased writing. Stopped! Just like that! *(snaps fingers)*

MAMA: *(turns to her)* That so?

MRS. CARTER: Yes. The reviews came out on his last book. Poor fellow.

MAMA: I'm sorry, mam . . . Mrs. Carter. They didn't like his book?

MRS. CARTER: Well enough . . . but Jeff's . . . well, Mr. Wiley is a genius. He says they missed the point! Lost the whole message! Did you read . . . do you . . . have you heard of *Lost My Lonely Way*?

MAMA: No, mam. I can't say I have.

MRS. CARTER: Well, it doesn't matter. It's profound. Real . . . you know. *(stands at the railing upstage)* It's about your people.

MAMA: That's nice.

MRS. CARTER: Jeff poured his complete self into it. Really delved into the heart of the problem, pulled no punches! He hardly stopped for his meals . . . And of course I wasn't here to see that he didn't overdo. He suffers so with his characters.

MAMA: I guess he wants to do his best.

MRS. CARTER: Zelma! . . . That's his heroine . . . Zelma! A perfect character.

MAMA: *(interested . . . coming out of her shell eagerly)* She was colored, mam?

MRS. CARTER: Oh yes! . . . But of course you don't know what it's about do you?

MAMA: No, miss . . . Would you tell me?

MRS. CARTER: *(leaning on the railing)* Well . . . she's almost white, see? Really you can't tell except in small ways. She wants to be a lawyer . . . and . . . and . . . well, there she is full of complexes and this deep shame you know.

MAMA: *(excitedly but with curiosity)* Do tell! What shame has she got?

MRS. CARTER: *(takes off her fur neckpiece and places it on bench with overnight bag)* It's obvious! This lovely creature . . . intelligent, ambitious, and well . . . she's a Negro!

MAMA: *(waiting eagerly)* Yes'm, you said that . . .

MRS. CARTER: Surely you understand? She's constantly hating herself. Just before she dies she says it!... Right on the bridge...

MAMA: (*genuinely moved*) How sad. Ain't it a shame she had to die?

MRS. CARTER: It was inevitable... couldn't be any other way!

MAMA: What did she say on the bridge?

MRS. CARTER: Well...just before she jumped...

MAMA: (*slowly straightening*) You mean she killed *herself*?

MRS. CARTER: Of course. Close your eyes and picture it!

MAMA: (*turns front and closes her eyes tightly with enthusiasm*) Yes'm.

MRS. CARTER: (*center stage on "White" side*) Now...! She's standing on the bridge in the moonlight... Out of her shabby purse she takes a mirror... and by the light of the moon she looks at her reflection in the glass.

MAMA: (*clasps her hands together gently*) I can see her just as plain.

MRS. CARTER: (*sincerely*) Tears roll down her cheeks as she says... almost! almost white... but I'm black! I'm a Negro! and then... (*turns to MAMA*) she jumps and drowns herself!

MAMA: (*opens her eyes and speaks quietly*) Why?

MRS. CARTER: She can't face it! Living in a world where she almost belongs but not quite. (*drifts upstage*) Oh it's so...so...tragic.

MAMA: (*carried away by her convictions... not anger... she feels challenged. She rises.*) That ain't so! Not one bit it ain't!

MRS. CARTER: (*surprised*) But it is!

MAMA: (*During the following she works her way around the railing until she crosses over about one foot to the "White" side and is face to face with MRS. CARTER.*) I know it ain't! Don't my friend Essie Kitredge daughter look just like a German or somethin'? She didn't kill herself! She's teachin' the third grade in the colored school right here. Even the bus drivers ask her to sit in the front seats cause they think she's white!... an'... an'... she just says as clear as you please... "I'm sittin' where my people got to sit by law. I'm a Negro woman!"

MRS. CARTER: (*uncomfortable and not knowing why*)... But there you have it. The exception makes the rule. That's proof!

MAMA: No such thing! My cousin Hemsly's as white as you!... an'... an' he never...

MRS. CARTER: (*flushed with anger... yet lost... because she doesn't know why*) Are you losing your temper? (*weakly*) Are you angry with me?

MAMA: (*stands silently trembling as she looks down and notices she is on the wrong side of the railing. She looks up at the "White Ladies Room" sign and slowly works her way back to the "Colored" side. She feels completely lost.*) No, mam. Excuse me please. (*with bitterness*) I just meant Hemsly works in the colored section of the shoe store... He never once wanted to kill his self! (*She sits down on the bench and fumbles for her newspaper. Silence.*)

MRS. CARTER: (*Caught between anger and reason... she laughs nervously.*) Well! Let's not be upset by this. It's entirely my fault you know. This whole thing is a completely controversial subject. (*silence*) If it's too much for Jeff... well naturally I shouldn't discuss it with you. (*approaching railing*) I'm sorry. Let *me* apologize.

MAMA: (*keeps her eyes on the paper*) No need for that, mam. (*silence*)

MRS. CARTER: (*painfully uncomfortable*) I've drifted away from... What started all of this?

MAMA: (*no comedy intended or allowed on this line*) Your brother, mam.

MRS. CARTER: (*trying valiantly to brush away the tension*) Yes... Well, I had to come down and sort of hold his hand over the reviews. He just thinks too much... and studies. He knows the Negro so well that sometimes our friends tease him and say he almost *seems* like... well you know...

MAMA: (*tightly*) Yes'm.

MRS. CARTER: (*slowly walks over to the "Colored" side near the top of the rail*) You know I try but it's really difficult to understand you people. However... I keep trying.

MAMA: (*still tight*) Thank you, mam.

MRS. CARTER: (*retreats back to "White" side and begins to prove herself*) Last week ... Why do you know what I did? I sent a thousand dollars to a Negro college for scholarships.

MAMA: That was right kind of you.

MRS. CARTER: (*almost pleading*) I know what's going on in your mind... and what you're thinking is wrong. I've... I've... eaten with Negroes.

MAMA: Yes, mam.

MRS. CARTER: (*trying to find a straw*)... And there's Malcom! If it weren't for the guidance of Jeff he'd never written his poems. Malcom is a Negro.

MAMA: (*freezing*) Yes, mam.

MRS. CARTER: (*gives up, crosses to her bench, opens her overnight bag and takes out a book and begins to read. She glances at MAMA from time to time. MAMA is deeply absorbed in her newspaper. MRS. CARTER closes her book with a bang... determined to penetrate the wall MAMA has built around her.*) Why are you going to New York?

MAMA: (*almost accusingly*) I got a daughter there.

MRS. CARTER: I lost my son in the war. (*silence... MAMA is ill at ease.*) Your daughter... what is she doing... studying?

MAMA: No'm, she's trying to get on stage.

MRS. CARTER: (*pleasantly*) Oh... a singer?

MAMA: No, mam. She's...

MRS. CARTER: (*warmly*) You people have such a gift. I love spirituals... "Steal Away," "Swing Low, Sweet Chariot."

MAMA: They are right nice. But Florence wants to act. Just say things in plays.

MRS. CARTER: A dramatic actress?

MAMA: Yes, that's what it is. She been in a colored moving picture, and a big show for two weeks on Broadway.

MRS. CARTER: The dear, precious child!... But this is funny... no! it's pathetic. She must be bitter... *really* bitter. Do you know what I do?

MAMA: I can't rightly say.

MRS. CARTER: I'm an actress! A dramatic actress... And I haven't really worked in six months... And I'm pretty well-known... And everyone knows Jeff. I'd like to work. Of course, there are my committees, but you see, they don't need me. Not really... not even Jeff.

MAMA: Now that's a shame.

MRS. CARTER: Now your daughter... you must make her stop before she's completely unhappy. Make her stop!

MAMA: Yes'm... why?

MRS. CARTER: I have the best of contacts and *I've* only done a few *broadcasts* lately. Of course, I'm not counting the things I just wouldn't do. Your daughter ... make her stop.

MAMA: A drama teacher told her she has real talent.

MRS. CARTER: A drama teacher! My dear woman, there are loads of unscrupulous whites up there that just hand out opinions for...

MAMA: This was a colored gentleman down here.

MRS. CARTER: Oh well!... And she went up there on the strength of that? This makes me very unhappy. (*puts book away in case, and snaps lock. silence*)

MAMA: (*getting an idea*) Do you really, truly feel that way, mam?

MRS. CARTER: I do. Please... I want you to believe me.

MAMA: Could I ask you something?

MRS. CARTER: Anything.

MAMA: You won't be angry, mam?

MRS. CARTER: (*remembering*) I won't. I promise you.

MAMA: (*gathering courage*) Florence is proud... but she's having it hard.

MRS. CARTER: I'm sure she is.

MAMA: Could you help her out some, mam? Knowing all the folks you do... maybe...

MRS. CARTER: (*rubs the outside of the case*) Well... it isn't that simple... but... you're very sweet. If only I could...

MAMA: Anything you did, I feel grateful. I don't like to tell it, but she can't even pay her rent and things. And she's used to my cooking for her... I believe my girl goes hungry sometime up there... and yet she'd like to stay so bad.

MRS. CARTER: (*looks up, resting case on her knees*) How can I refuse? You seem like a good woman.

MAMA: Always lived as best I knew how and raised my children up right. We got a fine family, mam.

MRS. CARTER: And I've no family at all. I've got to! It's clearly my duty. Jeff's books . . . guiding Malcom's poetry . . . It isn't enough . . . oh I know it isn't. Have you ever heard of Melba Rugby?

MAMA: No, mam. I don't know anybody much . . . except right here.

MRS. CARTER: (*brightening*) She's in California, but she's moving East again . . . hates California.

MAMA: Yes'm.

MRS. CARTER: A most versatile woman. Writes, directs, acts . . . everything!

MAMA: That's nice, mam.

MRS. CARTER: Well, she's uprooting herself and coming back to her first home . . . New York . . . to direct "Love Flowers" . . . it's a musical.

MAMA: Yes'm.

MRS. CARTER: She's grand . . . helped so many people . . . and I'm sure she'll help your . . . what's her name.

MAMA: Florence.

MRS. CARTER: (*turns back to bench, opens bag, takes out a pencil and an address book*) Yes, Florence. She'll have to *make* a place for her.

MAMA: Bless you, mam.

MRS. CARTER: (*holds handbag steady on rail as she uses it to write on*) Now let's see . . . the best thing to do would be to give you the telephone number . . . since you're going there.

MAMA: Yes'm.

MRS. CARTER: (*writing address on paper*) Your daughter will love her . . . and if she's a deserving girl . . .

MAMA: (*looking down as MRS. CARTER writes*) She's a good child. Never a bit of trouble. Except about her husband, and neither one of them could help that.

MRS. CARTER: (*stops writing, raises her head questioning*) Oh?

MAMA: He got killed at voting time. He was a good man.

MRS. CARTER: (*embarrassed*) I guess that's worse than losing him in the war.

MAMA: We all got our troubles passing through here.

MRS. CARTER: (*gives her the address*) Tell your dear girl to call this number about a week from now.

MAMA: Yes, mam.

MRS. CARTER: Her experience won't matter with Melba. I know she'll understand. I'll call her too.

MAMA: Thank you, mam.

MRS. CARTER: I'll just tell her . . . no heavy washing or ironing . . . just light cleaning and a little cooking . . . does she cook?

MAMA: Mam? (*slowly backs away from MRS. CARTER and sits down on bench*)

MRS. CARTER: Don't worry, that won't matter to Melba. (*silence. moves around the rail to "Colored" side, leans over MAMA*) I'd take your daughter myself, but

I've got Binnie. She's been with me for years, and I just can't let her go . . . can I?

MAMA: (*looks at MRS. CARTER closely*) No, mam.

MRS. CARTER: Of course she must be steady. I couldn't ask Melba to take a fly-by-night. (*touches MAMA's arm*) But she'll have her own room and bath, and above all . . . security.

MAMA: (*reaches out, clutches MRS. CARTER's wrist almost pulling her off balance*) Child!

MRS. CARTER: (*frightened*) You're hurting my wrist.

MAMA: (*looks down, realizes how tight she's clutching her, and releases her wrist*) I mustn't hurt you, must I.

MRS. CARTER: (*backing away rubbing her wrist*) It's all right.

MAMA: (*rises*) You better get over on the other side of that rail. It's against the law for you to be over here with me.

MRS. CARTER: (*frightened and uncomfortable*) If you think so.

MAMA: I don't want to break the law.

MRS. CARTER: (*keeps her eye on MAMA as she drifts around railing to bench on her side. gathers overnight bag*) I know I must look like a fright. The train should be along soon. When it comes, I won't see you until New York. These silly laws. (*silence*) I'm going to powder my nose. (*exits into "White ladies" room*

PORTER: (*singing offstage*)

MAMA: (*sits quietly, staring in front of her . . . then looks at the address for a moment . . . tears the paper into little bits and lets them flutter to the floor. She opens the suitcase, takes out notebook, an envelope and a pencil. She writes a few words on the paper.*)

PORTER: (*enters with broom and dust pan*) Number 42 will be coming along in nine minutes. (*When MAMA doesn't answer him, he looks up and watches her. She reaches in her bosom, unpins the check, smooths it out, places it in the envelope with the letter. She closes the suitcase.*) I said the train's coming. Where's the lady?

MAMA: She's in the *ladies'* room. You got a stamp?

PORTER: No. But I can get one out of the machine. Three for a dime.

MAMA: (*hands him the letter*) Put one on here and mail it for me.

PORTER: (*looks at it*) Gee . . . you writing Florence when you're going to see her?

MAMA: (*picks up the shoebox and puts it back on the bench*) You want a good lunch? It's chicken and fruit.

PORTER: Sure . . . thank you . . . but you won't . . .

MAMA: (*rises, paces up and down*) I ain't gonna see Florence for a long time. Might be never.

PORTER: How's that, Mrs. Whitney?

MAMA: She can be anything in the world she wants to be! That's her right. Marge can't make her turn back, Mrs. Carter can't make her turn back. *Lost My Lonely Way!* That's a book! People killing theyselves 'cause they look white but be black. They just don't know do they, Mr. Brown?

PORTER: Whatever happened don't you fret none. Life is too short.

MAMA: Oh, I'm gonna fret plenty! You know what I wrote Florence?

PORTER: No, mam. But you don't have to tell me.

MAMA: I said "Keep trying." . . . Oh, I'm going home.

PORTER: I'll take your bag. (*picks up bag and starts out*) Come on, Mrs. Whitney. (*PORTER exits*)

> (*MAMA moves around to "White" side, stares at sign over door. She starts to knock on "White Ladies" door, but changes her mind. As she turns to leave, her eye catches the railing; she approaches it gently, touches it, turns, exits. Stage is empty for about six or seven seconds. Sound of train whistle is heard in the distance. Slow curtain.*)

CURTAIN

Wine in the Wilderness (1969) ——

Alice Childress

CHARACTERS

BILL JAMESON	an artist aged thirty-three
OLDTIMER	an old roustabout character in his sixties
SONNY-MAN	a writer aged twenty-seven
CYNTHIA	a social worker aged twenty-five. She is SONNY-MAN'S wife.
TOMMY	a woman factory worker aged thirty

TIME: the summer of 1964. Night of a riot.
PLACE: Harlem, New York City, New York, U.S.A.

SCENE: A one room apartment in a Harlem tenement. It used to be a three room apartment but the tenant has broken out walls and is half finished with a redecorating job. The place is now only partly reminiscent of its past tawdry days, plaster broken away and lathing exposed right next to a new brick-faced portion of wall. The kitchen is now part of the room. There is a three-quarter bed covered with an African throw, a screen is placed at the foot of the bed to insure privacy when needed. The room is obviously black dominated, pieces of sculpture, wall hangings, paintings. An artist's easel is standing with a drapery thrown across it so the empty canvas beneath it is hidden. Two other canvases the same size are next to it; they too are covered and conceal paintings. The place is in a beautiful, rather artistic state of disorder. The room also reflects an interest in other darker peoples of the world . . . A Chinese incense-burner Buddha, an American Indian feathered war helmet, a Mexican serape, a Japanese fan, a West Indian travel poster. There is a kitchen table, chairs, floor cushions, a couple of box crates, books, bookcases, plenty of artist's materials. There is a small raised platform for model posing. On the platform is a backless chair.

The tail end of a riot is going on out in the street. Noise and screaming can be heard in the distance, . . . running feet, voices shouting over loudspeakers.

OFFSTAGE VOICES: Offa the street! Into your homes! Clear the street! (*the whine of a bullet is heard*) Cover that roof! It's from the roof!

(BILL is seated on the floor with his back to the wall, drawing in a large sketch pad with charcoal pencil. He is very absorbed in his task but flinches as he hears the bullet sound, ducks and shields his head with upraised hand, . . . then resumes sketching. The telephone rings; he reaches for phone with caution, pulls it toward him by the cord in order to avoid going near window or standing up.)

BILL: Hello? Yeah, my phone is on. How the hell I'm gonna be talkin' to you if it's not on? *(sound of glass breaking in the distance)* I could lose my damn life answerin' the phone. Sonny-man, what the hell you callin' me up for! I thought you and Cynthia might be downstairs dead, I banged on the floor and hollered down the air-shaft, no answer. No stuff! Thought yall was dead. I'm sittin' here drawin' a picture in your memory. In a bar! Yall sittin' in a bar? See there, you done blew the picture that's in your memory . . . No kiddin', they wouldn't let you in the block? Man, they can't keep you outta your own house. Found? You found who? Model? What model? Yeah, yeah, thanks, . . . but I like to find my own models. No! Don't bring nobody up here in the middle of a riot . . . Hey, Sonny-man! Hey!

(sound of yelling and rushing footsteps in the hall)

WOMAN'S VOICE: *(offstage)* Dammit, Bernice! The riot is over! What you hidin' in the hall for? I'm in the house, your father's in the house, . . . and you out there hidin' in the hall!

GIRL'S VOICE: *(offstage)* The house might burn down!

BILL: Sonny-man, I can't hear you!

WOMAN'S VOICE: *(offstage)* If it do burn down, what the hell you gon' do, run off and leave us to burn up by ourself? The riot is over. The police say it's over! Get back in the house!

(sound of running feet and a knock on the door)

BILL: They say it's over. Man, they oughta let you on your own block, in your own house . . . Yeah, we still standin', this seventy year old house got guts. Thank you, yeah, thanks but I like to pick my own models. You drunk? Can't you hear when I say not to . . . Okay, all right, bring her . . .

(frantic knocking at the door)

BILL: I gotta go. Yeah, yeah, bring her. I gotta go . . .

(BILL hangs up phone and opens the door for OLDTIMER. The old man is carrying a haul of loot . . . two or three bottles of liquor, a ham, a salami and a suit with price tags attached.)

BILL: What's this! Oh, no, no, no, Oldtimer, not here . . .

(faint sound of a police whistle)

BILL: The police after you? What you bring that stuff in here for?

OLDTIMER: *(runs past BILL to center as he looks for a place to hide the loot)* No, no they not really after me but . . . I was in the basement so I could stash this stuff, . . . but a fella told me they pokin' 'round down there : . . in the back yard pokin' 'round . . . the police doin' a lotta pokin' 'round.

BILL: If the cops are searchin' why you wanna dump your troubles on me?

OLDTIMER: I don't wanta go to jail. I'm too old to go to jail. What we gonna do?

BILL: We can throw it the hell outta the window. Didn't you think of just throwin' it away and not worry 'bout jail?

OLDTIMER: I can't do it. It's like... I'm Oldtimer but my hands and arms is somebody else that I don' know-a-tall.

(*BILL pulls stuff out of OLDTIMER'S arms and places loot on the kitchen table. OLDTIMER'S arms fall to his sides.*)

OLDTIMER: Thank you, son.

BILL: Stealin' ain't worth a bullet through your brain, is it? You wanna get shot down and drown in your own blood, ... for what? A suit, a bottle of whiskey? Gonna throw your life away for a damn ham?

OLDTIMER: But I ain't really stole nothin', Bill, cause I ain't no thief. Them others, ... they smash the windows, they run in the stores and grab and all. Me, I pick up what they left scatter in the street. Things they drop... things they trample underfoot. What's in the street ain't like stealin'. This is leavin's. What I'm gon' do if the police come?

BILL: (*starts to gather the things in the tablecloth that is on the table*) I'll throw it out the air-shaft window.

OLDTIMER: (*places himself squarely in front of the air-shaft window*) I be damn. Uh-uh, can't let you do it, Billy-Boy. (*grabs the liquor and holds on*)

BILL: (*wraps the suit, the ham and the salami in the tablecloth and ties the ends together in a knot*) Just for now, then you can go down and get it later.

OLDTIMER: (*getting belligerent*) I say I ain't gon' let you do it.

BILL: Sonny-man calls this "The people's revolution." A revolution should not be looting and stealing. Revolutions are for liberation.

(*OLDTIMER won't budge from before the window.*)

BILL: Okay, man, you win, it's all yours. (*walks away from OLDTIMER and prepares his easel for sketching*)

OLDTIMER: Don't be mad with me, Billy-Boy, I couldn't help myself.

BILL: (*at peace with the old man*) No hard feelin's.

OLDTIMER: (*as he uncorks bottle*) I don't blame you for bein' fed up with us, ... fella like you oughta be fed up with your people sometime. Hey, Billy, let's you and me have a little taste together.

BILL: Yeah, why not.

OLDTIMER: (*at the table pouring drinks*) You mustn't be too hard on me. You see, you talented, you got somethin' on the ball, you gonna make it on past these white folk, ... but not me, Billy-Boy, it's too late in the day for that. Time, time, time, ... time done put me down. Father Time is a bad white cat. Whatcha been paintin' and drawin' lately? You can paint me again if you wanta, ... no charge. Paint me 'cause that might be the only way I get to stay in the world after I'm dead and gone. Somebody'll look up at your paintin' and say, ... "Who's that?" And you say, ... "That's Oldtimer."

(*BILL joins OLDTIMER at table and takes one of the drinks.*)

OLDTIMER: Well, here's lookin' at you and goin' down me. (*gulps down drink*)

BILL: (*raising his glass*) Your health, Oldtimer.

OLDTIMER: My day we didn't have all this grants and scholarship like now. Whatcha been doin'?

BILL: I'm working on the third part of a triptych.

OLDTIMER: A what tick?

BILL: A triptych.

OLDTIMER: Hot-damn, that call for another drink. Here's to the trip-tick. Down the hatch. What is one-a-those?

BILL: It's three paintings that make one work . . . three paintings that make one subject.

OLDTIMER: Goes together like a new outfit . . . hat, shoes and suit.

BILL: Right. The title of my triptych is . . . "Wine in the Wilderness" . . . Three canvases on black womanhood . . .

OLDTIMER: (*eyes light up*) Are they naked pitchers?

BILL: (*crosses to paintings*) No, all fully clothed.

OLDTIMER: (*wishing it was a naked picture*) Man, ain' nothin' dirty 'bout naked pitchers. That's art. What you call artistic.

BILL: Right, right, right, but these are with clothes. That can be artistic too. (*uncovers one of the canvases and reveals painting of a charming little girl in Sunday dress and hair ribbon*) I call her . . . "Black Girlhood."

OLDTIMER: Awwwww, that's innocence! Don't know what it's all about. Ain't that the little child that live right down the street? Yeah. That call for another drink.

BILL: Slow down, Oldtimer, wait till you see this. (*He covers the painting of the little girl, then uncovers another canvas and reveals a beautiful woman, deep mahogany complexion; she is cold but utter perfection, draped in startling colors of African material, very "Vogue" looking. She wears a golden head-dress sparkling with brilliants and sequins applied over the paint.*) There she is . . . "Wine in the Wilderness" . . . Mother Africa, regal, black womanhood in her noblest form.

OLDTIMER: Hot damn. I'd die for her, no stuff, . . . Oh, man. "Wine in the Wilderness."

BILL: Once, a long time ago, a poet named Omar told us what a paradise life could be if a man had a loaf of bread, a jug of wine and . . . a woman singing to him in the wilderness. She is the woman; she is the bread; she is the wine; she is the singing. This Abyssinian maiden is paradise, . . . perfect black womanhood.

OLDTIMER: (*pours for BILL and himself*) To our Abyssinian maiden.

BILL: She's the Sudan, the Congo River, the Egyptian Pyramids . . . Her thighs are African mahogany . . . she speaks and her words pour forth sparkling clear as the waters . . . Victoria Falls.

OLDTIMER: Ow! Victoria Falls! She got a pretty name.

BILL: (*covers her up again*) Victoria Falls is a waterfall, not her name. Now, here's the one that calls for a drink. (*snatches cover from the empty canvas*)

OLDTIMER: (*stunned by the empty canvas*) Your... your pitcher is gone.

BILL: Not gone, ... she's not painted yet. This will be the third part of the triptych. This is the unfinished third of "Wine in the Wilderness." She's gonna be the kinda chick that is grass roots, ... no, not grass roots, ... I mean she's underneath the grass roots. The lost woman, ... what the society has made out of our women. She's as far from my African queen as a woman can get and still be female; she's as close to the bottom as you can get without crackin' up... She's ignorant, unfeminine, coarse, rude... vulgar... a poor, dumb chick that's had her behind kicked until it's numb... and the sad part is... she ain't together, you know, ... there's no hope for her.

OLDTIMER: Oh, man, you talkin' 'bout my first wife.

BILL: A chick that ain't fit for nothin' but to... to... just pass her by.

OLDTIMER: Yeah, later for her. When you see her, cross over to the other side of the street.

BILL: If you had to sum her up in one word it would be nothin'!

OLDTIMER: (*roars with laughter*) That call for a double!

BILL: (*beginning to slightly feel the drinks. He covers the canvas again.*) Yeah, that's a double! The kinda woman that grates on your damn nerves. And Sonny-man just called to say he found her runnin' 'round in the middle-a this riot; Sonny-man say she's the real thing from underneath them grass roots. A back-country chick right outta the wilds of Mississippi, ... but she ain't never been near there. Born in Harlem, raised right here in Harlem, ... but back country. Got the picture?

OLDTIMER: (*full of laughter*) When... when... when she get here let's us stomp her to death.

BILL: Not till after I paint her. Gonna put her right here on this canvas. (*pats the canvas, walks in a strut around the table*) When she gets put down on canvas, ... then triptych will be finished.

OLDTIMER: (*joins him in the strut*) Trip-tick will be finish... trip-tick will be finish ...

BILL: Then "Wine in the Wilderness" will go up against the wall to improve the view of some post office... or some library... or maybe a bank... and I'll win a prize... and the queen, my black queen will look down from the wall so the messed up chicks in the neighborhood can see what a woman oughta be... and the innocent child on the side of her and the messed up chick on the other side of her... MY STATEMENT.

OLDTIMER: (*turning the strut into a dance*) Wine in the wilderness... up against the wall... wine in the wilderness... up against the wall...

WOMAN FROM UPSTAIRS APT.: (*offstage*) What's the matter! The house on fire?

BILL: (*calls upstairs through the air-shaft window*) No, baby! We down here paintin' pictures! (*sound of police siren in distance*)

WOMAN FROM UPSTAIRS APT.: (*offstage*) So much-a damn noise! Cut out the noise! (*to her husband hysterically*) Percy! Percy! You hear a police siren! Percy! That a fire engine?!

BILL: Another messed up chick. (*gets a rope and ties it to OLDTIMER'S bundle*) Got an idea. We'll tie the rope to the bundle, . . . then . . . (*lowers bundle out the window*) lower the bundle outta the window . . . and tie it to this nail here behind the curtain. Now! Nobody can find it except you and me . . . Cops come, there's no loot. (*ties rope to nail under curtain*)

OLDTIMER: Yeah, yeah, loot long gone 'til I want it. (*makes sure window knot is secure*) It'll be swingin' in the breeze free and easy. (*There is knocking on the door.*)

SONNY-MAN: Open up! Open up! Sonny-man and company.

BILL: (*putting finishing touches on, securing knot to nail*) Wait, wait, hold on . . .

SONNY-MAN: And-a here we come!

> (*SONNY-MAN pushes the door open. Enters room with his wife CYNTHIA and TOMMY, SONNY-MAN is in high spirits. He is in his late twenties; his wife CYNTHIA is a bit younger. She wears her hair in a natural style; her clothing is tweedy and in good, quiet taste. SONNY-MAN is wearing slacks and a dashiki over a shirt. TOMMY is dressed in a mis-matched shirt and sweater, wearing a wig that is not comical, but is wiggy. She has the habit of smoothing it every once in a while, patting to make sure it's in place. She wears sneakers and bobby sox, carries a brown paper sack.*)

CYNTHIA: You didn't think it was locked, did you?

BILL: Door not locked? (*looking over TOMMY*)

TOMMY: You oughta run him outta town, pushin' open people's door.

BILL: Come right on in.

SONNY-MAN: (*standing behind TOMMY and pointing down at her to draw BILL'S attention*) Yes, sireeeeee.

CYNTHIA: Bill, meet a friend-a ours . . . this is Miss Tommy Fields. Tommy, meet a friend-a ours . . . this is Bill Jameson . . . Bill, Tommy.

BILL: Tommy, if I may call you that . . .

TOMMY: (*likes him very much*) Help yourself, Bill. It's a pleasure. Bill Jameson, well, all right.

BILL: The pleasure is all mine. Another friend-a ours, Oldtimer.

TOMMY: (*with respect and warmth*) How are you, Mr. Timer?

BILL: (*laughs along with others, OLDTIMER included*) What you call him, baby?

TOMMY: Mr. Timer, . . . ain't that what you say?

> (*They all laugh expansively.*)

BILL: No, sugar pie, that's not his name, . . . we just say . . . "Oldtimer," that's what everybody call him.

OLDTIMER: Yeah, they all call me that . . . everybody say that . . . OLDTIMER.

TOMMY: That's cute, . . . but what's your name?

BILL: His name is . . . er . . . er . . . What is your name?

SONNY-MAN: Dog-bite, what's your name, man?

> (*There is a significant moment of self-consciousness as CYNTHIA, SONNY-MAN and BILL realize they don't know OLDTIMER'S name.*)

OLDTIMER: Well, it's . . . Edmond L. Matthews.

TOMMY: Edmond L. Matthews. What's the L for?

OLDTIMER: Lorenzo, . . . Edmond Lorenzo Matthews.

BILL and SONNY-MAN: Edmond Lorenzo Matthews.

TOMMY: Pleased to meetcha, Mr. Matthews.

OLDTIMER: Nobody call me that in a long, long time.

TOMMY: I'll call you Oldtimer like the rest but I like to know who I'm meetin'.

> (*OLDTIMER gives her a chair.*)

TOMMY: There you go. He's a gentleman too. Bet you can tell my feet hurt. I got one corn . . . and that one is enough. Oh, it'll ask you for somethin'.

> (*general laughter. BILL indicates to SONNY-MAN that TOMMY seems right. CYNTHIA and OLDTIMER take seats near TOMMY.*)

BILL: You rest yourself, baby, er . . . er . . . Tommy. You did say Tommy.

TOMMY: I cut it to Tommy . . . Tommy-Marie; I use both of 'em sometime.

BILL: How 'bout some refreshment?

SONNY-MAN: Yeah, how 'bout that. (*pouring drinks*)

TOMMY: Don't yall carry me too fast, now.

BILL: (*indicating liquor bottles*) I got what you see and also some wine . . . couple-a cans-a beer.

TOMMY: I'll take the wine.

BILL: Yeah, I knew it.

TOMMY: Don't wanta start nothin' I can't keep up.

> (*OLDTIMER slaps his thigh with pleasure.*)

BILL: That's all right, baby, you just a wine-o.

TOMMY: You the one that's got the wine, not me.

BILL: I use this for cookin'.

TOMMY: You like to get loaded while you cook?

> (*OLDTIMER is having a ball.*)

BILL: (*as he pours wine for TOMMY*) Oh, baby, you too much.

OLDTIMER: (*admiring TOMMY*) Oh, Lord, I wish, I wish, I wish I was young again.

TOMMY: (*flirtatiously*) Lively as you are, . . . I don't know what we'd do with you if you got any younger.

OLDTIMER: Oh, hush now!

SONNY-MAN: (*whispering to BILL and pouring drinks*) Didn't I tell you! Know what I'm talkin' about. You dig? All the elements, man.

TOMMY: (*worried about what the whispering means*) Let's get somethin' straight. I didn't come bustin' in on the party, . . . I was asked. If you married and any wives or girl-friends round here . . . I'm innocent. Don't wanta get shot at, or jumped on. Cause I wasn't doin' a thing but mindin' my business! (*saying the last in loud tones to be heard in other rooms*)

OLDTIMER: Jus' us here, that's all.

BILL: I'm single, baby. Nobody wants a poor artist.

CYNTHIA: Oh, honey, we wouldn't walk you into a jealous wife or girl friend.

TOMMY: You paint all-a these pitchers?

(*BILL and SONNY-MAN hand out drinks.*)

BILL: Just about. Your health, baby, to you.

TOMMY: (*lifts her wine glass*) All right, and I got one for you . . . Like my grampaw used-ta say, . . . Here's to the men's collars and the women's skirts, . . . may they never meet.

(*general laughter*)

OLDTIMER: But they ain't got far to go before they do.

TOMMY: (*suddenly remembers her troubles*) Niggers, niggers . . . niggers . . . I'm sick-a niggers, ain't you? A nigger will mess up everytime . . . Lemmie tell you what the niggers done . . .

BILL: Tommy, baby, we don't use that word around here. We can talk about each other a little bit better than that.

CYNTHIA: Oh, she doesn't mean it.

TOMMY: What must I say?

BILL: Try Afro-Americans.

TOMMY: Well, . . . the Afro-Americans burnt down my house.

OLDTIMER: Oh, no they didn't!

TOMMY: Oh, yes they did . . . it's almost burn down. Then the firemen nailed up my door . . . the door to my room, nailed up shut tight with all I got in the world.

OLDTIMER: Shame, what a shame.

TOMMY: A damn shame. My clothes . . . Everything gone. This riot blew my life. All I got is gone like it never was.

OLDTIMER: I know it.

TOMMY: My transistor radio . . . that's gone.

CYNTHIA: Ah, gee.

TOMMY: The transistor . . . and a brand new pair-a shoes I never had on one time . . . (*raises her right hand*) If I never move, that's the truth . . . new shoes gone.

OLDTIMER: Child, when hard luck fall it just keep fallin'.

TOMMY: And in my top dresser drawer I got a my-on-ase jar with forty-one dollars in it. The fireman would not let me in to get it . . . And it was a Afro-American fireman, don'tcha know.

OLDTIMER: And you ain't got no place to stay.

(*BILL is studying her for portrait possibilities.*)

TOMMY: (*rises and walks around room*) That's a lie. I always got some place to go. I don't wanta boast but I ain't never been no place that I can't go back the second time. Woman I use to work for say . . . "Tommy, any time, any time you want a sleep-in place you come right here to me." . . . And that's Park Avenue, my own private bath and T.V. set . . . But I don't want that . . . so I make it on out here to the dress factory. I got friends . . . not a lot of 'em . . . but a few good ones. I call my friend-girl and her mother . . . they say . . . "Tommy, you come here, bring yourself over here." So Tommy got a roof with no sweat. (*looks at torn wall*) Looks like the Afro-Americans got to you too. Breakin' up, breakin' down, . . . that's all they know.

BILL: No, Tommy, . . . I'm re-decorating the place . . .

TOMMY: You mean you did this to yourself?

CYNTHIA: It's gonna be wild . . . brick-face walls . . . wall to wall carpet.

SONNY-MAN: She was breakin' up everybody in the bar . . . had us all laughin' . . . crackin' us up. In the middle of a riot . . . she's gassin' everybody!

TOMMY: No need to cry, it's sad enough. They hollerin' whitey, whitey . . . but who they burn out? Me.

BILL: The brothers and sisters are tired, weary of the endless get-no-where struggle.

TOMMY: I'm standin' there in the bar . . . tellin' it like it is . . . next thing I know they talkin' 'bout bringin' me to meet you. But you know what I say? Can't nobody pick nobody for nobody else. It don't work. And I'm standin' there in a mis-match skirt and top and these sneaker-shoes. I just went to put my dresses in the cleaner . . . Oh, Lord, wonder if they burn down the cleaner. Well, no matter, when I got back it was all over . . . They went in the grocery store, rip out the shelves, pull out all the groceries . . . the hams . . . the . . . the . . . the can goods . . . everything . . . and then set fire . . . Now who you think live over the grocery? Me, that's who. I don't even go to the store lookin' this way . . . but this would be the time, when . . . folks got a fella they want me to meet.

BILL: (*suddenly self-conscious*) Tommy, they thought . . . they thought I'd like to paint you . . . that's why they asked you over.

TOMMY: (*pleased by the thought but she can't understand it*) Paint me? For what? If he was gonna paint somebody seems to me it'd be one of the pretty girls they show in the beer ads. They even got colored on television now, . . . brushin' their teeth and smokin' cigarettes, . . . some of the prettiest girls in the world. He could get them, . . . couldn't you?

BILL: Sonny-man and Cynthia were right. I want to paint you.

TOMMY: (*suspiciously*) Naked, with no clothes on?

BILL: No, baby, dressed just as you are now.

OLDTIMER: Wearin' clothes is also art.

TOMMY: In the cleaner I got a white dress with a orlon sweater to match it, maybe I can get it out tomorrow and pose in that.

(*CYNTHIA, OLDTIMER and SONNY-MAN are eager for her to agree.*)

BILL: No, I will paint you today, Tommy, just as you are, holding your brown paper bag.

TOMMY: Mmmmmm, me holdin' the damn bag; I don' know 'bout that.

BILL: Look at it this way, tonight has been a tragedy.

TOMMY: Sure in hell has.

BILL: And so I must paint you tonight, . . . Tommy in her moment of tragedy.

TOMMY: I'm tired.

BILL: Damn, baby, all you have to do is sit there and rest.

TOMMY: I'm hongry.

SONNY-MAN: While you're posin' Cynthia can run down to our house and fix you some eggs.

CYNTHIA: (*gives her husband a weary look*) Oh, Sonny, that's such a lovely idea.

SONNY-MAN: Thank you, darlin'; I'm in there, . . . on the beam.

TOMMY: (*ill at ease about posing*) I don't want no eggs. I'm goin' to find me some Chinese food.

BILL: I'll go. If you promise to stay here and let me paint you, . . . I'll get you anything you want.

TOMMY: (*brightening up*) Anything I want. Now, how he sound? All right, you comin' on mighty strong there. "Anything you want." When last you heard somebody say that? . . . I'm warnin' you, now, . . . I'm free, single and disengage, . . . so you better watch yourself.

BILL: (*keeping her away from ideas of romance*) Now this is the way the program will go down. First I'll feed you, then I'll paint you.

TOMMY: Okay, I'm game, I'm a good sport. First off, I want me some Chinese food.

CYNTHIA: Order up, Tommy, the treat's on him.

TOMMY: How come it is you never been married? All these girls runnin' 'round Harlem lookin' for husbands. (*to CYNTHIA*) I don't blame 'em, 'cause I'm lookin' for somebody myself.

BILL: I've been married, married and divorced; she divorced me, Tommy, so maybe I'm not much of a catch.

TOMMY: Look at it this-a-way. Some folks got bad taste. That woman had bad taste.

(*All laugh except BILL who pours another drink.*)

TOMMY: Watch it, Bill, you gonna rust the linin' of your stomach. Ain't this a shame? The riot done wipe me out and I'm sittin' here ballin'! (*as BILL refills her glass*) Hold it, that's enough. Likker ain' my problem.

OLDTIMER: I'm havin' me a good time.

TOMMY: Know what I say 'bout divorce. (*slaps her hands together in a final gesture*) Anybody don' wantcha, . . . later, let 'em go. That's bad taste for you.

BILL: Tommy, I don't wanta ever get married again. It's me and my work. I'm not gettin' serious about anybody . . .

TOMMY: He's spellin' at me, now. Nigger, . . . I mean Afro-American . . . I ain' ask you nothin'. You hinkty, I'm hinkty too. I'm independent as a hog on ice, . . . and a hog on ice is dead, cold, well-preserved . . . and don't need a mother-grabbin' thing.

(*All laugh heartily except BILL and CYNTHIA.*)

TOMMY: I know models get paid. I ain' no square but this is a special night and so this one'll be on the house. Show you my heart's in the right place.

BILL: I'll be glad to pay you, baby.

TOMMY: You don't really like me, do you? That's all right, sometime it happen that way. You can't pick for nobody. Friends get to matchin' up friends and they mess up everytime. Cynthia and Sonny-man done messed up.

BILL: I like you just fine and I'm glad and grateful that you came.

TOMMY: Good enough. (*extends her hand. They slap hands together.*) You'n me friends?

BILL: Friends, baby, friends. (*putting rock record on*)

TOMMY: (*trying out the model stand*) Okay, Dad! Let's see 'bout this anything I want jive. Want me a bucket-a Egg Foo Yong, and you get you a shrimp-fry rice, we split that and each have some-a both. Make him give you the soy sauce, the hot mustard and the duck sauce too.

BILL: Anything else, baby?

TOMMY: Since you ask, yes. If your money hold out, get me a double order egg roll. And a half order of the sweet and sour spare ribs.

BILL: (*to OLDTIMER and SONNY-MAN*) Come on, come on. I need some strong men to help me bring back your order, baby.

TOMMY: (*going into her dance . . . simply standing and going through some boo-ga-loo motions*) Better get it 'fore I think up some more to go 'long with it.

(*The men vanish out of the door. Steps heard descending stairs.*)

TOMMY: Turn that off. (*CYNTHIA turns off record player.*) How could I forget your name, good as you been to me this day. Thank you, Cynthia, thank you. I like him. Oh, I like him. But I don't wanta push him too fast. Oh, I got to play these cards right.

CYNTHIA: (*a bit uncomfortable*) Oh, Honey, . . . Tommy, you don't want a poor artist.

TOMMY: Tommy's not lookin' for a meal ticket. I been doin' for myself all my life. It takes two to make it in this high-price world. A black man see a hard way to go. The both of you gotta pull together. That way you accomplish.

CYNTHIA: I'm a social worker . . . and I see so many broken homes. Some of these men! Tommy, don't be in a rush about the marriage thing.

TOMMY: Keep it to yourself, . . . but I was thirty my last birthday and haven't ever been married. I coulda been. Oh, yes, indeed, coulda been. But I don't want any and everybody. What I want with a no-good piece-a nothin'? I'll never forget what the Reverend Martin Luther King said . . . "I have a dream." I liked him sayin' it 'cause truer words have never been spoke. (*straightening the room*) I have a dream, too. Mine is to find a man who'll treat me just half-way decent . . . just to meet me half-way is all I ask, to smile, be kind to me. Somebody in my corner. Not to wake up by myself in the mornin' and face this world all alone.

CYNTHIA: About Bill, it's best not to ever count on anything, anything at all, Tommy.

TOMMY: (*This remark bothers her for a split second but she shakes it off.*) Of course, Cynthia, that's one of the foremost rules of life. Don't count on nothin'!

CYNTHIA: Right, don't be too quick to put your trust in these men.

TOMMY: You put your trust in one and got yourself a husband.

CYNTHIA: Well, yes, but what I mean is . . . Oh, you know. A man is a man and Bill is also an artist and his work comes before all else and there are other factors . . .

TOMMY: (*sits facing CYNTHIA*) What's wrong with me?

CYNTHIA: I don't know what you mean.

TOMMY: Yes you do. You tryin' to tell me I'm aimin' too high by lookin' at Bill.

CYNTHIA: Oh, no, my dear.

TOMMY: Out there in the street, in the bar, you and your husband were so sure that he'd like me and want to paint my picture.

CYNTHIA: But he does want to paint you; he's very eager to . . .

TOMMY: But why? Somethin' don't fit right.

CYNTHIA: (*feeling sorry for TOMMY*) If you don't want to do it, just leave and that'll be that.

TOMMY: Walk out while he's buyin' me what I ask for, spendin' his money on me? That'd be too dirty. (*She looks at books and takes one from shelf.*) Books, books, books everywhere. "Afro-American History." I like that. What's wrong with me, Cynthia? Tell me, I won't get mad with you, I swear. If there's somethin' wrong that I can change, I'm ready to do it. Eight grade, that's all I had of school. You a social worker; I know that means college. I come from poor people. (*examining the book in her hand*) Talkin' 'bout poverty this and poverty that and studyin' it. When you in it you don' be studyin' 'bout it. Cynthia, I remember my mother tyin' up her stockin's with strips-a rag 'cause she didn't have no garters. When I get home from school she'd say, . . . "Nothin' much here to eat." Nothin' much might be grits, or bread and coffee. I got sick-a all that, got me a job. Later for school.

CYNTHIA: The Matriarchal Society.

TOMMY: What's that?

CYNTHIA: A Matriarchal Society is one in which the women rule . . . the women have the power . . . the women head the house.

TOMMY: We didn't have nothin' to rule over, not a pot nor a window. And my papa picked hisself up and ran off with some finger-poppin' woman and we never hear another word 'til ten, twelve years later when a undertaker call up and ask if Mama wanta claim his body. And don'cha know, Mama went on over and claim it. A woman need a man to claim, even if it's a dead one. What's wrong with me? Be honest.

CYNTHIA: You're a fine person...

TOMMY: Go on, I can take it.

CYNTHIA: You're too brash. You're too used to looking out for yourself. It makes us lose our femininity... It makes us hard... it makes us seem very hard. We do for ourselves too much.

TOMMY: If I don't, who's gonna do for me?

CYNTHIA: You have to let the black man have his manhood again. You have to give it back, Tommy.

TOMMY: I didn't take it from him, how I'm gonna give it back? What else is the matter with me? You had school, I didn't. I respect that.

CYNTHIA: Yes, I've had it, the degrees and the whole bit. For a time I thought I was about to move into another world, the so-called "integrated" world, a place where knowledge and know-how could set you free and open all the doors, but that's a lie. I turned away from that idea. The first thing I did was give up dating white fellas.

TOMMY: I never had none to give up. I'm not soundin' on you. White folks, nothin' happens when I look at 'em. I don't hate 'em, don't love 'em,...just nothin' shakes a-tall. The dullest people in the world. The way they talk... "Oh, hooty, hooty, hoo"... Break it down for me to A, B, C's. That Bill... I like him, with his black, uppity, high-handed ways. What do you do to get a man you want? A social worker oughta tell you things like that.

CYNTHIA: Don't chase him... at least don't let it look that way. Let him pursue you.

TOMMY: What if he won't? Men don't chase me much, not the kind I like.

CYNTHIA: (*rattles off instructions glibly*) Let him do the talking. Learn to listen. Stay in the background a little. Ask his opinion... "What do you think, Bill?"

TOMMY: Mmmmm, "Oh, hooty, hooty, hoo."

CYNTHIA: But why count on him? There are lots of other nice guys.

TOMMY: You don't think he'd go for me, do you?

CYNTHIA: (*trying to be diplomatic*) Perhaps you're not really his type.

TOMMY: Maybe not, but he's mine. I'm so lonesome... I'm lonesome... I want somebody to love. Somebody to say... "That's all-right when the World treats me mean."

CYNTHIA: Tommy, I think you're too good for Bill.

TOMMY: I don't wanta hear that. The last man that told me I was too good for him... was tryin' to get away. He's good enough for me. (*straightening room*)

CYNTHIA: Leave the room alone. What we need is a little more sex appeal and a little less washing, cooking and ironing.

(*TOMMY puts down the room straightening.*)

CYNTHIA: One more thing, . . . do you have to wear that wig?

TOMMY: (*a little sensitive*) I like how your hair looks. But some of the naturals I don't like. Can see all the lint caught up in the hair like it hasn't been combed since know not when. You a Muslim?

CYNTHIA: No.

TOMMY: I'm just sick-a hair, hair, hair. Do it this way, don't do it, leave it natural, straighten it, process, no process. I get sick-a hair and talkin' 'bout it and foolin' with it. That's why I wear the wig.

CYNTHIA: I'm sure your own must be just as nice or nicer than that.

TOMMY: It oughta be. I only paid nineteen ninety five for this.

CYNTHIA: You ought to go back to using your own.

TOMMY: (*tensely*) I'll be givin' that some thought.

CYNTHIA: You're pretty nice people just as you are. Soften up, Tommy. You might surprise yourself.

TOMMY: I'm listenin'.

CYNTHIA: Expect more. Learn to let men open doors for you . . .

TOMMY: What if I'm standin' there and they don't open it?

CYNTHIA: (*trying to level with her*) You're a fine person. He wants to paint you, that's all. He's doing a kind of mural thing and we thought he would enjoy painting you. I'd hate to see you expecting more out of the situation than what's there.

TOMMY: Forget it, sweetie-pie, don' nothin' that's not suppose to.

(*sound of laughter in the hall. BILL, OLDTIMER and SONNY-MAN enter.*)

BILL: No Chinese restaurant left, baby! It's wiped out. Gone with the revolution.

SONNY-MAN: (*to CYNTHIA*) Baby, let's move, split the scene, get on with it, time for home.

BILL: The revolution is here. Whatta you do with her? You paint her?

SONNY-MAN: You write her . . . you write the revolution into a novel nine hundred pages long.

BILL: Dance it! Sing it! "Down in the cornfield Hear dat mournful sound . . . "

(*SONNY-MAN and OLDTIMER harmonize.*)

BILL: Dear old Massa am-a sleepin'. A-sleepin' in the cold, cold ground. Now for "Wine in the Wilderness!" Triptych will be finished.

CYNTHIA: (*in BILL's face*) "Wine in the Wilderness," huh? Exploitation!

SONNY-MAN: Upstairs, all out, come on, Oldtimer. Folks can't create in a crowd. Cynthia, move it, baby.

OLDTIMER: (*starting toward the window*) My things! I got a package.

SONNY-MAN: (*heads him off*) Up and out. You don't have to go home, but you have to get outta here. Happy paintin', yall.

(*One backward look and they all are gone.*)

BILL: Whatta night, whatta night, whatta night, baby. It will be painted, written, sung and discussed for generations.

(*Tommy notices nothing that looks like Chinese food. BILL is carrying a small bag and a container.*)

TOMMY: Where's the Foo-Yong?

BILL: They blew the restaurant, baby. All I could get was a couple-a franks and a orange drink from the stand.

TOMMY: (*tersely*) You brought me a frank-footer? That's what you think-a me, a frank-footer?

BILL: Nothin' to do with what I think. Place is closed.

TOMMY: (*quietly surly*) This is the damn City-a New York, any hour on the clock they sellin' the chicken in the basket, barbecue ribs, pizza pie, hot pastrami samitches; and you brought me a frank-footer?

BILL: Baby, don't break bad over somethin' to eat. The smart set, the jet set, the beautiful people, kings and queens eat frankfurters.

TOMMY: If a queen sent you out to buy her a bucket-a Foo-Yong, you wouldn't come back with no lonely-ass frank-footer.

BILL: Kill me 'bout it, baby! Go 'head and shoot me six times. That's the trouble with our women, yall always got your mind on food.

TOMMY: Is that our trouble? (*laughs*) Maybe you right. Only two things to do. Either eat the frank-footer or walk outta here. You got any mustard?

BILL: (*gets mustard from the refrigerator*) Let's face it, our folks are not together. The brothers and sisters have busted up Harlem, . . . no plan, no nothin'. There's your black revolution, heads whipped, hospital full and we still in the same old bag.

TOMMY: (*seated at the kitchen table*) Maybe what everybody need is somebody like you, who know how things oughta go, to get on out there and start some action.

BILL: You still mad about the frankfurter?

TOMMY: No. I keep seein' pitchers of what was in my room and how it all must be spoiled now. (*sips the orange drink*) A orange never been near this. Well, it's cold. (*looking at an incense burner*) What's that?

BILL: An incense burner, was given to me by the Chinese guy, Richard Lee. I'm sorry they blew his restaurant.

TOMMY: Does it help you to catch the number?

BILL: No, baby, I just burn incense sometime.

TOMMY: For what?

BILL: Just 'cause I feel like it. Baby, ain't you used to nothin'?

TOMMY: Ain't used to burnin' incent for nothin'.

BILL: (*laughs*) Burnin' what?

TOMMY: That stuff.

BILL: What did you call it?

TOMMY: Incent.

BILL: It's not incent, baby. It's incense.

TOMMY: Like the sense you got in your head. In-sense. Thank you. You're a very correctable person, ain't you.

BILL: Let's put you on canvas.

TOMMY: (*stubbornly*) I have to eat first.

BILL: That's another thing 'bout black women, they wanta eat 'fore they do anything else. Tommy, . . . Tommy, . . . I bet your name is Thomasina. You look like a Thomasina.

TOMMY: You could sit there and guess til your eyes pop out and you never would guess my first name. You might could guess the middle name but not the first one.

BILL: Tell it to me.

TOMMY: My name is Tomorrow.

BILL: How's that?

TOMMY: Tomorrow, . . . like yesterday and tomorrow, and the middle name is just plain Marie. That's what my father name me. Tomorrow Marie. My mother say he thought it had a pretty sound.

BILL: Crazy! I never met a girl named Tomorrow.

TOMMY: They got to callin' me Tommy for short, so I stick with that. Tomorrow Marie, . . . Sound like a promise that can never happen.

BILL: (*straightens chair on stand. He is very eager to start painting.*) That's what Shakespeare said, . . . "Tomorrow and tomorrow and tomorrow." Tomorrow, you will be on this canvas.

TOMMY: (*still uneasy about being painted*) What's the hurry? Rome wasn't built in a day, . . . that's another saying.

BILL: If I finish in time, I'll enter you in an exhibition.

TOMMY: (*loses interest in the food. She examines the room, and looks at portrait on the wall.*) He looks like somebody I know or maybe saw before.

BILL: That's Frederick Douglass. A man who used to be a slave. He escaped and spent his life trying to make us all free. He was a great man.

TOMMY: Thank you, Mr. Douglass. Who's the light colored man? (*indicates a frame next to the Douglass*)

BILL: He's white. That's John Brown. They killed him for tryin' to shoot the country outta the slavery bag. He dug us, you know. Old John said, "Hell no, slavery must go."

TOMMY: I heard all about him. Some folks say he was crazy.

BILL: If he had been shootin' at us they wouldn't have called him a nut.

TOMMY: School wasn't a great part-a my life.

BILL: If it was you wouldn't-a found out too much 'bout black history cause the books full-a nothin' but whitey, . . . all except the white ones who dug us, . . . they not there either. Tell me, . . . who was Elijah Lovejoy?

TOMMY: Elijah Lovejoy, . . . Mmmmmmmm. I don't know. Have to do with the Bible?

BILL: No, that's another white fella, . . . Elijah had a printin' press and the main thing he printed was "Slavery got to go." Well the man moved in on him, smashed his press time after time . . . but he kept puttin' it back together and doin' his thing. So, one final day, they came in a mob and burned him to death.

TOMMY: (*blows her nose with sympathy as she fights tears*) That's dirty.

BILL: (*as Tommy glances at titles in book case*) Who was Monroe Trotter?

TOMMY: Was he white?

BILL: No, soul brother. Spent his years tryin' to make it all right. Who was Harriet Tubman?

TOMMY: I heard-a her. But don't put me through no test, Billy. (*moving around studying pictures and books*) This room is full-a things I don' know nothin' about. How'll I get to know.

BILL: Read, go to the library, book stores, ask somebody.

TOMMY: Okay, I'm askin'. Teach me things.

BILL: Aw, baby, why torment yourself? Trouble with our women, . . . they all wanta be great brains. Leave somethin' for a man to do.

TOMMY: (*eager to impress him*) What you think-a Martin Luther King?

BILL: A great guy. But it's too late in the day for the singin' and prayin' now.

TOMMY: What about Malcolm X?

BILL: Great cat . . . but there again . . . Where's the program?

TOMMY: What about Adam Powell? I voted for him. That's one thing 'bout me. I vote. Maybe if everybody vote for the right people . . .

BILL: The ballot box. It would take me all my life to straighten you on that hype.

TOMMY: I got time.

BILL: You gonna wind up with a king size headache. The Matriarchy gotta go. Yall throw them suppers together, keep your husband happy, raise the kids.

TOMMY: I don't have a husband. Course, that could be fixed. (*leaving the unspoken proposal hanging in the air*)

BILL: You know the greatest thing you could do for your people? Sit up there and let me put you down on canvas.

TOMMY: Bein' married and havin' family might be good for your people as a race, but I was thinkin' 'bout myself a little.

BILL: Forget yourself sometime, sugar. On that canvas you'll be givin' and givin' and givin' . . . That's where you do your thing best. What you stallin' for?

TOMMY: (*returns to table and sits in chair*) I . . . I don't want to pose in this outfit.

BILL: (*patience wearing thin*) Why, baby, why?

TOMMY: I don't feel proud-a myself in this.

BILL: Art, baby, we talkin' art. Whatcha want . . . Ribbons? Lace? False eyelashes?

TOMMY: No, just my white dress with the orlon sweater, . . . or anything but this what I'm wearin'. You oughta see me in that dress with my pink linen shoes. Oh, hell, the shoes are gone. I forgot 'bout the fire . . .

BILL: Oh, stop fightin' me! Another thing . . . our women don't know a damn thing 'bout bein' feminine. Give in sometime. It won't kill you. You tellin' me how to paint? Maybe you oughta hang out your shingle and give art lessons! You too damn opinionated. You gonna pose or you not gonna pose? Say somethin'.

TOMMY: You makin' me nervous! Hollerin' at me. My mama never holler at me. Hollerin'.

BILL: I'll soon be too tired to pick up the brush, baby.

TOMMY: (*eye catches picture of white woman on the wall*) That's a white woman! Bet you never hollered at her and I bet she's your girlfriend . . . too, and when she posed for her pitcher I bet yall was laughin' . . . and you didn't buy her no frank-footer!

BILL: (*feels a bit smug about his male prowess*) Awww, come on, cut that out, baby. That's a little blonde, blue-eyed chick who used to pose for me. That ain't where it's at. This is a new day, the deal is goin' down different. This is the black moment, doll. Black, black, black is bee-yoo-tee-full. Got it? Black is beautiful.

TOMMY: Then how come it is that I don't feel beautiful when you talk to me?!!

BILL: That's your hang-up, not mine. You supposed to stretch forth your wings like Ethiopia, shake off them chains that been holdin' you down. Langston Hughes said let 'em see how beautiful you are. But you determined not to ever be beautiful. Okay, that's what makes you Tommy.

TOMMY: Do you have a girlfriend? And who is she?

BILL: (*now enjoying himself to the utmost*) Naw, naw, naw, doll. I know people, but none-a this "tie-you-up-and-I-own-you" jive. I ain't mistreatin' nobody and there's enough-a me to go around. That's another thing with our women, . . . they wanta latch on. Learn to play it by ear, roll with the punches, cut down on some-a this "got-you-to-the-grave" kinda relationship. Was today all right? Good, be glad, . . . take what's at hand because tomorrow never comes, it's always today.

   (*TOMMY begins to cry.*)

BILL: Awwww, I didn't mean it that way . . . I forgot your name. (*He brushes her tears.*) You act like I belong to you. You're jealous of a picture?

TOMMY: That's how women are, always studyin' each other and wonderin' how they look up 'gainst the next person.

BILL: (*a bit smug*) That's human nature. Whatcha call healthy competition.

TOMMY: You think she's pretty?

BILL: She was, perhaps still is. Long, silky hair. She could sit on her hair.

TOMMY: (*with bitter arrogance*) Doesn't everybody?

BILL: You got a head like a rock and gonna have the last word if it kills you. Baby, I bet you could knock out Mohamud Ali in the first round, then rare back and scream like Tarzan . . . "Now, I am the greatest!" (*He is very close to her and is amazed to feel a great sense of physical attraction.*) What we arguin' 'bout? (*looks her over as she looks away. He suddenly wants to put the conversation on a more intimate level. His eye is on the bed.*) Maybe tomorrow would be a better time for paintin'. Wanna freshen up, take a bath, baby? Water's nice n' hot.

TOMMY: (*knows the sound and turns to check on the look. She notices him watching the bed, and starts weeping.*) No, I don't. Nigger!

BILL: Was that nice? What the hell, let's paint the picture. Or are you gonna hold that back too?

TOMMY: I'm posin'. Shall I take off the wig?

BILL: No, it's part of your image, ain't it? You must have a reason for wearin' it.

(*TOMMY snatches up her orange drink and sits in the model's chair.*)

TOMMY: (*with defiance*) Yes, I wear it 'cause you and those like you go for long, silky hair, and this is the only way I can have some without burnin' my mother-grabbin brains out. Got it? (*She accidentally throws over container of orange drink in her lap.*) Hell, I can't wear this. I'm soaked through. I'm not gonna catch no double pneumonia sittin' up here wringin' wet while you paint and holler at me.

BILL: Bitch!

TOMMY: You must be talkin' 'bout your mama!

BILL: Shut up! Aw, shut-up! (*phone rings. He finds an African throw-cloth and hands it to her.*) Put this on. Relax, don't go way mad, and all the rest-a that jazz. Change, will you? I apologize. I'm sorry. (*He picks up phone.*) Hello, survivor of a riot speaking. Who's calling?

(*TOMMY retires behind the screen with the throw. During the conversation, she undresses and wraps the throw around her. We see TOMMY and BILL, but they can't see each other.*)

BILL: Sure, told you not to worry. I'll be ready for the exhibit. If you don't dig it, don't show it. Not time for you to see it yet. Yeah, yeah, next week. You just make sure your exhibition room is big enough to hold the crowds that's gonna congregate to see this fine chick I got here.

(*TOMMY's ears perk up.*)

BILL: You oughta see her. The finest black woman in the world . . . No, . . . the finest any woman in the world . . . This gorgeous satin chick is . . . is . . . black velvet moonlight . . . an ebony queen of the universe . . .

(*TOMMY can hardly believe her ears.*)

BILL: One look at her and you go back to Spice Islands . . . She's Mother Africa . . . You flip, double flip. She has come through everything that has been put on her . . .

(*He unveils the gorgeous woman he has painted . . . "Wine in the Wilderness." TOMMY believes he is talking about her.*)

BILL: Regal . . . grand . . . magnificent, fantastic . . . You would vote her the woman you'd most like to meet on a desert island, or around the corner from anywhere. She's here with me now . . . and I don't know if I want to show her to you or anybody else . . . I'm beginnin' to have this deep attachment . . . She sparkles, man, Harriet Tubman, Queen of the Nile . . . sweetheart, wife, mother, sister, friend . . . The night . . . a black diamond . . . A dark, beautiful dream . . . A cloud with a silvery lining . . . Her wrath is a storm over the Bahamas. "Wine in the Wilderness" . . . The memory of Africa . . . The now of things . . . but best of all and most important . . . She's tomorrow . . . she's my tomorrow . . .

(TOMMY is dressed in the African wrap. She is suddenly awakened to the feeling of being loved and admired. She removes the wig and fluffs her hair. Her hair under the wig must not be an accurate, well-cut Afro . . . but should be rather attractive natural hair. She studies herself in a mirror. We see her taller, more relaxed and sure of herself. Perhaps braided hair will go well with Afro robe.)

BILL: Aw, man, later. You don't believe in nothin'! *(He covers "Wine in the Wilderness." He is now in a glowing mood.)* Baby, whenever you ready.

(TOMMY emerges from behind the screen, dressed in the wrap, sans wig. He is astounded.)

BILL: Baby, what . . . ? Where . . . where's the wig?

TOMMY: I don't think I want to wear it, Bill.

BILL: That is very becoming . . . the drape thing.

TOMMY: Thank you.

BILL: I don't know what to say.

TOMMY: It's time to paint. *(She steps up on the model stand and sits in the chair. She is now a queen, relaxed and smiling her appreciation for his last speech to the art dealer. Her feet are bare.)*

BILL: *(mystified by the change in her)* It is quite late.

TOMMY: Makes me no difference if it's all right with you.

BILL: *(wants to create the other image)* Could you put the wig back on?

TOMMY: You don't really like wigs, do you?

BILL: Well, no.

TOMMY: Then let's have things the way you like.

BILL: *(has no answer for this. He makes a haphazard line or two as he tries to remember the other image.)* Tell me something about yourself, . . . anything.

TOMMY: *(now on sure ground)* I was born in Baltimore, Maryland and raised here in Harlem. My favorite flower is "Four O'clocks," that's a bush flower. My wearin' flower, corsage flower, is pink roses. My mama raised me, mostly by herself, God rest the dead. Mama belonged to "The Eastern Star." Her father was a "Mason." If a man in the family is a "Mason" any woman related to him can be an "Eastern Star." My grandfather was a member of "The Prince Hall Lodge." I had a uncle who was an "Elk," . . . a member of the "The Improved Benevolent Protective Order of Elks of the World": "The Henry Lincoln Johnson Lodge." You know, the white "Elks" are called "The Benevolent Protective Order of Elks" but black "Elks" are called "The Improved Benevolent Protective Order of Elks of the World." That's because the black "Elks" got copyright first but the white "Elks" took us to court about it to keep us from usin' the name. Over fifteen hundred black folk went to jail for wearin' the "Elk" emblem on their coat lapel. Years ago, ... that's what you call history.

BILL: I didn't know about that.

TOMMY: Oh, it's understandable. Only way I heard about John Brown was because the black "Elks" bought his farmhouse where he trained his men to attack the government.

BILL: The black "Elks" bought the John Brown Farm? What did they do with it?

TOMMY: They built a outdoor theater an put a perpetual light in his memory, ... and they buildin' cottages there, one named for each state in the union and ...

BILL: How do you know about it?

TOMMY: Well, our "Elks" helped my cousin go through school with a scholarship. She won a speaking contest and wrote a composition titled "Onward and Upward, O, My Race." That's how she won the scholarship. Coreen knows all that Elk history.

BILL: (*seeing her with new eyes*) Tell me some more about you, Tomorrow Marie. I bet you go to church.

TOMMY: Not much as I used to. Early in life I pledged myself to the A. M. E. Zion Church.

BILL: (*studying her face, seeing her for the first time*) A. M. E.?

TOMMY: A. M. E. That's African Methodist Episcopal. We split off from the white Methodist Episcopal and started our own in the year 1796. We built our first buildin' in the year 1800. How 'bout that?

BILL: That right?

TOMMY: Oh, I'm just showin' off. I taught Sunday School for two years and you had to know the history of A. M. E. Zion ... or else you couldn't teach. My great, great grandparents was slaves.

BILL: Guess everybody's was.

TOMMY: Mine was slaves in a place called Sweetwater Springs, Virginia. We tried to look it up one time but somebody at church told us that Sweetwater Springs had become a part of Norfolk ... so we didn't carry it any further ... As it would be a expense to have a lawyer trace your people.

BILL: (*throws charcoal pencil across room*) No good! It won't work! I can't work anymore.

TOMMY: Take a rest. Tell me about you.

BILL: (*sits on bed*) Everybody in my family worked for the Post Office. They bought a home in Jamaica, Long Island. Everybody on that block bought an aluminum screen door with a duck on it, ... or was it a swan? I guess that makes my favorite flower crab grass and hedges. I have a lot of bad dreams.

(*TOMMY massages his temples and the back of his neck.*)

BILL: A dream like suffocating, dying of suffocation. The worst kinda dream. People are standing in a weird looking art gallery; they're looking and laughing at everything I've ever done. My work begins to fade off the canvas, right before my eyes. Everything I've ever done is laughed away.

TOMMY: Don't be so hard on yourself. If I was smart as you I'd wake up singin' every mornin'.

(*There is the sound of thunder. He kisses her.*)

TOMMY: When it thunders that's the angels in heaven playin', with their hoops, rollin' their hoops and bicycle wheels in the rain. My mama told me that.

BILL: I'm glad you're here. Black is beautiful, you're beautiful, A. M. E. Zion, Elks, pink roses, bush flower, . . . blooming out of the slavery of Sweetwater Springs, Virginia.

TOMMY: I'm gonna take a bath and let the riot and the hell of living go down the drain with the bath water.

BILL: Tommy, Tommy, Tomorrow Marie, let's save each other, let's be kind and good to each other while it rains and the angels roll those hoops and bicycle wheels.

(*They embrace; after embrace and after rain music in as lights come down. As lights fade down to darkness, music comes in louder. There is a flash of lightening. We see TOMMY and BILL in each other's arms. It is very dark, music up louder, then softer and down to very soft. Music is mixed with the sound of rain beating against the window. Music slowly fades as gray light of dawn shows at window. Lights go up gradually. The bed is rumpled and empty. BILL is in the bathroom. TOMMY is at the stove turning off the coffee pot. She sets table with cups, saucers, spoons. TOMMY'S hair is natural; she wears another throw [African design] draped around her. She sings and hums a snatch of a joyous spiritual.*)

TOMMY: "Great day, Great day, the world's on fire, Great day . . . " (*calling out to BILL who is in the bath*) Honey, I found the coffee, and it's ready. Nothin' here to go with it but a cucumber and a Uneeda biscuit.

BILL: (*joyous yell from offstage*) Tomorrow and tomorrow and tomorrow! Good mornin', Tomorrow!

TOMMY: (*more to herself than to BILL*) "Tomorrow and tomorrow." That's Shakespeare. (*calls to BILL*) You say that was Shakespeare?

BILL: (*offstage*) Right, baby, right!

TOMMY: I bet Shakespeare was black! You know how we love poetry. That's what give him away. I bet he was passin'. (*laughs*)

BILL: (*offstage*) Just you wait, one hundred years from now all the honkeys gonna claim our poets just like they stole our blues. They gonna try to steal Paul Laurence Dunbar and LeRoi and Margaret Walker.

TOMMY: (*to herself*) God moves in a mysterious way, even in the middle of a riot.

(*a knock on the door*)

TOMMY: Great day, great day the world's on fire . . .

(*TOMMY opens the door. OLDTIMER enters. He is soaking wet. He does not recognize her right away.*)

OLDTIMER: 'Scuse me, I must be in the wrong place.

TOMMY: (*patting her hair*) This is me. Come on in, Edmond Lorenzo Matthews. I took off my hair-piece. This is me.

OLDTIMER: (*very distracted and worried*) Well, howdy-do and good mornin'. (*He has had a hard night of drinking and sleeplessness.*) Where Billy-Boy? It pourin' down some rain out there. (*makes his way to the window*)

TOMMY: What's the matter?

OLDTIMER: (*raises the window and starts pulling in the cord; the cord is weightless and he realizes there is nothing on the end of it.*) No, no, it can't be. Where is it? It's gone! (*looks out the window*)

TOMMY: You gonna catch your death. You wringin' wet.

OLDTIMER: Yall take my things in? It was a bag-a loot. A suit and some odds and ends. It was my loot. Yall took it in?

TOMMY: No. (*realizes his desperation. She calls to BILL through the closed bathroom door.*) Did you take in any loot that was outside the window?

BILL: (*offstage*) No.

TOMMY: He said "no."

OLDTIMER: (*yells out window*) Thieves, . . . dirty thieves . . . lotta good it'll do you
. . .

TOMMY: (*leads him to a chair, dries his head with a towel*) Get outta the wet things. You smell just like a whiskey still. Why don't you take care of yourself. (*dries off his hands*)

OLDTIMER: Drinkin' with the boys. Likker was everywhere all night long.

TOMMY: You got to be better than this.

OLDTIMER: Everything I ever put my hand and mind to do, it turn out wrong, . . . Nothin' but mistakes . . . When you don' know, you don' know. I don' know nothin'. I'm ignorant.

TOMMY: Hush that talk . . . You know lotsa things, everybody does. (*helps him remove wet coat*)

OLDTIMER: Thanks. How's the trip-tick?

TOMMY: The what?

OLDTIMER: Trip-tick. That's a paintin'.

TOMMY: See there, you know more about art than I do. What's a trip-tick? Have some coffee and explain me a trip-tick.

OLDTIMER: (*proud of his knowledge*) Well, I tell you, . . . a trip-tick is a paintin' that's in three parts . . . but they all belong together to be looked at all at once. Now . . . this is the first one . . . a little innocent girl . . . (*unveils picture*)

TOMMY: She's sweet.

OLDTIMER: And this is "Wine in the Wilderness" . . . The Queen of the Universe . . . the finest chick in the world.

TOMMY: (*She is thoughtful as he unveils the second picture.*) That' not me.

OLDTIMER: No, you gonna be this here last one. The worst gal in town. A messed-up chick that—that— (*He unveils the third canvas and is face to face with the almost blank canvas, then realizes what he has said. He turns to see the stricken look on TOMMY'S face.*)

TOMMY: The messed-up chick, that's why they brought me here, ain't it? That's why he wanted to paint me! Say it!

OLDTIMER: No, I'm lyin', I didn't mean it. It's the society that messed her up. Awwwwww, Tommy, don't look that-a-way. It's art, ... it's only art ... He couldn't mean you ... it's art ...

(*The door opens. CYNTHIA and SONNY-MAN enter.*)

SONNY-MAN: Anybody want a ride down ... down ... down ... downtown? What's wrong? Excuse me ... (*starts back out*)

TOMMY: (*blocking the exit to CYNTHIA and SONNY-MAN*) No, come on in. Stay with it ... "Brother" ... "Sister." Tell 'em what a trip-tick is, Oldtimer.

CYNTHIA: (*very ashamed*) Oh, no.

TOMMY: You don't have to tell 'em. They already know. The messed-up chick! How come you didn't pose for that, my sister? The messed-up chick lost her home last night, ... burnt out with no place to go. You and Sonny-man gave me comfort, you cheered me up and took me in, ... took me in!

CYNTHIA: Tommy, we didn't know you, we didn't mean ...

TOMMY: It's all right! I was lost but now I'm found! Yeah, the blind can see! (*She dashes behind the screen and puts on her clothing, sweater, skirt, etc.*)

OLDTIMER: (*goes to bathroom*) Billy, come out!

SONNY-MAN: Billy, step out here, please!

(*BILL enters shirtless, wearing dungarees.*)

SONNY-MAN: Oldtimer let it out 'bout the triptych.

BILL: The rest of you move on.

TOMMY: (*looking out from behind the screen*) No, don't go a step. You brought me here, see me out!

BILL: Tommy, let me explain it to you.

TOMMY: (*coming out from behind screen*) I gotta check out my apartment, and my clothes and money. Cynthia, ... I can't wait for anybody to open the door or look out for me and all that kinda crap you talk. A bunch-a liars!

BILL: Oldtimer, why you ...

TOMMY: Leave him the hell alone. He ain't said nothin' that ain' so!

SONNY-MAN: Explain to the sister that some mistakes have been made.

BILL: Mistakes have been made, baby. The mistakes were yesterday, this is today ...

TOMMY: Yeah, and I'm Tomorrow, remember? Trouble is I was Tommy to you, to all of you, ... "Oh, maybe they gon' like me." ... I was your fool, thinkin' writers and painters know moren' me, that maybe a little bit of you would rub off on me.

CYNTHIA: We are wrong. I knew it yesterday. Tommy, I told you not to expect anything out of this . . . this arrangement.

BILL: This is a relationship, not an arrangement.

SONNY-MAN: Cynthia, I tell you all the time, keep outta other people's business. What the hell you got to do with who's gonna get what outta what? You and Oldtimer, yakkin' and hakkin'. (*to OLDTIMER*) Man, your mouth gonna kill you.

BILL: It's me and Tommy. Clear the room.

TOMMY: Better not. I'll kill him! The "black people" this and the "Afro-American" . . . that . . . You ain't got no use for none-a us. Oldtimer, you their fool too. 'Til I got here they didn't even know your damn name. There's something inside-a me that says I ain' suppose to let nobody play me cheap. Don't care how much they know! (*She sweeps some of the books to the floor.*)

BILL: Don't you have any forgiveness in you? Would I be beggin' you if I didn't care? Can't you be generous enough . . .

TOMMY: Nigger, I been too damn generous with you already. All-a these people know I wasn't down here all night posin' for no pitcher, nigger!

BILL: Cut that out, Tommy, and you not going anywhere!

TOMMY: You wanna bet? Nigger!

BILL: Okay, you called it, baby, I did act like a low, degraded person . . .

TOMMY: (*combing out her wig with her fingers while holding it*) Didn't call you no low, degraded person. Nigger! (*to CYNTHIA who is handing her a comb*) "Do you have to wear a wig? Yes! To soften the blow when yall go up side-a my head with a baseball bat. (*going back to taunting BILL and ignoring CYNTHIA'S comb*) Nigger!

BILL: That's enough-a that. You right and you're wrong too.

TOMMY: Ain't a-one-a us you like that's alive and walkin' by you on the street . . . you don't like flesh and blood niggers.

BILL: Call me that, baby, but don't call yourself. That what you think of yourself?

TOMMY: If a black somebody is in a history book, or printed on a pitcher, or drawed on a paintin' . . . or if they're a statue, . . . dead, and outta the way, and can't talk back, then you dig 'em and full-a so much-a damn admiration and talk 'bout "our" history. But when you run into us livin' and breathin' ones, with the life's blood still pumpin' through us, . . . then you comin' on 'bout we ain' never together. You hate us, that's what! You hate black me!

BILL: (*stung to the heart, confused and saddened by the half truth which applies to himself*) I never hated you, I never will, no matter what you or any of the rest of you do to make me hate you. I won't! Hell, woman, why do you say that! Why would I hate you?

TOMMY: Maybe I look too much like the mother that give birth to you. Like the

Ma and Pa that worked in the post office to buy you a house and a screen door with a damn duck on it. And you so ungrateful you didn't even like it.

BILL: No, I didn't, baby. I don't like screen doors with ducks on 'em.

TOMMY: You didn't like who was livin' behind them screen doors. Phoney Nigger!

BILL: That's all! Dammit! Don't go there no more!

TOMMY: Hit me, so I can tear this place down and scream bloody murder.

BILL: (*somewhere between laughter and tears*) Looka here, baby, I'm willin' to say I'm wrong, even in fronta the room fulla people . . .

TOMMY: (*through clinched teeth*) Nigger.

SONNY-MAN: The sister is upset.

TOMMY: And you stop callin' me "the" sister, . . . if you feelin' so brotherly why don't you say "my" sister? Ain't no we-ness in your talk. "The" Afro-American, "the" black man, there's no we-ness in you. Who you think you are?

SONNY-MAN: I was talkin' in general er . . . my sister, 'bout the masses.

TOMMY: There he go again. "The" masses. Tryin' to make out like we pitiful and you got it made. You the masses your damn self and don't even know it. (*another angry look at BILL*) Nigger.

BILL: (*pulls dictionary from shelf*) Let's get this ignorant "nigger" talk squared away. You can stand some education.

TOMMY: You treat me like a nigger, that's what. I'd rather be called one than treated that way.

BILL: (*questions TOMMY*) What is a nigger? (*talks as he is trying to find word*) A nigger is a low, degraded person, any low degraded person. I learned that from my teacher in the fifth grade.

TOMMY: Fifth grade is a liar! Don't pull that dictionary crap on me.

BILL: (*pointing to the book*) Webster's New World Dictionary of the American Language, College Edition.

TOMMY: I don't need to find out what no college white folks say nigger is.

BILL: I'm tellin' you it's a low, degraded person. Listen. (*reads from the book*) Nigger, N-i-g-g-e-r, . . . A Negro . . . A member of any dark-skinned people . . . Damn. (*amazed by dictionary description*)

SONNY-MAN: Brother Malcolm said that's what they meant, . . . nigger is a Negro, Negro is a nigger.

BILL: (*slowly finishing his reading*) A vulgar, offensive term of hostility and contempt. Well, so much for the fifth grade teacher.

SONNY-MAN: No, they do not call low, degraded white folks niggers. Come to think of it, did you ever hear whitey call Hitler a nigger? Now if some whitey digs us, . . . the others might call him a nigger-lover, but they don't call him no nigger.

OLDTIMER: No, they don't.

TOMMY: (*near tears*) When they say "nigger," just dry-long-so, they mean educated you and uneducated me. They hate you and call you "nigger," I called you "nigger" but I love you. (*There is dead silence in the room for a split second.*)

SONNY-MAN: (*trying to establish peace*) There you go. There you go.

CYNTHIA: (*cautioning SONNY-MAN*) Now is not the time to talk, darlin'.

BILL: You love me? Tommy, that's the greatest compliment you could . . .

TOMMY: (*sorry she said it*) You must be runnin' a fever, nigger, I ain' said nothin' 'bout lovin' you.

BILL: (*in a great mood*) You did, yes, you did.

TOMMY: Well, you didn't say it to me.

BILL: Oh, Tommy, . . .

TOMMY: (*cuts him off abruptly*) And don't you dare say it now. I'm tellin' you, . . . it ain't to be said now. (*checks through her paper bag to see if she has everything. She starts to put on the wig, changes her mind, holds it to end of scene, turns to the others in the room.*) Oldtimer, . . . my brothers and my sister.

OLDTIMER: I wish I was a thousand miles away; I'm so sorry. (*He sits at the foot of the model stand.*)

TOMMY: I don't stay mad; it's here today and gone tomorrow. I'm sorry your feelin's got hurt, . . . but when I'm hurt I turn and hurt back. Somewhere, in the middle of last night, I thought the old me was gone, . . . lost forever, and gladly. But today was flippin' time, so back I flipped. Now it's "turn the other cheek" time. If I can go through life other-cheekin' the white folk, . . . guess yall can be other-cheeked too. But I'm going back to the nitty-gritty crowd, where the talk is we-ness and us-ness. I hate to do it but I have to thank you 'cause I'm walkin' out with much more than I brought in. (*goes over and looks at the queen in the "Wine in the Wilderness" painting*) Tomorrow-Marie had such a lovely yesterday.

(*BILL takes her hand; she gently removes it from his grasp.*)

TOMMY: Bill, I don't have to wait for anybody's by-your-leave to be a "Wine in the Wilderness" woman. I can be it if I wanta, . . . and I am. I am. I am. I'm not the one you made up and painted, the very pretty lady who can't talk back, . . . but I'm "Wine in the Wilderness." . . . alive and kickin', me . . . Tomorrow-Marie, cussin' and fightin' and lookin' out for my damn self 'cause ain' nobody else 'round to do it, dontcha know. And, Cynthia, if my hair is straight, or if it's natural, or if I wear a wig, or take it off, . . . that's all right; because wigs . . . shoes . . . hats . . . bags . . . and even this . . . (*She picks up the African throw she wore a few moments before . . . fingers it.*) They're just what . . . what you call . . . access . . . (*fishing for the word*) . . . like what you wear with your Easter outfit . . .

CYNTHIA: Accessories.

TOMMY: Thank you, my sister. Accessories. Somethin' you add on or take off. The real thing is takin' place on the inside . . . that's where the action is. That's "Wine in the Wilderness," . . . a woman that's a real one and a good one. And yall just better believe I'm it. (*She proceeds to the door.*)

BILL: Tommy.

(*TOMMY turns. He takes the beautiful queen, "Wine in the Wilderness" from the easel.*)

BILL: She's not it at all, Tommy. This chick on the canvas, . . . nothin' but accessories, a dream I drummed up outta the junk room of my mind. (*places the "queen" to one side*) You are and . . . (*points to OLDTIMER*) . . . Edmond Lorenzo Matthews . . . the real beautiful people, . . . Cynthia.

CYNTHIA: (*bewildered and unbelieving*) Who? Me?

BILL: Yeah, honey, you and Sonny-man, don't know how beautiful you are. (*indicates the other side of model stand*) Sit there.

SONNY-MAN: (*places cushions on the floor at the foot of the model stand*) Just sit here and be my beautiful self. (*to CYNTHIA*) Turn on, baby, we gonna get our picture took. (*CYNTHIA smiles.*)

BILL: Now there's Oldtimer, the guy who was here before there were scholarships and grants and stuff like that, the guy they kept outta the schools, the man the factories wouldn't hire; the union wouldn't let him join.

SONNY-MAN: Yeah, yeah, rap to me. Where you goin' with it, man? Rap on.

BILL: I'm makin' a triptych.

SONNY-MAN: Make it, man.

BILL: (*indicating CYNTHIA and SONNY-MAN*) On the other side, Young Man and Woman, workin' together to do our thing.

TOMMY: (*quietly*) I'm goin' now.

BILL: But you belong up there in the center, "Wine in the Wilderness" . . . that's who you are. (*moves the canvas of "the little girl" and places a sketch pad on the easel*) The nightmare, about all that I've done disappearing before my eyes. It was a good nightmare. I was painting in the dark, all head and no heart. I couldn't see until you came, baby. (*to CYNTHIA, SONNY-MAN and OLDTIMER*) Look at Tomorrow. She came through the biggest riot of all, . . . somethin' called "Slavery," and she's even comin' through the "now" scene, . . . folks laughin' at her, even her own folks laughin' at her. And look how . . . with her head high like she's poppin' her fingers at the world. (*takes up charcoal pencil and tears old page off sketch pad so he can make a fresh drawing*) Aw, let me put it down, Tommy. "Wine in the Wilderness," you gotta let me put it down so all the little boys and girls can look up and see you on the wall. And you know what they're gonna say? "Hey, don't she look like somebody we know?"

(*TOMMY slowly returns and takes her seat on the stand. TOMMY is holding the wig in her lap. Her hands are very graceful looking against the texture of the wig.*)

BILL: And they'll be right, you're somebody they know . . . (*He is sketching hastily. There is a sound of thunder and the patter of rain.*) Yeah, roll them hoops and bicycle wheels.

(*Music in low; music up higher as BILL continues to sketch.*)

CURTAIN

SONIA SANCHEZ (1934–   )

Sister Son/ji (1969)

BIOGRAPHY AND ACHIEVEMENTS

Sonia Sanchez was born on September 9, 1934, in Birmingham, Alabama, to Wilson L. and Lena Jones Driver. She earned a B.A. from Hunter College (now Hunter College of the City University of New York) in 1955. She is the mother of three children: Anita, Morani, and Mungu.

Sanchez has served in a number of academic positions, including staff member at the Downtown Community School in San Francisco, California, from 1965 to 1967; instructor at San Francisco State College (now University) from 1966 to 1968; assistant professor at the University of Pittsburgh from 1969 to 1970; assistant professor at Rutgers University in New Brunswick, New Jersey, from 1970 to 1971; assistant professor of Black literature and creative writing at Manhattan Community College of the City University of New York from 1971 to 1973; and associate professor of Afro-American Studies at the University of Massachusetts in Amherst from 1972 to 1973.

Sanchez has been the recipient of a host of impressive awards, including the P.E.N. Writing Award in 1969, the National Institute of Arts and Letters Grant in 1970, a National Endowment of Arts fellowship, and an American Book Award for poetry in the 1978–79 academic year.

Ms. Sanchez is currently an associate professor at Temple University of Philadelphia.

Sonia Sanchez is a major figure in the development of African American theater. As early as the 1960s she was blending poetry with drama and creating a place for her provocative poemplays on the American stage. The nontraditional structure of her dramatic pieces expresses the violence and turmoil of blacks in America. The language is precise and extremely visual. She manipulates the militant black street speech to underscore the impoverishment of the black masses. She has become increasingly popular with international audiences because of her plea for justice for women and people of color around the globe.

Sanchez has been a leading American poet since the 1960s, with the publication of such volumes of poetry as *Homecoming* (1969), *We a BaddDDD People* (1970), *It's a New Day: Poems for Young Brothers and Sisters* (1971), *Love Poems* (1973), *A Blues Book for Blue Black Magical Women* (1974), *I've Been A Woman* (1978), *Home Girls and Handgrenades* (1984), and *Generations: Selected Poetry: 1969–1985* (1986).

Sanchez brings the same poignancy of her poems to her theater pieces. She is the author of several noteworthy poemplays: *The Bronx is Next*, first produced in New York City at Theater Black on October 3, 1970; *Uh Huh, But How Do It Free Us*, 1970; *Sister Son/ji*, first produced off-Broadway at the New York Shakespeare Festival Public Theater in 1972; *Dirty Hearts*, 1972; *Malcolm/Man Don't Live Here No Mo*, 1972; and *I'm Black When I'm Singing, I'm Blue When I Ain't* (1982).

Sanchez denounces imperialism, capitalism, racism and sexism, and reminds America that the tumultuous times of the 1960s may come again if people of color and women are not allowed the freedom to choose their destinies.

SYNOPSIS AND ANALYSIS: *SISTER SON/JI*

This play opens with the protagonist on stage made up to appear to be in her fifties. Music begins to play, but Sister Son/ji commands, "turn off that god/damn music. this is not my music/day. i'll tell u when to play music to soothe my savage sounds."

Sister Son/ji's sounds, indeed, are savage throughout the play. She chooses to remember her life's struggle and rationalizes her right to do so by saying, "rememberings are for the near/dead/dying. for death is made up of past actions/deeds and thoughts." Sister Son/ji regresses to her youth and then gradually progresses through her life until she returns to her fifties. As she tells of different phases of her life, she shows signs of aging in her gestures and speech.

She wipes off her make up, takes off her gray wig, puts on a straightened black one, a wide belt, a necklace and an ankle bracelet as she moves to her youth of 18 or 19. Once there, she recalls a painful experience at a white college where the professor invalidated her along with two other black students by refusing to learn their names. The professor was able to remember everyone else's name except the names of the three black female students. Sister Son/ji tells how she walked out of the class in protest of forced invisibility. She also recalls losing her virginity in the back seat of her boyfriend's new car while at Hunter College.

Sister Son/ji moves to another level of her growth, demonstrated by the removal of her straightened wig and the addition of large hoop earrings, as she listens to a tape of activist Malcolm X. She begins to preach black nationhood, advocating that black women should stop seeing black men as their enemies and start supporting them as blacks and work toward establishing healthy relationships based upon mutual love and respect.

Sister Son/ji's public life is fuller than her private life. Though she and her companion rally to free blacks from injustices, their very own house is crumbling. She begs her lover to spend time with her and to leave the barhopping, alcohol, marijuana, and drugs alone. She tells him it is hypocritical to preach togetherness of black people if they themselves cannot unite as a family.

Her pleas go unheard as she moves into the next stage where she is alone, confused, and pregnant, conditions exacerbated by her anger at white racists. She moves to still another phase when she describes her part in the revolution of the 1960s. She tells of how she lost a child, a thirteen-year-old warrior, in the revolution. She says with pride that death must come in order for there to be life or freedom.

Sister Son/ji returns to her fifties not as a defeated woman but as one who has been a part of the struggle and who dared as she says, "to pick up the day and shake its tail until it became evening." She ends questioning whether young blacks will continue to struggle and dare to demand a new day.

Sonia Sanchez's play is one of the most significant portrayals of the Black Power Movement of the 1960s. This compact one-act drama poignantly captures the spirit of this revolutionary time.

Sister Son/ji, a surrealistic drama, cautions that the key to survival for African Americans is for them to learn to love themselves and each other. This play is extremely timely and relevant, given the constant statistics that show that many blacks, both children and adults, do not like their blackness. Many blacks measure beauty by the models used by world media, i.e., thin, blonde, blue-eyed, middle-class or wealthy men and women. Many blacks hate themselves or certainly have a difficulty seeing pride in their beautiful black bodies and minds. Sister Son/ji serves as a healer to blacks when she says, "Listen. listen. did u hear those blk/words of that beautiful/ blk/warrior/prince—did u see his flashing eyes and did u hear his dagger/ words. cuz if u did then u will know as i have come to know. u will change—u will pick up yr/roots and become yr/self again—u will come home to blk/ness for he has looked blk/people in the eye and said welcome home. yr/beautiful/blkness/awaits u."

Not only does Sanchez suggest that many blacks are burdened by selfhate, but she also offers advice about how blacks can learn to love themselves. She suggests that it must begin at home with the family. She argues that black men and women must spend time with each other and refuse to go the route that some of their parents took by allowing the man the option of abandoning his family in the name of black manhood. Sanchez, serving as a minister, preaches that blacks can heal themselves by not allowing themselves to be seduced by such evils as liquor, drugs, and illicit affairs. Sister Son/ji begs, "Stay home with me and let us start building true blk/ lives—let our family be a family built on mutual love and respect."

Sanchez also advises that the key to survival for blacks is through separation of the races. During the 1960s there was much debate about the merits or demerits of allowing liberal whites to fight alongside blacks in the battle for civil rights. Sanchez's position was clear, particularly in her reference to whites as devils, beasts, and death. For any black man who insists on keeping his white female companion, Sister Son/ji preaches that he should be excluded from the revolution, at best, or sent to "certain death if he tries to keep her." She maintains that a white woman's whiteness can do nothing but pollute blackness and bring destruction. Sister Son/ji's advice to the black man who feels sorry for a liberal white female is to "send her back to her own kind. Let her liberalize them."

Sanchez, while not being anti-man, is certainly pro-woman. Her description of the heroine's first sexual experience is sensitively characterized. Sister Son/ji represents many women in her apprehension and fear of the first sex act. Like many women, Sister Son/ji's reluctance is based upon her religious upbringing which does not condone premarital intercourse. Though she tells her lover that she is frightened and is trembling, he marches to his own drummer, one that turns a deaf ear to Sister Son/ji's "i feel the cold air on my thighs. how shall i move my love; i keep missing the beat of yr/ fast/movements. is it time to go already?" Sanchez seems to be telling men that women need time and tenderness.

Sanchez not only uses *Sister Son/ji* as an instrument to teach blacks how to love themselves and each other but she also embodies the African spirit in this play's heroine. Sister Son/ji, in a number of instances in the play, resorts to African chants to help empower herself and the warriors of the revolution. The play also contains music, much of which is in the form of drums, which links Sister Son/ji to the tom-toms of Africa.

Another excellent example of Sanchez's connection to Africa is the structure of the plot. Ancient African mythology, particularly the hieroglyphics of ancient Egypt, suggests that the Afrocentric approach to life is one that reveres the cyclical nature of things. Ancient Africans wrote solutions to their problems on pyramid walls because they knew that future generations would face their problems. The fact that the heroine, who is in her fifties, regresses back to her teens and then moves back in the direction of the present, clearly illustrates that this cyclical odyssey is, in part, a manifestation of the African spirit of survival. Her journey leads her to wholeness as she looks back on the struggles of her life. The heroine's spirit is timeless.

Though *Sister Son/ji* is a play about the suffering of oppressed black people, it is also a play about survival and triumph. The heroine looks back on her life with pride, knowing that she gave her life in an effort to free blacks to live as human beings.

NOTE

For more information about Sanchez's life and works, see *Contemporary Authors*, vols. 33–36, First Revision.

Sister Son/ji (1969) ───────────

Sonia Sanchez

CHARACTER

SISTER SON/JI   dressed in shapeless blk/burlap dress, blk/
                                leotards & stockings; gray/natural wig—is
                                made to look in her fifties.

SCENE

The stage is dark except for a light directed on the middle of the stage where there is a dressing/room/table with drawers/and chair—a noise is heard offstage—more like a deep/guttural/laugh mixed with the sound of two/slow/dragging feet—as a figure moves and stops, back to the audience, the stage lightens.

TIME

Age and now and never again.

SISTER SON/JI: (*as she turns around, the faint sound of music is heard*) not yet. turn off that god/damn music. this is not my music/day. i'll tell u when to play music to soothe my savage sounds. this is my quiet time. my time for reading or thinking thoughts that shd be thought. (*pause*) now after all that talk, what deep thoughts shd i think today. Shall they be deeper than the sounds of my blk/today or shall they be louder than the sounds of my white/yesterdays. (*moves to the dressing/table and sits in the chair*) Standing is for young people. i ain't young no mo. My young days have gone, they passed me by so fast that i didn't even have a chance to see them. What did i do with them? What did i say to them? do i still remember them? Shd i remember them? hold on Sister Son/ji—today is tuesday. Wed. is yr/day for remembering. tuesday is for reading and thinking thoughts of change.

Hold on! hold on
for what? am i not old? older than the mississippi hills i settled near. Ain't time
and i made a truce so that i am time

a blk/version of past/ago & now/time.

no, if i want
to i shall remember.

rememberings are for the old.

What else
is left them? My family is gone. all my beautiful children are buried here in
mississippi.

Chausiku. Mtume. Baraka.
Mungu./brave warriors. DEAD.

Yes. rememberings are
for the near/dead/dying.

for death is made up of past/
actions/deeds and thoughts. (*rises*)

So. fuck the hold/
ons today. i shall be a remembered Sister Son/ji. today i shall be what i was/
shd have been and never can be again. today i shall bring back yesterday as it
can never be today.

as it shd be tomorrow.

(*She drags her chair back to the dressing table and opens the drawer—her movements
are still slow-oldish—she takes off her gray/wig and puts on a straightened/blk/wig—
stands and puts on a wide belt, a long necklace and a bracelet on her right ankle. As
she sits and begins to remove the make/up of old age from her face her movements
quicken and become more active. A recording of Sammy Davis Jr. singing "This is
my beloved" is heard and she joins in—*)

SISTER SON/JI: "strange spice from the south, honey from the dew drifting,
imagine this in one perfect one and this is my beloved. And when he moves
and when he talks to me, music—ah-ah-mystery—"

(*hums the rest as she takes off all the make/up and puts on some lipstick. When she
stands again she is young—a young/negro/woman of 18 or 19. She picks up a note/
book and begins to run across the stage.*)

SISTER SON/JI: i'm coming nesbitt. i'm coming. Hey. thought i'd never catch
u— how are u? (*looks down for she has that shyness of very young women who are
unsure/uncertain of themselves and she stretches out her hand and begins to walk—a
lover's walk.*) yeah. i'm glad today is friday too. that place is a mad/house.
hunter college indeed. do u know nesbitt that that ole/bitch in my political
theory course couldn't remember my name and there are only 12 of us in the
class—only 3 negroes—as different as day and night and she called out Miss
Jones, Miss Smith, Miss Thomas and each time she looked at the three of us
and couldn't remember who was who. Ain't that a drag? But she remembered
the ofays' names/faces and they all look like honey. (*turns and faces him*) you

know what i did? u know what i did nesbitt? i stood up, picked up my note/ book and headed for the door and u know she asked where i was going and i said out of here—away from u because u don't even know my name unless i raise my hand when u spit out three/blk/names—and she became that flustered/ red/whiteness that ofays become, and said but u see it's just that—and i finished it for her—i sd it's just that we all look alike. yeah. well damn this class (*i wanted to say fuck this class honey but she might have had a heart/attack/rt/there in class*) i said damn this class. i'm a human being to be remembered just like all these other human beings in this class. and with that i walked out. (*is smiling as she turns her head*) what did u say? am i going back? no honey. how/why shd i return? she showed me no respect. none of the negroes in that class was being respected as the individuals we are. just three/big/blk/masses of blk/woman- hood. that is not it. can't be. (*stops walking*).

Uh-huh. i'll lose the credit for that course but i'll appeal when i'm a senior and u know what i'll write on that paper. i'll write the reason i lost these three credits is due to discrimination, yes. that's what i'll say and . . .

oh

honey. yes. it might have been foolish but it was right. after all at some point a person's got to stand up for herself just a little and . . . oh. u have a surprise. what? there? that's yrs? boss. o it's boss. (*jumps up and down*) Nesbitt yr/father is the nicest man. what a beautiful car. now u can drive up from Howard on weekends. yes. i'd like that. Let's go for a ride, u know upstate N.Y. is pretty this time of yr. where we headed for?

Yes. i do love u nesbitt. i've told u so many times but i'm scared to do it because i might get pregnant; i'm scared of the act, i guess u're right in saying that i'm against it becuz it has not been sanctioned by church/marriage and . . .

i'm trembling nesbitt.

i

feel the cold air on my thighs. how shall i move my love; i keep missing the beat of yr/fast/movements.

is it time to

go already? that's rt. we do have to go to yr/father's/dance. how do i look?

any different? i thought not. i'm

ready to go.

(*softly*) nesbitt do u think after a first love each succeeding love is a repetition?

(*The stage darkens and SON/JI moves to the dressing table and sits. Then a tape of Malcolm's voice is heard and SON/JI adds a long skirt, removes the straightened/ wig and puts on large/hoop/earrings.*)

SISTER SON/JI: racist? brothers & sisters. he is not the racist here in white/america. he is a beautiful/blk/man who talks about separation cuz we must move there. no more fucking SIT/ins-toilet/ins-EAT/ins—just like he says—the time for ins is over and the time for outs is here. out of this sadistic/masochistic/society that screams its paleface over the world. the time for blk/nationhood is here. (*gets up and moves forward*)

Listen. listen. did u hear those blk/words of that
beautiful/blk/warrior/prince—
Did u see his flashing eyes and did u hear his dagger/words. cuz if u did then u will know as i have come to know. u will change—u will pick up yr/roots and become yr/self again—u will come home to blk/ness for he has looked blk/people in the eye and said

welcome home. yr/beautiful/blkness/awaits u. here's my hand brother/sister— welcome. Home. (*stage lightens*)

brother Williams. this blk/power/conference is outa sight. i ain't never seen so many heavee/blk/people together. i am learning too much. this morning i heard a sister talk about blk/women supporting their blk/men. listening to their men, sacrificing, working while blk/men take care of bizness, having warriors and young sisters. i shall leave this conference brother with her words on my lips. i will talk to sisters abt loving their blk/men and letting them move in tall/ straight/lines toward our freedom. yes i will preach blk/love/respect between blk/men and women for that will be the core/basis of our future in white/ america.

But. why do u have to split man. u've been out all this week to meetings. can't we have some time together. the child is in bed. and i don't feel like reading. it's just 11 PM. can't we talk/touch. we hardly talk any more. i'm afraid that one day we'll have nothing to say to each other.

yes. i know u're tired. i know that the brothers are always on yr/case where u're organizing; and u need to unwind from the week but i want to unwind with u. i want to have a glass of wine with u and move into yr/arms; i want to feel u moving inside of me. we haven't made love in weeks man and my body feels dead, unalive. i want to talk abt our past/future—if we have one in this ass/hole country. Don't go. Stay home with me and let us start building true blk/lives—let our family be a family built on mutual love and respect. Don't leave me man i've been by myself for weeks. we need time together. blk/people gots to spend all their spare time together or they'll fall into the same traps their fathers and mothers fell into when they went their separate ways and one called it retaining their manhood while the other called it just plain/don't/care/about/family/hood. a man is a man in a house where a woman/ children cry out for a man's presence—where young warriors can observe their father's ways and grow older in them—where young sisters can receive the smiles of their fathers and carry their smiles to their future husbands. Is there time for all this drinking—going from bar to bar. Shouldn't we be getting ourselves together—strengthening our minds, bodies and souls away from drugs, weed, whiskey and going out on Saturday nites. alone. what is it all about or is the rhetoric apart from the actual being/doing? What is it all about if the doings do not match the words?

(*The stage becomes dark with only a spotlight on SISTER SON/JI's face and since she is constantly moving on the stage, sometimes she is not seen too clearly.*)

SISTER SON/JI: (*is crooning softly*) hee. haa. haa. THE HONKIES ARE COMING
TO TOWN TODAY. HOORAY. HOORAY. HOORAY.

THE CRACKERS ARE COMING TO
TOWN TODAY. TODAY. TODAY. HOORAY.

where
are u man? hee hee. hee. the shadow knows. we are our brother's keepers. we
must have an undying love for each other. it's 5 AM in the morning.

i am scared of voices moving
in my head.

ring-around-the-honkies-a-
pocketful-of-gunskerboomkerboomwehavenopains.

the child is moving
inside of me. where are you? Man yr/son moves against this silence. he kicks
against my silence.

Aaaaaaah. Aaaaaaah.
Aaaaaah. oh. i must keep walking. man, come fast. come faster than the speed
of bullets—faster than the speed of lightning and when u come we'll see it's
SUPER-BLOOD. HEE. HEE. HAA. FOOLED U DIDN'T IT? Ahhh—go
way. go way voices that send me spinning into nothingness. Ah. aah. aaaah.
aaaaah. Aaaaaah. aAaaAaah. Aaaaah. Aaaaaah. AaAaah. AaaaaaaaaaaaaaaaaaaaaH.
(*SISTER SON/JI falls on her knees and chants.*)

What is my name o blk/prince in what house do
I walk while i smell yr/distant smells
how have i come into this land
by what caravan did i cross the
desert of yr/blk/body?

(*SISTER SON/JI finally moves to dressing/table. Her walk is slower, almost oldish.
She rests her head. Then the sound of drums is heard mixed with a Coltrane sound.
SISTER SON/JI puts her hands over her ears to drown out the sounds but they
grow louder and she lifts her head, removes her jewelry, removes the long skirt, puts
on a gun and belt, ties a kerchief around her head and puts a baby/carrier on her back.
The music subsides.*)

SISTER SON/JI: do u think they will really attack us? what abt world opinion?
no, i hadn't noticed that they had a new administration. newer and better fascist
pigs. So we must send all the children away. will i help take them? but will i
have enough time to get back and help. good. Ahh—u think it'll be a long/
drawn/out fight. are we well prepared mume?—come children. Malika-
Nakawa-Damisi, Mungu, Mjumbe, Mtume, Baraka. come. the trucks are ready
to take us on our trip. make sure u have yr/lunches and canteens. make sure
u have yr/identification tags. where is our drummer?

Mwenge play us yr/songs as
we leave.

i shall return soon mume. i shall return soon. (*The sounds of guns/helicopters are heard.*)

So the war is becoming unpopular. and many devils are refusing to fight us. good. mume. can we trust the devils who have come to fight on our side? the women and i don't mind the male/devils here but the female/devils who have followed them. they shd not be allowed here. what happens to them when the one they are following is killed. It will become a problem if we don't send them packing. rt. away.

Ah. that sounds like a heavy attack. It is. women. sisters. Let us sing the killing/song for our men. let us scream the words of dying as we turn/move against the enemy. (*SISTER SON/JI moves as she chants.*)

OOOOU-WAH
OOOOU-WAH
OOOU-OOOU-OOOU-WAH-WAH-WAH-
OOOU-OOOU-OOOU-WAH-WAH-WAH-
EEYE-YO
EEYE-YO
EEYE-EEYE-EEYE-YO-YO-
EEYE-EEYE-EEYE-YO-YO-

Is it true that Mungu is here? But. he is only thirteen. a child. He's still a child mume. He's as tall as u mume but he's still a boy. send him back. all the other warriors are fifteen. are we—do we need soldiers that badly. Mume. please send him back. he's just a boy. he's just my little boy.

he's not so tall stretched out on the ground. the bullets have taken away his height. Mungu. Mungu. Mungu. can u hear me?

do my words go in and out yr/bullet/holes till they finally rest inside u? Mungu. Mungu. Mungu. My first warrior. i love u my little one even as u stare yr/death stare. SCREAM-HEY-SCREAM-HEY.

Yes. u. death. i'm calling yr/name. why not me? Stay away from my family. i've given u one son—one warrior for yr/apprenticeship. git stepping death for our tomorrows will be full of life/living/births.

if he keeps the devil/woman then he shd be made to leave. Yes. he must go. Mume. tell me what are all these deaths for, with more likely to come? so he can feel sorry for a devil/woman and bring her whiteness among all this BLK/NESS.

he feels sorry for her. and what abt our teachings. have we forgotten so soon that we hate devils. that we are in a death/struggle with the beasts. if she's so good. so liberal. send her back to her own kind. Let her liberalize them. Let her become a camp follower to the hatred that chokes white/america. yes i wd vote to send yr/partner to certain death if he tries to keep her.

these mississippi hills will not give up our dead. my son/our son did not die for integration. u must still remember those ago/yrs when we had our blk/ white period. they died for the right of blk/children to run on their own land and let their bodies explode with the sheer joy of living. of being blk/and many children have died and these brown hills and red gullies will not give up our dead.

                                                                                    and neither

will i.

(The sounds of guns, planes are heard. SISTER SON/JI moves slowly to the dressing/table. The war/sounds decrease and a sound like Coltrane mixed with drums begin slowly, tiredly. She puts on the gray/haired/wig, takes off the gun and baby carrier—and puts on the make/up of all the yrs she has gathered. Then she turns around in the chair and stares at the audience.)

SISTER SON/JI: Death is a five o'clock door forever changing time. And wars end. Sometimes too late. i am here. still in mississippi. Near the graves of my past. We are at peace. the state supports me and others like me and i have all the time i want to do what all old/dying people do. Nothing. but i have my memories. *(rises)* Yes. hee. hee. i have my sweet/astringent memories becuz we dared to pick up the day and shake its tail until it became evening. a time for us. blk/ness. blk/people. Anybody can grab the day and make it stop. can u my friends? or may be it's better if i ask:

                                    will you?

CURTAIN

SYBIL KEIN (1939–   )

Get Together (1970)

BIOGRAPHY AND ACHIEVEMENTS

Sybil Kein (named Consuela Moore at birth) was born on September 29, 1939, in New Orleans to Augustine Boudreaux Moore and Frank Moore. Along with twelve brothers and sisters, she grew up in the seventh ward of New Orleans, an area historically inhabited by the jens du couleur (free men of color, or Creoles). Kein, a Creole of Color, (of Native American, African, and French ancestry,) spoke a French patois as a first language and recalls having a great deal of difficulty learning to speak English when she began grammar school.

She attended Corpus Christi Elementary, a school that historically educated the Creoles of Color of New Orleans. While in attendance at this private Catholic school, Kein studied dancing and music. She made her debut on the stage at the age of three when she performed at a dance recital. Though dancing intrigued her, it was from musical instruments, particularly the viola, that she derived a strong sense of self. She greatly admired the Creoles of Color jazz musicians of the seventh ward. Like them, she wanted to tell of the lives of Creoles of Color through music.

She continued the study of musical instruments at Xavier Preparatory School, from which she graduated, and at Xavier University in New Orleans where she earned a bachelor of arts in instrumental music in 1958. By then, Kein had mastered the viola, violin, cello, string base, guitar, and piano. She had also begun writing plays and poems and working on ways to complement them with Creole songs and music.

Kein's determination to succeed at a career was tested after the birth of her three children, Elizabeth, David, and Susan, and after her divorce. Always pushing herself to achieve, Kein enrolled at the University of New Orleans (formerly Louisiana State University at New Orleans) where she earned a master's degree in theater arts and communication in 1972. Three years later Kein graduated from the University of Michigan at Ann Arbor with a doctorate in American ethnic literature.

Combining her skills in dance, music, and theater, Kein has been performing her poetry and Creole ballads for over twenty years. Currently she is a full professor at the University of Michigan-Flint, where she has taught English and theater since 1972.

A performing artist, poet, playwright, scholar, and recording artist, Sybil Kein has spent two decades researching the history and culture of Louisiana Creoles of Color as well as writing poems and plays about them. She has published several volumes of poetry, including *Visions from the Rainbow* (1979), *Gumbo People: Poesie Creole de La Nouvelle-Orleans 1981, and Delta Dancer*, 1984. Generally, her poetry is written in both Creole and English. Her poems and critical essays on Creole culture and Ethnic American literature have appeared in *Essence, Black American Literature Forum, Callaloo, New Orleans Review,* and *Obsidian*. Additionally, Kein has produced several Creole sound recordings, including *Poetry and Music by Sybil Kein*, by the National Federation of Community Broadcasters Program Service, 1979, and *Serenade Creole* by Mastertracks, 1987.

As poetic as she is dramatic, Kein has written twenty-eight plays. Crediting Eugene Ionesco, Samuel Beckett, Douglass Turner Ward, and Lorraine Hansberry as her principal influences, she has had ten plays produced: *Saints and Flowers*, 1965 (also produced in Wien, Austria); *Projection One*, 1966; *The Black Box*, 1967; *The Christmas Holly*, 1967; *Deep River Rises*, 1970; *The Reverend*, 1970; *Get Together*, 1970; *When I Grow Up!*, 1974; *Rogues Along the River Flint*, 1977; and *River Rogues*, 1979.

Kein's plays, both comedies and tragicomedies, treat a variety of subjects, including slavery, miscegenation, the color line, the dilemma of mulattos, teenage pregnancy, and stereotypes among blacks and whites. Her plays, saturated with wit, are important in the development of African American theater because of the local color and have helped make regionalist drama fashionable.

Kein has received a host of awards for her poetry and plays, including Best Playwright, Louisiana State University of New Orleans, 1970; The Avery Hopwood Award for poetry, Ann Arbor, 1975; the Creative Achievement Award, the University of Michigan, 1978; the AMOCO Foundation Award, 1979; Michigan Association of Governing Boards Award, 1982; and the Michigan Council of the Arts Artist Award, 1981 and 1990. In May 1989, she lectured at the Sorbonne in Paris on Louisiana Creole language and again at the Sorbonne in December 1989 on New Orleans Jazz funerals at the International Conference on Ethnic Festivals in America. Named Chercheur Associe (associate research scholar) for 1990 at the Centre d'Etudes Afro-americaines of Universite de la Sorbonne nouvelle, Kein researched early French writers to look for their use of Creole in their writings.

Sybil Kein, who skillfully blends music and poetry to form provocative drama, has the potential for energizing American theater.

SYNOPSIS AND ANALYSIS: *GET TOGETHER*

Operating around coexisting sets, this play opens with the Doolikes, a white family, on Set I and the Markems, a black family, on Set II. Both families can be seen simultaneously as they alternate delivering lines. Both Mrs. Doolike and Mrs. Markem are crying over the death of an uncle. Each husband tries to console his wife in her time of mourning, while reminding her that she has not seen her uncle in many years. Each wife abruptly stops crying when her husband reminds her of the sizable inheritance that has been left to her by her uncle.

As soon as the women are reminded of their inheritance, they remember that they have guests coming. Mrs. Doolike and her family are expecting a black man who is a new aide to the mayor. They boast that now that they have money, they can invite blacks to their house. Mr. Doolike says, "We don't have to act the way we used to in order to be accepted. We can afford to be a little uh—'discriminating'—." On the other hand, Mrs. Markem and her family are expecting a white man who is a new aide to the mayor.

The Markems and Doolikes are very nervous about impressing their guests and go out of their way to imitate what they consider "white" and "black" behavior, tastes, customs, and rituals. Each family makes changes, actually reversals, in decor, meals, dress, language, dance, and children.

In an attempt to prepare for their white guest, the Markems remove all doilies and scarves from their furniture as well as remove their loud-colored curtains. On the other hand, the Doolikes bring in doilies and scarves to cover their furniture and redecorate their home to appeal to their black guest.

Mrs. Doolike almost becomes hysterical when she realizes that she does not know what kinds of food black people eat. Her mother-in-law, Mother Doolike, suggests "Sam's the Man Catering Service." Similarly, Mrs. Markem comes up with the idea to hire a catering service to prepare a "seven plate meal." Her mother-in-law, Mama Markem, tells her that she will never be able to pull off the evening if she does not know that it is a "seven course meal" she's ordering.

Once the question of the meals is settled, the women plan the appropriate attire that their family should wear to dinner. Mrs. Doolike dresses in an African robe, and her husband and children wear dashikis. Mrs. Markem and her daughter dress in flamboyant after-five dresses, and Mr. Markem and his son dress in suits.

Language is also a concern for both families. The Doolikes wish to learn the latest slang. From their son, they learn to use such phrases as "Yeah, you right!", "You can dig it!", "Foxy man foxy!", and "Where you at?". Similarly, the Markems are busy trying to "watch" their speech by using very formal language, some of which results in hypercorrection. For example, when Mr. Markem says that whites "shore eat funny," Mrs. Markem falls victim to hypercorrection with, "They shore eats funny." She is trying too hard to speak what she considers is "good" English.

Not only do they modify their language, but they also learn new dances. The Doolikes practice doing the watusi, while the Markems display their expertise at ballroom dancing.

Perhaps the most humorous reversal centers around the children. The Doolikes only have two children but rush out to borrow four or five more from neighbors who are having a birthday party because they assume that blacks believe in having a half dozen or more children per couple. On the other hand, the Markems, who have six or more children, send all but two away, particularly those children who have black sounding names, such as Annie Mae, Sammy, and Joe.

Once each family has made all of the necessary reversals, the guests arrive. Much to the surprise of the Doolikes, Mr. White, a black man, is the antithesis of what they expected. He is cultured, refined, suave, sophisticated, and well dressed. When the Doolikes offer him white lightning and chitterlings, Mr. White runs out, saying he is going to faint.

On the other hand, when Mr. Brown, a white man, arrives at the Markems, they are shocked to discover that he is dressed like a typical country politician with a wide hat, sloppy clothes, cigar, and a wide grin. When he is offered filet mignon, broccoli au gratin, and mushroom soup, Mr. Brown gasps and demands greens and chitterlings. He extinguishes his cigar on their table and marches out.

While both families are reeling from disappointment over failed expectations, Dotty, daughter of the Markems, walks in with her white boyfriend, Ludwig Highbachker, and Doris, daughter of the Doolikes, comes in with her black boyfriend, Ebeneezer Johnson. The play ends with the adults wondering if the children know more than they do about getting along in interracial situations.

When *Get Together* was first produced in 1970 in New Orleans, audiences enjoyed watching their biases revealed as foolish because of Kein's deft handling of humor. She made whites and blacks laugh at the stereotypes each had of the other.

Kein's ingenius manipulation of coexisting sets allows two plays about the same issues to go on simultaneously. The plot is easy to follow because what one family gives up the other accepts as appropriate. For example, when the Markems discard the doilies and the Doolikes decorate their living area with the very same doilies, a sense of continuity is set that remains through the end of the play. The audience knows early in the play that a series of reversals will take place as each family prepares for a guest of a different race.

Kein's central message in *Get Together* is that blacks and whites are not very different from each other. They both want good health, economic security, safety for their children, and acceptance by society. Kein demonstrates that Mr. Brown, the white politician, enjoys what black people like in terms of food and clothes. In the same breath, the audience realizes that Mr. White, a black man, has every bit as much right to like champagne, filet mignon, and broccoli au gratin as the white Doolikes. Kein suggests that it is in poor taste to label people and assume what their preferences are simply because of the color of their skin.

The play ends very optimistically in that the young ones seem to understand better than their parents that in order for one race to know the other there must be a coming together without the racial bars that prevent genuine communication. Both Doris and Dotty are free of the pretentiousness and presumptuousness of their parents. They make no changes in their lifestyles in order to accommodate their racially different companions.

In addition to the spoof on the groundless distrust that whites and blacks have of each other, the play also hints that very often these blacks and whites are related, albeit distantly, to each other. For example, it seems apparent that Kein is striving for a double entendre when both Mrs. Doolike and Mrs. Markem bemoan the loss of Uncle Richmond and Uncle Richie, respectively. Richmond and Richie could possibly be one and the same; this would underscore Kein's inference that because of miscegenation, blacks and whites are inextricably linked.

There are at least two instances where Kein pokes fun at blacks who give up parts of themselves in order to be accepted by mainstream America. In one instance, Mr. Markem tells his son not to bring his bicycle in the house because, "We don't act like that no more." Another case in point is the Markems shooing away their children who have black-sounding names. These characters go to great length to deny their heritage in order to impress their white guest.

Whites are not free from Kein's barbs either. Kein seems particularly bent on pointing the finger at those whites who boast that their maid is like one of the family. When Mother Doolike gets hysterical at the news that the black maid, Clara, has been given the day off because a black man is coming to dinner, the audience is aware that Clara is not treated as if she is a member of the family.

Kein also pokes fun at those whites who claim to be liberal but who inadvertently show themselves to be racist. For example, when Mr. Brown arrives for dinner, he says to the Markems, "Please to meet all yall. And you just call me Jason—'Mr.' Jason that is, he—he!" Though he has come to socialize, by insisting on a formal title he never lets them know that they are his equal.

Get Together, though it chastises both blacks and whites, challenges them to accept each other's similarities and differences and to learn to bridge the gap between the races.

NOTE

For more information about subjects treated by Sybil Kein, see Violet Harrington Bryan, "Evocations of Place and Culture in the Works of Four Contemporary Black Louisiana Writers: Brenda Osbey, Sybil Kein, Elizabeth Brown-Guillory, and Pinkie Gordon Lane, *Louisiana Literature* (Fall 1987), pp. 49–59.

Details about Sybil Kein's life and works are based upon a phone interview with her on September 8, 1989.

Get Together (1970) ─────────────

Sybil Kein

CHARACTERS

MR. MARKEM
MRS. MARKEM
DORIS MARKEM   Their 18–Year–Old Daughter
A. J. MARKEM   Alvin Jacob, Their 13–Year–Old Son
MR. JASON BROWN   A Mayor's Aide
LUDWIG HIGHBACHKER
MR. DOOLIKE
MRS. DOOLIKE
MOTHER DOOLIKE
DOTTY DOOLIKE   18 Years Old
A. J. DOOLIKE   13 Years Old
MR. GERALD WHITE   A Mayor's Aide
EBENEEZER JOHNSON

N.B.: All members of the Markem family are Negro.

Mr. Gerald White and Mr. Ebeneezer Johnson are also black.

All members of the Doolike family are white.

Mr. Ludwig Hibachker and Mr. Jason Brown are also white.

SCENE

The stage is divided into two sets. In Set I—a sofa, chair, tables, lamps, radio and a rocking chair. Typical middle-class living room is seen on both sets. They should be identical with one exception, i.e., on Set I doilies are used profusely (on tables, chairs, etc., as well as flowered curtains if able to use) and an old T.V. set.

On Set II a dining room set—6 chairs, a large table, and a buffet—all elegantly decorated on Set I and set up like a kitchen on Set II (i.e., kitchen type table cloth, etc.). Set I and II should be side by side with a partition of some type separating them. Lights should be arranged so that one or the other set can be blacked out when called for by the script.

ACT I

SCENE OPENS: The double living room sets are seen—no characters on set—the sets are muted a bit to indicate evening. The twin clocks indicate five o'clock.
NOTE: At some points the dialogue from the two sets must blend and the actors should time the wording so that the pace will not be lost.
Enter MRS. MARKEM and MRS. DOOLIKE—one at a time: MRS. DOOLIKE first, then MRS. MARKEM. Their actions are the same. Each walks in, looks around, takes a picture from a table, sits on the chair and sobs—softly at first, then quite a bit—staggering the sounds so that they are almost answering each other. They keep this up for a few minutes then cry softly into a handkerchief and put the pictures back down. Doors are heard closing.
Enter MR. MARKEM and MR. DOOLIKE—MR. MARKEM first then MR. DOO-LIKE.

MR. MARKEM: Why honey, some more tears? (*MRS. MARKEM takes the picture up and cries harder*). Come on now, he's been buried a week and besides, it's the Lord's will—

MR. DOOLIKE: Cry for the living, honey, not the dead. (*Both put their hands on their wives' shoulders and try to comfort them.*)

MRS. DOOLIKE: My poor Uncle Richmond!

MRS. MARKEM: My poor Uncle Richie!

MR. DOOLIKE: Oh come on dear—

MR. MARKEM: Honey, please—(*they continue sobbing and holding the pictures.*)

MRS. DOOLIKE: He was such a good man!

MRS. MARKEM: He shore was good to me!

MR. DOOLIKE: That he was!

MR. MARKEM: Shore was!

 (*They cry some more—the two husbands are getting a little disgusted with the scene.*)

MR. DOOLIKE: Please stop it—All this is not necessary—

MR. MARKEM: We have a guest for dinner, remember?

MR. DOOLIKE: (*trying again*) We've got to get ready.

MR. MARKEM: Tonight is special.

MR. DOOLIKE: Pull yourself together—

MR. MARKEM: Enough crying—

MR. DOOLIKE: After all, you hardly knew him—

MR. MARKEM: You hadn't seen him since you were three!

MR. DOOLIKE: He lived a long life!

MR. MARKEM: Drank himself to death at age 96—(*They cry a long time then.*)

MR. DOOLIKE: Oh well—remember–

MR. MARKEM AND MR. DOOLIKE: (*shout*) The Money! (*The women stop crying suddenly and then smile.*)

MRS. MARKEM: We is rich! (*They embrace briefly.*)

MRS. DOOLIKE: Oh, I must get ready. Indeed I did forget. Oh dear, the dinner! Whatever am I going to do?

MR. MARKEM: Mr. Brown, the Mayor's aide, is coming to dinner at 8 o'clock—and you know what he is!

MRS. MARKEM: Oh yes—what are we going to do? I haven't had time to really do all the things I wanted to—the furniture, the food, the—oh!—that T.V. set has got to go!

MRS. DOOLIKE: We've got to make him feel at home. After all, he is quite an important person you know, and we have to let him know that we are not like everybody else! Bring the T.V. in here.

MR. MARKEM: Yes, yes, just think of that—a mayor's aide—right here in our house—right here eating at my table with me and my family—Look—we got to make him feel that he's not out of place—After all, we are not like everybody else—(*takes a large roll of money out of his pockets*)

MR. DOOLIKE: The days are gone when we had to be careful who we invited to dinner—(*takes money out of his pocket*) Yes, we can afford to be uh—*discriminating*?

MRS. DOOLIKE: You know dear—this place is—is—(*looks around*) not bright enough—not enough life—(*exits*)

MRS. MARKEM: (*looks around*) A few changes here and there—get rid of those horrible scarves and junk. (*She takes away the doilies and frills. exit*)

MRS. DOOLIKE: What we need is some of these! (*She puts doilies and scarves where MRS. MARKEM had them.*)—and maybe a nice bright—

MRS. MARKEM: This has got to go—(*She takes a curtain down and exits.*)

MRS. DOOLIKE: (*brings in curtain*) Curtain! (*They are busy rearranging until SET II looks like SET I.*)

MRS. DOOLIKE: (*sits down to view*) There!

MRS. MARKEM: (*sits down to view*) There!

MR. DOOLIKE: It looks—

MRS. MARKEM: —Different!

MR. DOOLIKE: That's the word—different! By the way dear—what are you preparing for dinner?

MRS. MARKEM: Oh the menu—I almost forgot—

MR. MARKEM: The men-who?

MRS. DOOLIKE: I must do something simple—

MRS. MARKEM: A seven plate meal!

MR. DOOLIKE: —That sounds fine—but what?

MR. MARKEM: Seven plates, huh?

MRS. MARKEM: Oh, I don't know—you know how they eat.

MRS. DOOLIKE: Oh their culinary customs are so quaint—I think I had better get a recipe—

MR. MARKEM: Yeh—they shore eat funny—

MRS. MARKEM: (*correcting him*) They shore eats funny—I'm going to get some recipes—

MR. DOOLIKE: "Culinary customs"—Dear, I think your language is a little ostentatious. You should be a little more earthy in your choice of words—

MRS. DOOLIKE: Sorry dear—I'll try to remember—

(*Blackout Set II*)

MR. MARKEM: What do you mean—eats funny? What's wrong with eat funny?

MRS. MARKEM: You got to watch the way you talk—after all, we got standing in the community, (*to his face*) You dig?

MR. MARKEM: O.K. But they shore eat funny.

MAMA MARKEM: (*enters*) Evening Son, Daughter. (*She sits in rocker and takes off her shoes.*) Boy, I'm tired today.

MRS. MARKEM: Mama, you always tired!

MAMA MARKEM: So what—ain't I got a right? I works all day you know. I ain't like some people. (*glares at her*)

MRS. MARKEM: But I told you—you ain't got to work no more, we got money now—

MAMA MARKEM: Ain't none of mine. (*takes off stockings*)

MR. MARKEM: Mama, you know what's ours is yours.

MAMA MARKEM: The way you spending it, ours is going to be all gone before yours gets to see any of it!

MRS. MARKEM: Mama, we having an important guest for dinner tonight.

MAMA MARKEM: Oh? Is this why you got the place looking like—(*looks on back rocker*). What you do with my embroidered scarf I had on the rocker?

MRS. MARKEM: Well, since we can afford to redecorate, we can afford to—

MAMA MARKEM: Pay me for my scarf I hope—I made it with my own hands.

MR. MARKEM: Look Mama, if you could help the missus with dinner, I'll take you downtown and buy you that new coat you been wanting.

MAMA MARKEM: Help her with the dinner—well, what she cooking?

MRS. MARKEM: A seven plate meal—

MAMA MARKEM: A seven plate—you mean a seven course meal—who the hell is coming—and how the hell are you gonna cook it if you can't even say it right? Come on, let's see what we can do—no wait-(*She sits down again.*)—wait-(*to MR. MARKEM*) I already bought my new coat—it's been in lay-away for six months and I'll be getting it out before the weather changes—you cook your own dinner—

MRS. MARKEM: But Mama—

MR. MARKEM: Please, you gotta—

MAMA MARKEM: Do nothing I don't feel like—remember—we got uh money—

MRS. MARKEM: Well, at least tell me what I should have on the menu.

MAMA MARKEM: Well! Ain't we fancy—a menu! and I speck you gonna hire a butler to serve it—ha ha you two is too much—ha ha—well—(*gets up*) I'm going upstairs and rest my nerves—have fun children—or should I say "tally-ho" and stuff like that—he he! (*exits. During the above, MR. MARKEM reads a newspaper, then folds it to talk, then reads it again, etc.*)

MR. MARKEM: Oh shucks!

MRS. MARKEM: Wait, I have it! What do you call those people who cook for you and fix things?

MR. MARKEM: A colored maid?

MRS. MARKEM: No! No! That's not what I mean stupid; you know a business—

MR. MARKEM: A colored maid service! But we can't have no colored maid.

MRS. MARKEM: No! It sounds like colored. "Colored Service?" "Cattered?" "Catering?" That's it—a Catering service. (*exits*)

MR. MARKEM: Huh?

DORIS MARKEM: (*enters*) Hi Daddy. (*She kisses him.*)

MR. MARKEM: Glad you home, sugar—we got a problem—you got to get your thinking cap on and help us—the mayor's aide is coming to dinner and we got to have everything just right—you know—to impress—

DORIS MARKEM: Oh? The mayor's aide? Nice. How old is he? Is he groovy, you know?

MR. MARKEM: He's my age and he ain't groovy—I mean he's a respectable man—besides, he's—

DORIS MARKEM: (*interrupting*) Oh! Oh! I almost forgot—I got a new boyfriend, Daddy.

MR. MARKEM: Who is he?

DORIS MARKEM: His name is Ludwig Highbachker and he's—well you'll meet him tonight—he's picking me up at 9:30. Gee, it's getting late. Mama, you need some help? (*exits*)

MR. MARKEM: Highbachker? Ludwig?

A. J. MARKEM: (*enters riding his bike in and almost hits his father*) Hi, Daddy—Can I get a new bike?

MR. MARKEM: Hey! just a minute boy—didn't I tell you not to bring your bike in here? We don't act like that no more.

A. J.: We don't?

MR. MARKEM: No!

A. J.: Oh! Well, can I get a new bike? Huh? With an electric horn and a high seat and—

MR. MARKEM: (*interrupting*) Ok, ok, but get that out of here and go wash up and put your suit on—we got company for dinner.

A. J.: Huh? A suit?

MR. MARKEM: You heard me.

A. J.: Oh shucks—what kinder jive dinner is this? A suit! Shucks!

MR. MARKEM: Where's the other kids?

A. J.: Out playing in the yard—

MR. MARKEM: Well, go tell 'em I said to get upstairs and bathe.

A. J.: Bathe? Just to eat?

MR. MARKEM: You heard me! Git!

A. J.: O.K. I'm going—Oh boy! (*exits*)

MRS. MARKEM: (*enters. She brings in special suits for him to try on.*) Well, I got dinner taken care of—here, try these, (He does—one at a time.) Now let's see—the furniture is set—the dinner's planned—the kids—Oh my lawd!

MR. AND MRS. MARKEM: *The kids!* (*pause. They both sit down.*)

MR. MARKEM: What we gonna do?

MRS. MARKEM: We got too many. (*pause*)

MR. MARKEM: What we gonna do?

MRS. MARKEM: We shouldn't have more than 2 or 3. What we gonna do?

MR. MARKEM: Well, we could get rid of some of 'em.

MRS. MARKEM: (*sharply*) What do you mean?

MR. MARKEM: I mean—uh—send some of 'em to Aunt Mabel's—

MRS. MARKEM: Oh! Well, which ones?

MR. MARKEM: Well, let's be democratic about it and pull names. That's it—we'll pull names!

MRS. MARKEM: Good idea. (*goes to a small table—gets paper and a pen—brings them back to the sofa—sits down and quickly writes names on paper—tears it into strips and places them in a nearby ashtray*) You first—(*to her husband*)

MR. MARKEM: O.K. (*pulls a name and reads*) Sammy!

MRS. MARKEM: (*pulls a name and reads*) Joe! (*pause*)

MR. MARKEM: Wait—this ain't right—

MRS. MARKEM: Yeh—it ain't right—(*pause*) Let's do it again.

MR. MARKEM: (*pulls and reads*) A. J.—

MRS. MARKEM: (*pulls and reads*) Annie Mae—

MR. MARKEM: Oh hell—this ain't never gonna work!

MRS. MARKEM: Yeh—you right! Let's send everybody but Doris and—and—and—

MR. MARKEM: (*interrupting*) my oldest son Alvin Jacob!

MRS. MARKEM: Who is Alvin Jacob?

MR. MARKEM: A. J., stupid!

MRS. MARKEM: Oh that's right—Doris and Alvin Jacob—that sounds real high class!

MR. MARKEM: Course it does (*He picks out a formal suit.*) and I'm gonna look real high class in this. How's this?

MRS. MARKEM: Great! (*She brings out an elaborate after-5 dress.*) And this is me, Darling!

MR. MARKEM: Yeh, you right. (*quickly*) I mean—ah charming, my deah! Shall we go?

MRS. MARKEM: My steemed pleasure suh'. (*blackout on Set I; lights on Set II*)

MRS. DOOLIKE: (*enters*) Mother, darling—how are you? Did you enjoy your bridge meeting?

MOTHER DOOLIKE: Oh yes, it was simply lovely—you know it was Louise's turn to have the meeting at her house, and as usual, the food was simply terrible. The hors d'oeuvres tasted like left-overs from last night's party, and I just knew I'd catch some awful disease—there was dust all over the place—it was simply filthy—but of course, she does have "children" still running around and at her age too! I tell you—(*suddenly notices her son isn't listening and addresses her attention to him*) Son, you look a little tired—is anything wrong?

MR. DOOLIKE: Not tired, Mother—worried—

MOTHER DOOLIKE: Oh! What's the problem?

MR. DOOLIKE: Well, we're having a rather distinguished and unique guest for dinner tonight and we've got to make sure everything's prepared just right.

MOTHER DOOLIKE: Oh! Who is your guest?

MRS. DOOLIKE: Mr. White, the mayor's aide.

MOTHER DOOLIKE: Oh! (*as if she knows*) Well, what's the problem?

MRS. DOOLIKE: We're having trouble planning the menu, we can't decide what to wear, the house isn't the way it should be—oh gee, Mother, everything's WRONG! (*almost in tears*) We even had to get rid of the maid for today!

MOTHER DOOLIKE: Get rid of the MAID! Why that's terrible. Oh my God, that's terrible! (*as if suddenly realizing the significance of what she's just repeated*) How on earth will we get all of this work done without Clara—she's just like one of the family. (*She sits down to meditate on the new crisis for a bit, then turns to her daughter-in-law.*) What time is he coming?

MRS. DOOLIKE: 8 o'clock . . .

MOTHER DOOLIKE: (*rising from the chair*) Well, don't worry dear—I'll help—I know just the place to call—"Sam's the Man Catering Service." It specializes in just that type of "specialty." As for the other problems, we'll just have to take care of them one at a time. Anyway, we'd better hurry if he's due here at 8 o'clock. Let's get started! (*They exit.*)

DOTTY DOOLIKE: (*enters*) Hi Dad—What's up? (*She kisses him on the cheek.*)

MR. DOOLIKE: Hello dear—we've got a guest coming for dinner tonight at 8 o'clock.

DOTTY: Oh—who is it?

MR. DOOLIKE: The mayor's aide—he's—

DOTTY: (*interrupting*) Oh! marvelous! Yes, I've heard of him—oh gee Dad, and his picture's been in the newspapers and everything—boy—won't the kids in school be just green with envy when they find out that he was here at my house for dinner. Oh boy! Hey Dad, guess what? I got a new boyfriend—He is just divine, and we're going out tonight and his name is Ebeneezer Johnson, the president of our class and everything and—

MR. DOOLIKE: (*interrupting*) Dotty, all that's fine, but we've got a few problems about tonight's dinner party. Run into the kitchen and see if you can help your mother out with some of the planning like a good girl.

DOTTY: (*excitedly*) O.K. Dad—shall do! Oh boy—tonight's gonna be something else! (*exits*)

MR. DOOLIKE: (*disgustedly*) "Something else!" It sure will be if we don't get something going soon towards getting ready for it. (*as if just hearing it*) Ebeneezer Johnson? Who in the world would name a child—oh well—I got my own problems. I wonder where Andrew Jonathan is. (*to himself*) I'd better get him squared away about tonight before anymore problems develop. (*goes to the foot of stairs and yells upstairs*) ANDREW! Andrew Jonathan—Come here a moment, son, I want to talk with you.

ANDREW: Coming, Dad! (*runs downstairs with a broken spring in his hand*) Dad, I've got a problem. The mainspring on my Ajax computer set is broke and I can't fix it—would you get me another one please? The set is completely useless without it, and I was in the middle of programming a special—

MR. DOOLIKE: (*as if he hasn't heard a word his son's said*) Son, I want to talk with you a minute.

ANDREW: Sure, Dad—what is it? (*He sits down.*)

MR. DOOLIKE: Son, we're having a dinner guest this evening—the mayor's aide—and we must have our manners up to par.

ANDREW: Sure, Dad, I understand. I'll get my brown suit ready and—

MR. DOOLIKE: No–No, that won't do, I'm afraid. Dotty and your mother are getting something special for us to wear.

ANDREW: Oh they are? Well what is it?

MR. DOOLIKE: Something simple—but fashionable—I trust their good taste. But I want you to help me with something else.

ANDREW: What kind of dinner is this? You're not going to wear a suit either?

MR. DOOLIKE: No—well, not exactly, but anyway what I'm getting at is that tonight we'll have to be extra careful about our speech. After all, the mark of intelligence is that a person can be flexible in all things.

ANDREW: What are you trying to tell me, Dad?

MR. DOOLIKE: Well, son, huh—I mean are you familiar with any of the current "quaint expressions" going around town?

ANDREW: (*puzzled*) "Quaint expressions!" What do you mean, Dad?

MR. DOOLIKE: I mean the new "slang" expressions one hears nowadays.

ANDREW: (*looking enlightened*) Oh! You mean stuff like "Where you at?" and "I can dig it"—

MR. DOOLIKE: (*excitedly*) Yes!—that's it! And what's this new one? "Yes, you're correct!" uh—

ANDREW: Dad, it's "Yeah you right!"

MR. DOOLIKE: Fine, son, fine—now I want you to help me to memorize these expressions as soon as possible.

ANDREW: But Dad—we're going to sound so—

MR. DOOLIKE: (*interrupting*) Never mind, son—do as I say—Now you know about your mother's inheritance.

ANDREW: Yes, dad, but—

MR. DOOLIKE: Well, now that we've got money, we can afford to do as we please—we don't have to act the way we used to in order to be accepted. We can afford to be a little uh—"discriminating"—

ANDREW: Well, it sounds boring to me but I'll do it. I mean, "I can dig it!"

MR. DOOLIKE: Yeah—you right! Good boy.

MR. DOOLIKE: (*enters*) Everything is coming along fine—the meal's being taken care of by an expert caterer and—oh! by the way, Mother's not feeling well— she has a terrible headache. I don't believe she'll be able to make the dinner party. Here—Dotty said try these on. (*She hands them a variety of bell-bottom pants—plaids, stripes, polka dots, etc., large mod ties, loud silk suits, shirts, etc. He looks disdainfully, then starts trying them on, one at a time—they all look kind of ridiculous.*)

MRS. DOOLIKE: (*to herself while he's trying on the clothes*) Let's see now—dinner's taken care of—the house we want to get decorated properly, the children—

MR. AND MRS. DOOLIKE: (*together*) Oh my heavens, the children?

MRS. DOOLIKE: Oh dear!

MR. DOOLIKE: We don't have enough! (*pause*)

MRS. DOOLIKE: Oh dear!

MR. DOOLIKE: We haven't time to—

MRS. DOOLIKE: Well, I should say not! How dare you even think about such things! Anyway, it's impossible.

MR. DOOLIKE: How many do we need?

MRS. DOOLIKE: At least four more!

MR. DOOLIKE: Yes—it's impossible.

MRS. DOOLIKE: Wait, the Simms next door are having a birthday party—there should be lots of children there.

MR. DOOLIKE: Oh good—maybe we can borrow a few—

MRS. DOOLIKE: It's just for tonight—I'm sure they won't mind.

MR. DOOLIKE: Well, it would sure help us out a lot.

MRS. DOOLIKE: Then it's settled! I'll go over and speak to Mrs. Simms about it. How are you coming with the clothes?

MR. DOOLIKE: (*holds up something loud and colorful*) How's this?

MRS. DOOLIKE: Oh it's in! It's in!

MR. DOOLIKE: You mean "You can dig it!"

MRS. DOOLIKE: "Yeah you right!" (*goes to get her long, African type gown*) Look at me!

MR. DOOLIKE: Absolutely fascinating! I mean—Foxy man, foxy!

MRS. DOOLIKE: Oh sock it to me!

MR. DOOLIKE: Uh, yeah you right! Shall we day-part? (*motions to door*)

MRS. DOOLIKE: This is gonna be—

MR. DOOLIKE: Outa sight! (*exits*)

END ACT I

ACT II–SET I: An elaborate dining room—complete with lace tablecloth—table set for a 7–course meal—a radio is inconspicuously left on the table in the rear of set but is visible.
ACT II–SET II: An elaborate dining room—however, the table here is set with a red and white checkered cloth obviously for a "simple" meal! A radio is also on a small table in the rear of set. As in Set I, it is visible but not turned on.
ENTER SET I: MRS. MARKEM is dressed "to kill" complete with wig, "after–5" attire, iridescent stockings and jeweled heel shoes. She looks around—obviously well pleased with everything—goes to table to adjust a plate, then notices the radio. She turns on some symphonic music and waltzes around the room—then.
ENTER SET II: MRS. DOOLIKE—She is dressed in a long dashiki with an African headdress—sandals and a tiki around her neck. She smiles—obviously pleased with herself— moves to the table to adjust a plate—notices the radio and turns on the latest rock music— fakes a rock dance—then.

MR. AND MRS. DOOLIKE: (*enter*)

MR. MARKEM: Darling! (*They dance ballroom style.*) Darling!

MR. DOOLIKE: Wan tu watusi? (*They dance rock style.*)

A. J. MARKEM: (*enters. He's dressed in a full dress suit complete with appropriate accessories. He watches them a moment and then sits down disgusted.*)

ANDREW: (*enters. Dressed in sandals and a dashiki and dark pants—he watches his parents a minute then sits down disgusted. after dancing ends*)

A. J. MARKEM: What was that supposed to be?

MRS. MARKEM: Ballroom dancing, dear—you must learn it—

A. J.: Oh no! You ain't gittin' me to do that sissy stuff—

MRS. MARKEM: Shut up, son, you ain't got no say in the matter.

A. J.: Oh shucks! When we gonna eat—I'm starving.

MRS. MARKEM: Now you remember your language—

MR. MARKEM: Your maw's right! I mean, your mother is correct.

A. J.: I'm still starving.

MRS. MARKEM: Alvin Jacob!

A. J.: Alvin Jacob! (*as if he has never heard the name before.*)

(*mimed conversation for a while.*)

SET II—

ANDREW: That's odd, Mother—what do you call it?

MRS. DOOLIKE: It's called the "watusi." You should learn it, dear.

ANDREW: You really don't expect me to do that do you?

MR. DOOLIKE: We do expect you to do that, as you call it.

MRS. DOOLIKE: Now—let's not forget your words—

MR. DOOLIKE: Your Mother is right—I mean your mama knows what's happening—you dig!

ANDREW: Good grief—O.K. dad—when are we going to eat?

MRS. DOOLIKE: That's more like it.

ANDREW: Well—when are we going to eat??

DOTTY AND DORIS: (*both call from upstairs*) It's almost 8 o'clock and I'm ready! (*Enters DOTTY in her dashiki on SET II and DORIS in her "after 5" on SET I.*)

MRS. MARKEM AND MRS. DOOLIKE: BEAUTIFUL! (*Pause. Both daughters pose—four strange children follow DOTTY in to the scene—they are all wearing dashikis.*)

MRS. DOOLIKE: And here are the children? (*She goes over to them—they back away from her afraid.*) Oh! what's wrong? Are you hungry? (*They shake their heads "no."*) You're not?

(*bell rings on both sets. Everyone is struck dumb for a minute—then*)

MRS. MARKEM AND MRS. DOOLIKE: Here he is! (*They answer doors at the same time.*)

MRS. MARKEM: (*at door*) Mr. Brown, I presume—

MR. BROWN: How yal folks? (*He is dressed like the typical southern country politician—wide hat, sloppy clothes, smoking a cigar, and showing a wide grin.*)

MRS. DOOLIKE: Oh Mr. White—Where you at baby?

MR. WHITE: (*Very sophisticated, suave, well-dressed and quite intelligent looking.*) I beg your pardon, madam!

MR. DOOLIKE: Come on in, brother—what's happening?

MR. MARKEM: A pleasure to have you in our home—do come in.

MR. BROWN: The pleasure is all mine. Ah just loves to sociate with yal kinda people (*He drops ashes on the floor. He sees the table and rubs his hands together.*) Wow Wee! Looksa here! Looks like we gonna have some good eatin! (*sucks his lips*)

MR. WHITE: Am I in the right house? I mean—you are Mr. and Mrs. Doolike?

MR. DOOLIKE: We shore is, son. Make yourself at home! Take your shoes off—

MR. WHITE: Huh!

MRS. DOOLIKE: Sit down, Mr. White—Don't be bashful—as you can see—we just "down home folks"—(*MR. WHITE is obviously confused, but nonetheless plays along.*)

MR. WHITE: Well—thank you—I guess—

MR. MARKEM: Sit down—everybody—let's get together and introduce one another.

MR. DOOLIKE AND MR. MARKEM: My wife (*indicates—all answer with a nod*)

> My daughter—Dotty Doolike
> Doris Markem
> My son—A. J. Doolike
> Alvin Jacob Markem

MR. DOOLIKE: and (*indicating children*) and—

CHILD I: I wanna go home!

CHILD II: I wanna go back to the party!

CHILD III: I want some more ice cream!

CHILD IV: I have to go to the bathroom—real bad! (*He runs out door—all the other children follow him.*)

MR. WHITE: What in the world is going on?

MR. BROWN: Well ain't that nice—pleased to meet all yall. And you just call me Jason—"Mr." Jason that is, he-he!

MRS. DOOLIKE: Oh dear! (*embarrassed*) Well, er—(*laughs it off nervously*) of course, you know how children are. I imagine you must have come from a large family. By the way what's your first name? Whitey?

MR. WHITE: My name is "Gerald" not Whitey—"Mr. White" if you please—(*very indignantly*)

MR. DOOLIKE: Yeah—well, we're very informal over here.

MR. MARKEM: Well, Jason—How's politics?

MR. BROWN: Oh fine! fine! Say, I was talking to his honor the other day, and—

MR. DOOLIKE: You've uh—seen the mayor lately?

MR. BROWN: He's looking for a good boy for—

MR. WHITE: Er—if you're interested in politics, I guess we can discuss the possibility of a position on—

MR. WHITE AND MR. BROWN: The Human Relations Committee.

MR. MARKEM: I sure would appreciate whatsoever you can, "suh."

MR. DOOLIKE: Yeah bruh! That's what's happening—

DORIS: Mr. Jason, we honored to have you dine with us.

ALVIN JACOB: Yeah—are you ready to eat suh!

MRS. MARKEM: (*embarrassed*) Children! Please—er Mr. Jason—would like something to drink before we dines? Champagne? Sauterne? A little Drambuie?

MR. BROWN: Oh not for me—you got any white lightning!

MR. MARKEM: Now you talking my language!

MRS. MARKEM: But we bought Champagne! (*to her husband*) Stupid!

MRS. DOOLIKE: What you drinking, Whitey? Corn liquor, Thunderbird—white lightning!

MR. WHITE: "Mr. White," please! And no thank you regarding the liquor—a nice cordial would be fine—

MRS. DOOLIKE: A cordial! Oh dear—but I bought—I mean I thought you'd like some—

MR. DOOLIKE: (*interrupting*) I have just the thing here—(*goes to buffet. Drinks are served but not drunk.*)

ANDREW JONATHAN: I'm hungry!

DOTTY: Oh Mr. White—you're such a charming man—we're really pleased to have you over.

MR. WHITE: Thank you, my dear—

MR. MARKEM: I propose a toast—(*All raise their glasses.*) To men everywhere—

MR. DOOLIKE: May they all—

MR. MARKEM: be able like us—

MR. DOOLIKE: to sit down together—

MR. MARKEM: at the table of brotherhood—

MR. DOOLIKE: in understanding—

MR. MARKEM: so that there may be—

MR. MARKEM AND MR. DOOLIKE: Peace in our times! (*They touch glasses after the speech and all drink—the guests on both sets begin coughing and choking after drinking.*)

MR. MARKEM: (*indignant*) This ain't no white lightning—damn it! What the hell is this?

MR. WHITE: What on earth is this?

MR. MARKEM: (*quickly*)—Ah! bring on the food—

MRS. MARKEM AND MRS. DOOLIKE: Coming up. (*They exit and return with covered dishes and place them on the tables.*)

MRS. MARKEM: Guestes first—

MRS. DOOLIKE: Dig in everybody—(*Dishes are passed around until everyone is served—then.*)

MR. BROWN: (*looking at his plate*) You all expect me to eat this stuff? Where's the greens and taters?

MR. WHITE: I hate to say it—but i just can't eat this whatever this is.

MR. DOOLIKE: What's the matter? Don't you like chitterlings?

MR. MARKEM: But suh! This here is the finest filley migyong you could buy anywhere.

MR. BROWN: But I'm used to that good old home cookin' that you folks so famous for—you mean you ain't got no greens and chitterlings!

MR. WHITE: Chitterlings? What on earth is a "chitterling"? I never heard of it— it looks—"nauseating!"

MRS. DOOLIKE: Nauseating! but all your people eat "soul food" don't they?

MRS. MARKEM: Surely a man of your caliba is used to steaks and broccolli-o-grottin and mushroom soup and—

MR. BROWN: Just looking at this stuff makes me sick. (*He puts his cigar out on the table.*)

MR. MARKEM: (*excitedly*) Look what he did! (*He points at the smoking tablecloth.*)

MR. WHITE: That smell—oh—I think I'm going to faint.

DORIS: I can't eat it, either—I had a big lunch—excuse me—I have a date. (*She leaves quickly.*)

ALVIN JACOB: Ach! I'm gonna throw up—(*He runs off holding his mouth.*)

ANDREW: Ooh! I'm gonna throw up—(*He runs off holding his mouth.*)

DOTTY: I'm sorry Mother—I just can't go through with this—(*to MR. WHITE*) Pardon me—I have to uh get dressed. (*She exits.*)

MRS. MARKEM: Oh lawdy!

MRS. DOOLIKE: Oh heavens!

MR. MARKEM: (*indignant*) Suh! We went to all this trouble and you ain't even polite enough to partake of our dinner—why, you act like you—you—colored or something.

MR. BROWN: (*getting up*) What! I didn't come here to be insulted! Colored huh? Goodnight! (*leaves in a huff*)

MR. DOOLIKE: Now look here, sir—we have gone out of our way just to please you. The least you could do is eat our meal. What are you trying to prove anyway? Are you one of those colored people who try to act like they're white?

MR. WHITE: Really! I have had quite enough of this! Please excuse me—I have an urgent appointment. (*He leaves in a dignified huff.*)

MR. AND MRS. DOOLIKE AND MR. AND MRS. MARKEM: (*together*) What did we do wrong? (*They sit down bewildered—the bell rings on both sets. MAMA MARKEM answers the door on Set I offstage.*)

MAMA MARKEM: (*calling from offstage*) Hey son—they got some strange boy at the door asking for Doris—what he want with Doris? (*MAMA calls to DORIS.*)—What the hell is this?

(*MOTHER DOOLIKE answers the door offstage Set II.*)

MOTHER DOOLIKE: (*from offstage*) You have a date with whom? Oh no! Dotty— Dotty—how could you—

(*DORIS and DOTTY enter with two young men—they stand—unseen at the rear of sets while MAMA MARKEM enters—her hair in rollers—wearing a robe and large fuzzy slippers saying:*)

MAMA MARKEM: Son-of-a-gun them young folks is something else—(*to MR. and MRS. MARKEM*) Well—how was your famous dinner?

MRS. MARKEM: Oh Mama—everything went wrong.

MR. MARKEM: Yeah—after we spent all that money—that stupid son-of-a-gun wouldn't even eat! (*as if amazed*) He left!

MAMA MARKEM: (*looking at the food*) Well if you served me junk like that, I'd leave too—I sho wouldn't eat it. It's enough to give a good horse the running offs.

MOTHER DOOLIKE: (*enters*) Well, I guess if it must be—it must be—(*to MR. and MRS. DOOLIKE*) How was your dinner, darlings? I'm sorry I couldn't make it but I've been having my headaches again.

MRS. DOOLIKE: Oh I'm so embarrassed—it didn't work—he excused himself and left, Mother.

MOTHER DOOLIKE: No wonder! (*looking at the food*) Is this the famous "Soul Food?" Oh God—it smells like garbage—you didn't eat any of it did you? The poor fellow—this food is obscene!

MRS. MARKEM: Mama, what are we gonna do?

MAMA MARKEM: Go to the refrigerator and pull out them greens and chitterlings and taters I cooked yesterday—maybe a "decent" meal will make you feel better—(*exits*)

MR. DOOLIKE: I guess we just failed to communicate.

MOTHER DOOLIKE: Well son—it wasn't your fault—you tried—maybe a good meal will make you feel better. I'll call "La Cuisine Francaise" and have them send something special over. (*exits*)

MR. AND MRS. MARKEM AND MR. AND MRS. DOOLIKE: (*all together*) Oh Dear! We'll never get together!

DORIS: (*bringing her date frontstage*) Mother—I've been waiting to introduce you, but we have to run.

DOTTY: (*comes frontstage with her date*) We'll miss the movie entirely if we don't leave now

(*All four kids say "goodnight"—girls drag their boyfriends offstage hurriedly.*)

MR. MARKEM: Well I'll be a son-of-a-gun—He's white!

MR. DOOLIKE: Good Heavens! He's a Negro!

MRS. MARKEM: I wonder—

MRS. DOOLIKE: If—

MR. MARKEM: They know something—

MR. DOOLIKE: We don't know!

CURTAIN

ELIZABETH BROWN-GUILLORY (1954–   )

Mam Phyllis (1985)

BIOGRAPHY AND ACHIEVEMENTS

Elizabeth Brown-Guillory was born on June 20, 1954, in Lake Charles, Louisiana, to Marjorie Savoie Brown and Leo Brown. Along with seven siblings, she grew up in rural Church Point, Louisiana, having grandparents and parents who spoke Creole or a French patois. She attended Our Mother of Mercy Catholic School through eighth grade and graduated from Church Point High School with distinction in 1972.

She earned a B.A. in 1975 and an M.A. in 1977 in English from the University of Southwestern Louisiana (USL). She began studying play-writing seriously at USL, under the direction of English professor and founder of The Eavesdrop Theater Paul Nolan. Her play *Bayou Relics* was first produced at The Eavesdrop Theater in 1976. She earned a Ph.D. in English and American literature in 1980 at Florida State University in Tallahassee.

She has taught at the University of South Carolina at Spartanburg and at Dillard University in New Orleans. She is currently an associate professor of English at the University of Houston. She is married to Lucius M. Guillory, a middle-school principal, and is the mother of one child, Lucia Elizabeth.

Elizabeth Brown-Guillory is the author of five produced plays: *Bayou Relics, Mam Phyllis, Somebody Almost Walked Off With All Of My Stuff, Marry Me, Again,* and *Snapshots of Broken Dolls*. Two have been published by the Colorado Springs–based Contemporary Drama Service: *Bayou Relics* (1983) and *Snapshots of Broken Dolls* (1987), the latter produced off-Broadway in 1986.

Brown-Guillory's plays explore with pathos and comedy the lives of the elderly. Though the children of the elderly are usually the subjects of satire, they are sometimes given redeeming qualities. These insensitive children go on to learn how to heal old wounds. She also writes about the habits, beliefs, mannerisms, and values of the Louisiana Creoles of Color.

While continuing to write for the stage, Brown-Guillory has published a host of critical essays on American writers and is the author of a critical book, *Their Place on the Stage: Black Women Playwrights in America*, (Greenwood Press, 1988). She is at work on a book on playwright and novelist Alice Childress.

SYNOPSIS AND ANALYSIS: *MAM PHYLLIS*

This 1930s three-act comedy is set in a small rural Louisiana town where the blacks, or Creoles of Color, are of African, French, and Indian descent. The action takes place on coexisting sets with one area of the stage designated as Mam Phyllis's home and the other as the living space of the Philmore family.

Maggie is shallow and upper middle class. During the apex of the depression, she spends her time sampling wine and chastising her husband for spending too much time at their hardware store.

In scene two, Mam Phyllis receives a visit from her best friend and principal agitator, Sister Viola, who has come to tell Mam Phyllis the news that there is going to be a retreat with a special priest, but Mam Phyllis has already heard the news from Brother Jesse. When Mam Phyllis teases her about having a crush on Brother Jesse, Sister Viola boasts to Mam Phyllis that her mother always told her to stay away from dark-skinned men because they are evil. Mam Phyllis tells her, "Don't you know you can't put all Negro men in a jar and label it 'no account.' " Mam Phyllis changes the subject, only to have Sister Viola start up an equally offensive conversation. Sister Viola begins to throw barbs at the white women that Mam Phyllis has nursed. When Mam Phyllis tells Sister Viola that she does not feel like listening to gossip, Sister Viola reminds her that she was not always a saint and storms out.

Mam Phyllis later tells her niece, Helena, about the little charcoal baby that she let die. She tells how one night in a dream she saw a little black baby sitting at the foot of her bed, crying that he was not rich or white but that he needed her because he was dying. She ran six miles through the farmlands only to find the charcoal baby dead. Since that time, she has gone to aid birthing women regardless of whether they could pay her. Act I ends with Herman, Helena's boyfriend, coming over to find out if Helena has told Mam Phyllis that she is quitting college, temporarily, to get married.

Act II opens with Mam Phyllis ignoring Maggie's whining about Charles and the hardware store. Feeling desperate, Mam Phyllis tells her that Helena wants to quit college. She also tells Maggie she's thinking of giving up nursing and asks to leave work early.

In the subsequent scene, Sister Viola tells Mam Phyllis that she heard from Brother Jesse that she was not feeling well and that she came to help out. Only instead of easing Mam Phyllis 's burden, she berates her for overworking herself all across town on both sides of the tracks. Eyeing the shabby surroundings, she tells Mam Phyllis that she is a fool and that maybe she will get her reward in heaven because it will not be on earth. She also tells Mam Phyllis that she heard Helena was going to run off with Sam Martin's boy. She flings at Mam Phyllis, "I know if a niece of mine talked 'bout marryin' somebody as black and ugly as Sam Martin's boy, I'd poison her and throw her in the gully."

Mam Phyllis eases Sister Viola out of her home just before Helena returns. Helena tries to convince Mam Phyllis to let her get married. When Mam Phyllis realizes that she is unable to persuade Helena not to get married, she seemingly acquiesces.

Feeling a little sorry for herself, she tells Helena she is thinking of giving up nursing because old age has crept up on her. Her self pity is short-lived as Viola runs in with news that Shirley Birthmoor has gone into labor and is calling for Mam Phyllis. Act II ends with Mam Phyllis rushing out on another errand of mercy.

Act III opens three years later with Charles and Maggie discussing Mam Phyllis's memorial service. Charles comments that he counted 240 roses and "That's why Coloreds can't get nowhere . . . too busy wasting money on funerals." Feeling slighted, Maggie complains that there "just isn't enough love in the Colored community." Charles responds with, "There's only so much . . . people like you and me can do to uplift the race." They speak of Mam Phyllis as a credit to her race and in the same breath race to the bedroom to "sing in the clouds."

Herman and Helena, now expecting a child, have returned for the memorial but are ostracized by the community. Sister Viola comes over to visit, crying "I was so sorry to see her go. But, like my po Momma used to say, better her than me." She demands to know why Helena abandoned Mam Phyllis for the past three years.

On Sister Viola's way out, she eyes what appears to be the ghost of Mam Phyllis. She goes racing back to Helena and Herman who tell her that all she is having are fainting spells and that Madame Babineaux, the root doctor, can help. Not long after Herman goes to get Madame Babineaux, Mam Phyllis enters with the news that she has been across the bayou visiting an old cousin.

Mam Phyllis immediately sees that Helena is pregnant and all the old disappointment disappears as the two are reunited. With the help of Helena, Mam Phyllis and Sister Viola reconcile.

Mam Phyllis imperceptibly links the regional to the national and universal. The play captures the culture of Southwestern Louisiana Creoles of Color while dealing with such broad issues as aging, reconciliation, love, and ambition.

It is the culture of the characters that gives distinctiveness to the play. Southwestern Louisiana blacks are known for their strong belief in Catholicism and Hoodoo, for their hospitality and emphasis on food as a social institution, for their intraracial biases, for their unique relationship with Cajuns, for their emphasis on education, and for their good humor.

One of the dominant characteristics of the culture is its emphasis on religiosity. When the deviant Sister Viola walks onto the stage, her first concern is to tell Mam Phyllis that Monsignor Ledeaux from Opelousas is going to lead a special retreat in the community. Mam Phyllis, who is truly religious, teaches Helena to be Christian by her daily actions and by telling her of the pain and sorrow she once felt when she refused to nurse a woman who could not pay for her services. The story of the little charcoal baby illustrates Mam Phyllis's repentance and shows the depths of her goodness.

Mam Phyllis is also a play about religious intolerance. Many Creoles of Color traditionally have been very narrow minded and outspoken about those in their community who are not of their faith. Charles and Maggie are particularly obnoxious about the Protestant minister who is allowed to preach Mam Phyllis's memorial service. They are appalled that Father O'Henry allowed someone of a different religion to taint their Catholic pulpit.

Mam Phyllis also draws attention to the beliefs of many Louisiana Creoles of Color in Hoodoo or Voodoo practices brought by Africans to America. There remains a tenacious group who believes that good spells or remedies can be used to counteract bad spells or hexes. Many of them manage to combine both their faith in Catholicism and Hoodoo in order to survive difficult times.

Madame Babineax, referred to several times in the play, is a root doctor or someone who gives "treatments" to Creoles of Color. During the first half of the century, many blacks turned not to a doctor but to a medicine woman or conjurer or healer to cure ailments of various kinds. When Mam Phyllis leaves work early and is not feeling well, Helena offers to go get help from Madame Babineaux. When Sister Viola has what appear to be fainting spells, Herman goes to get a remedy from Madame Babineaux. Those who believe in the magic often give witness to the fact that spells or remedies are worked in conjunction with the aid of Catholic prayers.

Mam Phyllis underscores the emphasis that Creoles of Color place on food and eating. Numerous French dances or La-Las are held in conjunction with such "eating" celebrations as the Rice, Frog, Yambolee (sweet potato), and Crawfish festivals. Sister Viola's habit of eating a little taste as she weaves in and out of everybody's home best represents the black Creole's penchant for using food as a socializing mechanism. They visit each other frequently, cook a tremendous amount of food, and socialize over several servings. Sister Viola talks of having blackberry pie and ham hocks and beans at Martha-Mae's house; Helena says that she has had okra gumbo and dried shrimp at Cousin Mary's, and Maggie brags of her gourmet cooking. The play contains numerous other references to food.

Brown-Guillory demonstrates that food is not only used to welcome someone but that it serves as a device to curtail offensive conversation. Practically every time Sister Viola opens her mouth, Mam Phyllis or Helena offers her gingerbread. Gingerbread, then, becomes synonymous with "hold your tongue."

Though the Creoles of Color in the play are a hospitable group, they are not without their intraracial biases, particularly Sister Viola and the Philmores all of whom are fair skinned. Sister Viola is repulsed by Brother Jesse who she says is blue-black. Similarly, she criticizes Herman, calling him black and ugly. It is Mam Phyllis who tries to teach the incorrigible Sister Viola that not only does she not like dark-skinned blacks or whites but that she does not love herself either. The Philmores are also prejudiced; they despise not only dark-skinned blacks but poor ones as well. They apparently would like to "class off," but find themselves connected to blacks because of their hardware store which serves blacks primarily.

Mam Phyllis, on another level, captures the unique relationship that blacks and whites share in Southwestern Louisiana. The Cajuns, French-speaking descendants of Nova Scotians, and the Creoles of Color traditionally have worked closely to survive in the community. They work each other's land, share the festivals, and generally are friendly with each other. These two groups in past decades were bound together because of the farmlands and had to work as teams in order to withstand the hurricanes, droughts, and other natural hazards. Mam Phyllis, who works both sides of the tracks, is loved by all, even if Sister Viola reminds her that racism exists. Also, Sister Viola recalls that there were whites at Mam Phyllis's memorial, even if they did stand off in the corner. There is evidence in the play to support the contention that whites and blacks in Southwestern Louisiana not only tolerate but care for each other.

One of the strongest elements of the black Creole culture is its emphasis on education. *Mam Phyllis* revolves around securing an education for Helena, the first in four generations to go to college. Mam Phyllis works as a nurse/midwife for years in order to pay for Helena's college. The entire community has a vested interest in this young girl's education. When she announces that she plans to get married before she finishes college, the entire community is wounded.

Generally speaking, the overall tone of the play suggests the good nature of the Creoles of Color. They laugh a great deal and enjoy life to the fullest. Nearly all of the characters in *Mam Phyllis* are witty, particularly Mam Phyllis and Sister Viola. Violet Harrington Bryan argues that "Brown-Guillory presents us with a sense of the language, habits, and values of the religious, race conscious, Cajun/Creole small-town community in which she grew up. She points out the strengths of the people and their conventions but criticizes their limitations with humor" (p. 56). Brown–Guillory has captured the flavor and idioms of a group of people whose culture continues to have a significant impact on other cultures in America.

NOTE

For more information about Brown–Guillory's life and works see Bernard L. Peterson, Jr., *Contemporary Black American Playwrights and Their Plays* (Westport, CT.: Greenwood Press, 1988) and *International Who's Who of Professional and Business Women*, First Edition, (Cambridge, England: Melrose Press, 1989); see also Violet Harrington Bryan, "Evocations of Place and Culture in the Works of Four Contemporary Black Louisiana Writers: Brenda Osbey, Sybil Kein, Elizabeth Brown–Guillory, and Pinkie Gordon Lane," *Louisiana Literature*, (Fall 1987).

Mam Phyllis (1985) ⸻

Elizabeth Brown-Guillory

CHARACTERS

MAM PHYLLIS	A black woman of 70 years, she loves deeply the families she serves. Warm and dignified, she wears a floor length pleated dress, an apron, and round granny glasses. Protective and yet gentle, she commands the respect of all in her roles as nurse, guardian, and friend.
MAGGIE PHILMORE	An attractive, fair-skinned upper middle-class woman in her early thirties. She is vain, shallow, and haughty. Her main goal in life is to become a gourmet cook and an expert wine taster.
CHARLES PHILMORE	A tall, handsome, fair-skinned upper middle-class man in his forties. A business man, he owns a hardware store. Like his wife, he is insipid, shallow, and affected.
SISTER VIOLA	A fair-skinned black woman of 75 years, she is the friend of Mam Phyllis. A woman who lashes out with venom as easily as she blinks her eyes, Sister Viola evokes laughter as she comments on "delicate" matters. She never lets the audience forget that gossip makes the world go around.
HELENA	A young black woman of 20 years, she seems worried and shy most of the time. Helena often looks at the world through rose-tinted glasses. She is the niece of Mam Phyllis.
HERMAN	A young black man of 21 years, he is the fiance of Helena. He is a good country fellow who mainly wants a wife and family.

SCENE

A small town in Southwest Louisiana.

TIME

Winter of 1930.

ACT I

SCENE I: Two co-existing sets face the audience. To the left MAM PHYLLIS' living area consists of one rocking chair, one small chair, one small table, and two chairs. To the right, the PHILMORE family area consists of a loveseat, a rocking chair, an endtable, one lamp, one liquor table, and plants, a setting reflective of "affectation."
AT RISE: It is early evening. MAGGIE PHILMORE, wearing an elegant lounger and slippers, sits sipping wine as she looks at the several bottles before her on the endtable. She is a little tipsy.

MAGGIE: Mam Phyllis, could you hand me that bottle of wine on the breakfast table?

MAM PHYLLIS: (*enters wearing a long skirt and an apron and carrying a bottle of wine and a load of diapers to be folded*) Child, what you doin'?

MAGGIE: I'm tickling my palate with some of California's finest brews.

MAM PHYLLIS: So, you gettin' drunk, eh. (*sits and begins folding diapers*)

MAGGIE: (*condescending*) Of course not! This is a new challenge of mine.

MAM PHYLLIS: Looks to me like that "challenge" is almost empty.

MAGGIE: Never you mind. It's high time I learned the difference between white and red, dry and extra dry, chablis and sherry.

MAM PHYLLIS: It's not my place, so I'll keep my mouth shut.

MAGGIE: (*She pours more wine.*) No, go on.

MAM PHYLLIS: Child. I'm here to help you. A woman in yo condition shouldn't be soppin' up liquor.

MAGGIE: Mam Phyllis, my baby is three weeks old. I'm absolutely fine.

MAM PHYLLIS: See what I mean. You don't listen to what I say. I don't want to be the blame when your flesh hangs and sags.

MAGGIE: Don't be ridiculous. You've got me wearing a corset day and night. Nothing would dare hang or sag on me. (*She sips more wine.*)

MAM PHYLLIS: Just the same. You too hardheaded. You don't listen to a thang I say.

MAGGIE: That's not true.

MAM PHYLLIS: It is. I keep tellin' you to rest so you can get cured.

MAGGIE: (*She bursts out laughing.*) I'm not a ham or something. Cured. You're too much, Mam Phyllis. (*rises and begins exercising*)

MAM PHYLLIS: I didn't go to college like you, but you know what I mean, child.

MAGGIE: You're much too serious all the time.

MAM PHYLLIS: Child, there's a depression goin' on out there. Can't help but be serious. Got soup lines from church steps to city hall.

MAGGIE: Yeah, Charles says business has been extra slow at the hardware store. He said 1930 is a year he's going to scratch off his calendar.

MAM PHYLLIS: Business been slow for everybody. And President Hoover says his hands are tied. (*chuckling*) Hoover sure ain't no mover.

MAGGIE: (*sighing*) Charles says Hoover ought to quit saying what he's going to do and do it.

MAM PHYLLIS: (*annoyed by MAGGIE's exercising*) Child, will you quit that. Come sit and rest yourself.

MAGGIE: (*sitting on the sofa*) Oh, all right.

MAM PHYLLIS: Poor colored folks are goin' hungry all over these United States.

MAGGIE: (*ignoring MAM PHYLLIS*) It's a good thing Charles knows his business. Our store keeps a roof over our head. Truth is, we haven't felt the pinch too much.

MAM PHYLLIS: Child, you got plenty to be thankful for.

MAGGIE: (*sighing*) I know. Charles keeps telling me we're rich colored folks and we got a reputation to uphold. (*She sips.*)

MAM PHYLLIS: (*looking over her glasses*) You won't have much of a reputation, you keep gettin' drunk.

MAGGIE: I beg your pardon. How shall I put it? I'm becoming a connoisseur of wine.

MAM PHYLLIS: Still gettin' drunk to me.

MAGGIE: (*offering wine to MAM PHYLLIS*) Want a sip?

MAM PHYLLIS: Nooooooo, child. I got to sleep tonight.

MAGGIE: (*looking at watch again*) Charles is late again. (*She sighs and sips.*)

MAM PHYLLIS: Now, don't go gettin' upset . . . make the blood rush to yo head.

MAGGIE: (*tense and irritated*) I'm fine. Really, I'm fine.

MAM PHYLLIS: (*gesturing to leave*) Now, child, maybe I done overstayed my welcome.

MAGGIE: I'm sorry. It's my nerves.

MAM PHYLLIS: It's that wine.

MAGGIE: Come on, let's be friends. You're one of the few people in this town I can talk to.

MAM PHYLLIS: Don't try to butter me up.

MAGGIE: (*She sips and says in baby talk.*) Come on, Mammy Phyllis.

MAM PHYLLIS: I just want you to rest yourself so you can help out with the baby pretty soon.

MAGGIE: Why? You're not quitting are you?

MAM PHYLLIS: Not today.

MAGGIE: (*alarmed*) When?

MAM PHYLLIS: I can't keep runnin' between here and Miss Shifer's house. You most cured. She just had her baby.

MAGGIE: Well, I'd think you'd want to help your own kind before runnin' off to some white lady who'd just as soon look the other way than speak to coloreds.

MAM PHYLLIS: Now, child, I'm gonna let that remark pass. I can see you not feelin' well today.

MAGGIE: Well, Charles will have to get someone else to help out.

MAM PHYLLIS: That's between you and Charles.

MAGGIE: (*ignoring MAM PHYLLIS, rises, moves behind sofa*) I'm going to be too busy with my garden club.

MAM PHYLLIS: (*hearing keys jingling*) Sounds like somebody's at the door.

MAGGIE: And the next thing I simply must learn is gourmet cooking. Anybody who's worth her salt in my circles is a gourmet cook.

MAM PHYLLIS: Child, you feelin' ok?

MAGGIE: (*sipping wine*) I'm just super duper. Charles is darn late tonight, again.

MAM PHYLLIS: He'll be here directly. Come sit down and rest yourself.

MAGGIE: Is little Betty sleeping?

MAM PHYLLIS: Sure is. You wanta go take a nap with her?

MAGGIE: (*almost shouting*) No! (*lowering her voice*) Sorry, Mam Phyllis. My nerves are raw.

MAM PHYLLIS: (*picking up diapers to leave*) I can't tie you down. You a grown woman. (*exiting*) Evenin', Charles.

CHARLES: (*enters wearing a three piece suit, carrying a newspaper, a ledger, and a pen*) Evening to you, Mam Phyllis. (*moves to kiss MAGGIE*) How was your day, darling? How's little Betty?

MAGGIE: It was . . .

CHARLES: (*before MAGGIE can speak*) I had a horrendous day trying to sell anything. (*sits down and begins writing in ledger*) I was lucky to sell a few utensils and gadgets for making preserves.

MAGGIE: Want some wine? (*She pours some for herself.*)

CHARLES: (*ignoring her*) I can tell you business is dwindling. And did you hear about Mr. Richmond? I just heard he threw himself out of the window this morning.

MAGGIE: (*sips wine*) Charles, do you love me?

CHARLES: Yep, he was all crumpled up under a garbage can, I heard.

MAGGIE: Charles, am I fat?

CHARLES: I'm glad I didn't make his mistake. No siree. I called in all my shares months ago. No siree, I'm not worried about this depression just yet. I can squeeze a dollar out of a turnip.

MAGGIE: Charles, we never hug anymore.

CHARLES: The whole thing'll blow over any day. I just have to keep on selling. (*indignant*) And do you know that low down, trashy Billy-Bob came in the store wanting credit.

MAGGIE: (*insistent*) Charles, do you love me or not?

CHARLES: That no good scoundrel had nerve to say "yea, we colored folks got to stick together." (*as if clearing his hands*) I'll stick his together.

MAGGIE: (*shouting*) Charles!

CHARLES: I don't even want that wino in my store. It's funny how coloreds are always wanting credit. Well, I need every penny I can get. I have bills like everybody else, and credit doesn't pay bills.

MAGGIE: (*shouting*) Charles Philmore the Third, you're making me crazy.

CHARLES: (*as if noticing MAGGIE for the first time*) Darling, don't raise your voice. Women of breeding don't shout. It's so common.

MAGGIE: (*pouting*) Well, stop ignoring me.

CHARLES: (*noticing her bottles of wine*) And what are all these bottles?

MAGGIE: (*boasting*) I'm learning about wines.

CHARLES: Well, good for you. It's about time you took up something worthwhile to amuse yourself.

(*enters MAM PHYLLIS with coat and cap*)

MAM PHYLLIS: I'll be seein' you, Maggie. Be back day after tomorrow . . . unless you need me sooner.

MAGGIE: OK . . . but wait. Charles'll take you home.

CHARLES: Sure, let me finish this . . .

MAM PHYLLIS: No, don't you fret none. Brother Jesse's outside waitin' for me.

MAGGIE: Is that old coot still living?

MAM PHYLLIS: Course he is.

MAGGIE: I've lost touch with a whole lot of folk. Oh well.

MAM PHYLLIS: (*aside*) And what a shallow well it is. (*to MAGGIE*) Night, Maggie.

MAGGIE: (*kisses MAM PHYLLIS on both cheeks—affected*) Goodnight, darling.

MAM PHYLLIS: Night, Charles.

CHARLES: (*looking up from books*) Goodnight. Got to finish these entries. (*MAM PHYLLIS exits as MAGGIE watches, pours more wine, sips, hiccups loudly, and sighs.*)

(BLACKOUT)

(End of Scene I)

SCENE II: Lapse of time of about 30 minutes. Lights rise on MAM PHYLLIS' family area. MAM PHYLLIS enters and places coat and hat on chair. She moves to rocker and begins to sing a powerful, gut-level spiritual.

MAM PHYLLIS:

> No more weeping and wailing
> No more weeping and wailing
> I'm going home to meet Jesus
> I'm going home to meet my Lord
> No more sorrow and pain
> No more sorrow and pain
> I'm going home to meet my Jesus
> I'm going home to meet my Lord
> No more . . .

(*SISTER VIOLA enters and touches MAM PHYLLIS on the shoulder as she is singing and startles her. She takes off coat and hat and sits down.*)

SISTER VIOLA: Child, God sho done blessed you when he gived you that voice.

MAM PHYLLIS: (*out of breath*) Sister Viola, you shouldn't go around scarin' people the way you do. (*touching her chest*) My heart ain't strong as it used to be.

SISTER VIOLA: (*laughing*) The back door was unlatched and I didn't want to disturb you right away. Is you gonna sing that song tomorrow night at the retreat?

MAM PHYLLIS: I'm thinkin' about it. I haven't decided yet.

SISTER VIOLA: Sho hopes you do. Guess who I heard gonna be at church tomorrow night?

MAM PHYLLIS: (*reaching for knitting needles and yarn*) You must be talkin' about Monsignor Ledeaux from Opelousas.

SISTER VIOLA: (*quickly*) How you know that?

MAM PHYLLIS: Brother Jesse told me.

SISTER VIOLA: (*letting out a yelp*) Ohooooo child, that's a gossipin' man. Child, don't tell that man nothin' less you want the whole congregation to know 'bout it.

MAM PHYLLIS: (*raising an eyebrow at SISTER VIOLA's remark*) I don't think he was gossipin'.

SISTER VIOLA: Jest the same, Brother Jesse gossip too much. Remember when old man Cholly's daughter got with a baby, Brother Jesse was the first one whoopin and hollerin' 'bout how the young generation goin' to hell. I tell you he don't do nothin' but gossip.

MAM PHYLLIS: (*chuckling*) Look at the pepper callin' the okra long mouth. You sure do know a whole lot about Brother Jesse. (*jokingly*) Who knows, maybe you might be taking' a likin' to Brother Jesse.

SISTER VIOLA: (*excited*) Child, no. Brother Jesse smell like yesterday! I don't fool 'round with buzzards, me!

MAM PHYLLIS: (*jokingly*) Sister Viola, hush yo fuss.

SISTER VIOLA: Child, my po momma told me to stay clear of dark skinned men 'cause they ain't no account.

MAM PHYLLIS: (*reproachfully*) Why Sister Viola, I didn't know your momma lived with every dark skinned man on earth.

SISTER VIOLA: (*shocked*) Say what?

MAM PHYLLIS: Don't you know you can't put all Negro men in a jar and label it "no account!"

SISTER VIOLA: (*snobbishly*) I didn't say all Nigra men was no account. (*with emphasis*) I said dark-skinned men was no account. They jest as evil as the day is long, child.

MAM PHYLLIS: (*nonchalantly*) I guess your paw was no account and evil then?

SISTER VIOLA: (*defensively*) What you say, child? No, not my paw!

MAM PHYLLIS: Shame on you for believin' in such foolishness.

SISTER VIOLA: (*slightly angry*) I was jest sayin' what po momma said. Course I don't believe none a that stuff. How could I be a good Christian woman, goin' to church often as I do, and not love my own peoples?

MAM PHYLLIS: (*wanting to change the subject*) Sister Viola, would you like some gingerbread and coffee?

SISTER VIOLA: You got some coffee made?

MAM PHYLLIS: I can make some. I just came from Maggie's house, and I haven't had a chance to do too much here yet.

SISTER VIOLA: I ain't got time to wait for no coffee to make. I want to stop on off at Rose for a spell before I get home. Jest gimme a piece of gingerbread. I'll take it with me.

MAM PHYLLIS: This here is some fresh gingerbread. I brought Miss Shifer and Maggie a piece.

SISTER VIOLA: How they doin'?

MAM PHYLLIS: They doin' fine. I guess.

SISTER VIOLA: What you mean?

MAM PHYLLIS: (*sits down*) Miss Shifer too much in a hurry to get back to the newspaper, and Maggie . . . well, Maggie . . . almost on her feet again.

SISTER VIOLA: Guess they won't be needin' you too much longer if they cured.

MAM PHYLLIS: I guess not.

SISTER VIOLA: (*rises and starts snooping*) What you heard from Miss Shifer's cousin lately? What she been doin'?

MAM PHYLLIS: Who? (*eyeing SISTER VIOLA who checks for dust and looks in the cupboard*)

SISTER VIOLA: The one that hate colored folks so much?

MAM PHYLLIS: I don't reckon I know who you talkin' about.

SISTER VIOLA: Yeah, you know. Her paw used to run that store on the cornder.

MAM PHYLLIS: You must be talkin' about Miss Speakwell—old Mr. Speakwell's gal.

SISTER VIOLA: That's the one! I saw her on the street the other day, and she most broke her neck lookin' the other way. And to think, she used to not have a pot nee window to throw it out.

MAM PHYLLIS: (*chuckling*) Gracious almighty, I don't know where you get some of the things you come up with, Viola.

SISTER VIOLA: Well?

MAM PHYLLIS: Well what?

SISTER VIOLA: What Miss Speakwell been up to lately? Her and Miss Shifer cousins, ain't they?

MAM PHYLLIS: She's Mr. Shifer's cousin. Truth is, Miss Shifer and Miss Speakwell don't get along too good. They always disagreein' on one thing or another.

SISTER VIOLA: (*sitting down*) I'm not one for gossipin' but, child, let me tell you what I heard one time 'bout Miss Speakwell.

MAM PHYLLIS: (*attempting to quiet SISTER VIOLA*) Now, Sister Viola.

SISTER VIOLA: (*not heeding MAM PHYLLIS*) I heard she hates coloreds so much 'cause they ain't actin' the way they did in slavery.

MAM PHYLLIS: Sister Viola, what you talkin' about?

SISTER VIOLA: You know Sarah-Mae, don't you?

MAM PHYLLIS: Sarah-Mae Johnson?

SISTER VIOLA: Yes, child. (*rattling on in her usual rapid fashion*) Sarah-Mae, you know, work for Miss Montgomery. Child, one day Miss Speakwell came over to visit Miss Montgomery. Sarah-Mae say . . .

MAM PHYLLIS: Sister Viola, I don't know if I wants to hear this.

SISTER VIOLA: Sarah-Mae say Miss Speakwell runnin' colored folks down. Jest talkin' 'bout coloreds like a dog. Said Nigras are imitative people. Said some Nigras actin' and speakin' like they white. Said how she hate to see a Nigra put on airs.

MAM PHYLLIS: People like that need to pray, child.

SISTER VIOLA: Pray my big toe. Folks like that don't pray. (*pretends she's putting her foot on somebody's neck*) They too busy studyin' ways to put they foot on your neck.

MAM PHYLLIS: Now, Viola. That's not a Christian thing to say.

SISTER VIOLA: Maybe not, but it's the God's-honest truth. (*pause*) I shouldn't ought to say nothin', but I'ma tell you anyway. Yo name came up. Sarah-Mae said . . .

MAM PHYLLIS: I don't know if I wanta hear all this. I'm tired and hungry. Helena will be home soon, and I need to cook.

SISTER VIOLA: (*rattling off*) Sarah-Mae brung me the news. Miss Speakwell said you wasn't no common Mammy. Said yo paw was a minister and he taught you hisself. Said it's amazin' how edgumacation didn't make you lazy and no 'count. Child, I tell you them white people cross the tracks sho do sing yo praises through the cornders of they mouth.

MAM PHYLLIS: *(getting up and reaching for more knitting yarn)* You sure do get all kinds a news. I don't put much stock in hear-say.

SISTER VIOLA: *(feeling hurt)* You sayin' I'm lyin'?

MAM PHYLLIS: Don't put words in my mouth. I'm just sayin' I go by what I hear and see on my own.

SISTER VIOLA: Child, you sho do love them white people. I believes you love 'em bettern you love yo own. Sometimes you act like they good to eat.

MAM PHYLLIS: Sister Viola, didn't you say you wanted to stop off at Rose's house before it gets too late?

SISTER VIOLA: *(rising)* I gets the message. Now you puttin' me out.

MAM PHYLLIS: *(frustrated)* Oh, for Christ's sake, Viola.

SISTER VIOLA: *(angrily)* I wouldn't talk about Christ if I was you. *(pointing her finger)* You wasn't always no saint, child.

MAM PHYLLIS: *(with deep anger)* Viola, you done overstayed you welcome. Now go on 'bout you business.

SISTER VIOLA: *(exiting angrily)* I was leavin' this possum hole anyway. *(HELENA enters as SISTER VIOLA is leaving. HELENA has on an overcoat, a blue skirt, and a red turtleneck sweater. She kisses MAM PHYLLIS.)*

HELENA: Evenin', Sister Viola.

SISTER VIOLA: Ain't got time to talk, child, especially if people gonna be uppity. *(She exits.)*

HELENA: *(sits)* What's gotten into Sister Viola?

MAM PHYLLIS: Oh, you know how she is. She don't stop 'til she wears out her welcome.

HELENA: Who was she criticizin' today?

MAM PHYLLIS: Everybody! But, never mind about Sister Viola. I'm late startin' supper.

HELENA: Don't need to fix nothin' for me, Mam Phyllis. I ate at cousin Mary's house. She had some good old okra gumbo, with dried shrimp and tasso... and sausage.

MAM PHYLLIS: *(rocking and chuckling)* I was hungry, but Sister Viola made me lose my appetite.

HELENA: Oh, before I forget. I got a message for you.

MAM PHYLLIS: Well, what is it, child?

HELENA: The lady down the street from cousin Mary is havin' a baby in a few weeks.

MAM PHYLLIS: What lady, child?

HELENA: Shirley Birthmoor.

MAM PHYLLIS: Oh yeah . . . poor child havin' another baby.

HELENA: Cousin Mary said she almost died after she had her last baby. She wants to know if you can help out.

MAM PHYLLIS: (*to herself*) A tiny lil bit of a woman.

HELENA: Cousin Mary told me Shirley and her husband can't pay you.

MAM PHYLLIS: (*waving her hand*) Never mind.

HELENA: But they willin' to give you a few chickens if you help out for awhile.

MAM PHYLLIS: Tomorrow, you tell cousin Mary that I'll be there when Shirley need me. That poor girl is just worn out from havin' too many babies and not enough money to feed half of 'em.

HELENA: You mean you don't mind not gettin' paid?

MAM PHYLLIS: Not anymore, I don't. I did once—a long time ago.

HELENA: What's the matter, Mam?

MAM PHYLLIS: I'm fine, child. It's just that Shirley make me go back thirty years.

HELENA: Huh?

MAM PHYLLIS: Baby, about thirty years ago, some colored folks down the road needed a nurse. I was young then, kinda selfish.

HELENA: Selfish? Not you!

MAM PHYLLIS: God's-honest-truth. They sent for me, but I wouldn't go 'cause they didn't have money to pay me.

HELENA: So what happened?

MAM PHYLLIS: That night, way in the middle of the night, I started to dream. A little charcoal baby sat at the foot of my bed. He was naked as a bird. He said (*in a broken child's voice*), "Mam Phyllis, my maw and paw . . . ain't white and they ain't rich, but we need you just the same. I'm dyin', Mam Phyllis, I'm dyin'.' "

HELENA: Mam, I bet you went all to pieces.

MAM PHYLLIS: Couldn't even scream. I jumped straight out the bed, grabbed a few things, and started runnin' down the road. I musta run 'bout five or six miles before I came to these folks' house.

HELENA: You didn't have a buggy? Where was Uncle Walter?

MAM PHYLLIS: Po Walter was in Heaven, child. And I never did learn how to handle a buggy.

HELENA: You weren't scared out there?

MAM PHYLLIS: (*crying softly*) Not atall, child. The only thing that kept runnin' through my mind was, "Suffer the little children to come unto me, and harm them not."

HELENA: So, what happened?

MAM PHYLLIS: He was dead. (*pauses and wipes eyes*) The little charcoal baby had died.

HELENA: (*hugs MAM PHYLLIS*) It wasn't your fault.

MAM PHYLLIS: (*defensively*) Yes it was!

HELENA: How?

MAM PHYLLIS: Cause I was selfish. (*pauses*) For years I couldn't get that little charcoal baby out of my mind. I could see his little brown-stained palms reachin' out to me. And the sadness in his eyes. Oh, the sadness in his eyes cut right to my heart.

HELENA: It musta been hard keepin' all this inside.

MAM PHYLLIS: Folks didn't let me forgit. They used to whisper. "There go Mam Phyllis. She let colored babies die, and she cuddle lil white babies."

HELENA: (*angry*) That sounds like Sister Viola.

MAM PHYLLIS: She spoke her piece; she spoke it to everybody she knew and to some she didn't even know.

HELENA: Sister Viola's gossip; she just plain mean. With her rotten tongue.

MAM PHYLLIS: She's like all gossipers; she mixes an ounce of truth with a pound of lies.

HELENA: Yeah, but Sister Viola ought to mind her own business.

MAM PHYLLIS: Back then I tried to find excuses, too. I said to myself, "Phyllis Givins, you don't have to take chickens and pigs for your work."

HELENA: That's right.

MAM PHYLLIS: Then the old devil would say, "Yeah, 'cause you know them colored folks just give you the oldest and toughest chickens in the yard."

HELENA: (*laughing*) Mam, that old devil musta been kin to Sister Viola.

MAM PHYLLIS: (*chuckling*) All right, lil Miss Viola.

HELENA: Huh, not me. (*pause*) But, Mam, you gotta forgive yourself.

MAM PHYLLIS: I did. But it wasn't 'til I asked God to forgive me, child. (*pause*) Now, I go to anybody who needs nursin'... money or no money... and I give my best. (*A knock is heard, and the mood changes.*)

HELENA: I'll get it.

MAM PHYLLIS: I wonder who comin' here at this late hour?

HELENA: Oops, I forgot. That's probably Herman. He said he was comin' over tonight.

MAM PHYLLIS: He don't know how to come courtin' at a decent hour? Go on and answer the door, child. (*HELENA opens the door and in steps HERMAN, wearing a stocking cap, overcoat, blue jeans, and a plaid cotton flannel shirt.*)

HERMAN: (*shivering as he talks*) Evenin' to you, Mam Phyllis. (*romantically*) Hi, Lena. (*shivering again*) I got icicles on my tongue. Even pneumonia wouldn't come out tonight.

MAM PHYLLIS: Chere, what you doin' here? It's too cold for you to be out on the road like this.

HERMAN: I guess you right.

HELENA: (*standing awkwardly in the background and signaling to HERMAN not to say anything to MAM PHYLLIS about their plans*) Want some coffee and gingerbread?

HERMAN: Maybe later, Lena.

MAM PHYLLIS: Well, I guess I'll turn in and leave you two young folks to talk about whatever it was that got Herman out of a warm house into this cold.

HELENA: (*going over to kiss MAM PHYLLIS*) Sleep well.

HERMAN: Night, Mam Phyllis. I won't stay too long.

MAM PHYLLIS: (*as she is exiting*) You better not. I'm not too old to take a broom to anybody when I get riled up.

HERMAN: Yes, mam! (*HERMAN and HELENA embrace for a split second. He picks her up and spins her around and then HELENA breaks away and straightens her garments.*) Girl, you make me crazy, don't you know!

HELENA: Mam Phyllis would have a conniption fit if she saw us.

HERMAN: (*slightly disappointed*) Lena, how come you didn't tell her?

HELENA: Tonight wasn't right. She had a lot on her mind. I just couldn't up and tell her that I'm not going back to college next semester.

HERMAN: (*disappointed but holding her chin up with his hand*) Well, I don't suppose you told her we gettin' married, either? (*HELENA moves to rocker and HERMAN follows and stands behind her rubbing her shoulders and massaging her neck.*)

HELENA: I just couldn't, I told you. I get tongue-tied around Mam Phyllis.

HERMAN: Just tell her the truth. Tell her you made up your mind. You not goin' back to New Orleans next week.

HELENA: (*a little annoyed*) It's not that simple, Herman. I'm the first one in four generations to go to college. Before momma died, Mam Phyllis promised she'd send me to college. She's nursed a whole lot of women to put me through these first two years of college.

HERMAN: (*also getting annoyed*) It's not like you won't finish. As soon as I can save up enough money, we can move to New Orleans. I'll get a job farmin' like I got now, or I'll do odd jobs. Trust me, Lena.

HELENA: She'll never stand for it. That woman'll twist you to bits first.

HERMAN: Mam Phyllis was married once. She gotta have some kinda understandin'.

HELENA: I'm tellin' you she won't. She'd kill to keep me in college. No, we have to find another way.

HERMAN: (*moving to get his coat which he points at her as he talks*) I'm not gonna leave here unless you promise me you'll talk to Mam Phyllis tomorrow. Tomorrow's her day off, huh?

HELENA: Yeah, but . . .

HERMAN: No buts, Ok?

HELENA: Ok! Ok! I'll do what I can. Now, you'd better go.

HERMAN: (*moves to hold her*) Just a little while longer.

HELENA: (*jokingly*) You better get out of here 'cause Mam Phyllis swings a mean broom.

HERMAN: (*He kisses HELENA before he exits.*) See you tomorrow. (*tenderly*) Love you, Lena.

HELENA: Love you, too. Now get on out of here.

HERMAN: Ok, ok, I'm going! (*She plops in the rocking chair after he exits.*)

HELENA: I got to have courage! What's the worse thing she can do? (*pause*) She can kill me! That's what she'll do!

(BLACKOUT)
(END OF SCENE II)
(END OF ACT I)

ACT II

TIME: *Two days later*
SCENE I: *The PHILMORE family area*
AT RISE: *MAM PHYLLIS has just fed the PHILMORE baby and is rocking her and singing "Precious Lord." She handles the baby with great care and it is evident that she loves the baby. MAGGIE enters with a robe on.*

MAGGIE: Good morning, Mam Phyllis.

MAM PHYLLIS: Mornin'.

MAGGIE: (*baby talk*) Good morning my precious little bundle of joy. Mommy loves you. Mam Phyllis loves you too. See, naughty Mommy is a sleepy head, but Mam Phyllis won't let you go hungry, will you Mam Phyllis? But Mommy wouldn't be so tired if Daddy wouldn't be such a potato head.

MAM PHYLLIS: How you feelin' today, Maggie? (*quickly*) And don't go bad-mouthin' Charles so early in the mornin'. That man would give his right arm for you and little Betty.

MAGGIE: (*sits and begins reading paper*) Yeah, but he won't give us a good minute. Boy, husbands are something else.

MAM PHYLLIS: (*burping baby*) I wish my Walter was still here.

MAGGIE: That's the first time I've heard you talk about your husband.

MAM PHYLLIS: That's cause my Walter's died before you were born, child. God rest his soul. I still miss him.

MAGGIE: He must have died young?

MAM PHYLLIS: He did. My Walter came down with pneumonia, wasn't a thing anybody could do to save him. I asked God. Child, how I begged God, but I guess He saw fit to take him.

MAGGIE: (*nonchalantly*) He was good to you, huh? (*begins fussing with plant and then begins primping with hand mirror*)

MAM PHYLLIS: Honey, that man was God-sent. He used to say to me, "Phyllis, if you up and die on me, I don't know what I'd do or where I'd go, but no place on God's earth would be far enough."

MAGGIE: Is that so?

MAM PHYLLIS: Sure thing. And I'd say, "Shucks, Walter, I bet you'd have some little gal in here before I was in the ground good."

MAGGIE: You wouldn't?

MAM PHYLLIS: I would. And he'd say, "Don't talk like that, Phyllis, 'cause if something' was to happen to you, I'd crawl in that there cornder and collect dust."

MAGGIE: All man, wasn't he?

MAM PHYLLIS: Yep. He was quite a man, and I don't mind braggin' on him. He was a man, not a boy. Boys don't know how to love. They got little chicken hearts; they selfish.

MAGGIE: Well, Charles has been acting selfish around here lately. I was up half the night.

MAM PHYLLIS: Wasn't nothin' wrong with little Betty, huh?

MAGGIE: No, but that husband of mine. I could scream.

MAM PHYLLIS: Child, I don't wanta get in you business.

MAGGIE: Mam, I want him to notice me, but he's so preoccupied with that silly hardware store.

MAM PHYLLIS: I don't wanta put my nose where it don't belong, I tell you.

MAGGIE: But Mam, if you had a husband like Charles, what would you do?

MAM PHYLLIS: Honey, that man don't have to blow in my face at night, so I can't say what I'd do.

MAGGIE: You never agree with anything I say.

MAM PHYLLIS: Child, I never have lived my life by agreein'. I just try to see things from all sides. When you get my age, you don't just see the straight and narrow.

MAGGIE: (*rising and moving behind the sofa*) Well, I'm fed up with him.

MAM PHYLLIS: That's why you were totin' them wine bottles around the other day?

MAGGIE: That had nothing to do with Charles. I really do need to know all about etiquette. In my circles, one can't afford to be in the dark.

MAM PHYLLIS: (*rocking baby*) Um hum.

MAGGIE: It's true. It's not easy being well off. There are so many pressures. Why, I have so much to learn about what to serve with which meals. It's incredible.

MAM PHYLLIS: Um hum.

MAGGIE: Charles is on a cloud. Not in touch with the real world.

MAM PHYLLIS: Um hum.

MAGGIE: (*sits on sofa edge*) Last night, I fixed—with my own two little creole hands—Lobster a la King, steamed broccoli and squash, and pecan praline.

MAM PHYLLIS: I'm proud of you.

MAGGIE: Well, you're the only one. Charles sure wasn't.

MAM PHYLLIS: Um hum.

MAGGIE: All he could talk about was who wanted credit and whose shop was closing next. That lobster could have been a baboon sitting on his plate for all he noticed. (*silence*) What's wrong? You're not listening, Mam Phyllis.

MAM PHYLLIS: I'm a little tired, but I'm ok.

MAGGIE: You seem like you're in the clouds. Are you sure you're ok?

MAM PHYLLIS: (*rising*) Let me put this baby in the bed 'cause I get mad enough to die when I think about what that niece of mine wants to do.

MAGGIE: (*flippantly*) Trouble at home, huh?

MAM PHYLLIS: The worst kind. Can I get somethin' for you while I'm up? (*exits*)

MAGGIE: I knew something was wrong. (*remembering the question*) Oh, yes, could you get my hair brush on your way back?

MAM PHYLLIS: (*from offstage*) The orange one or the small blue one?

MAGGIE: The small blue one. It's on the cedar chest in my room. (*sighing*) It's so hard when you have to listen to the problems of your hired help. But if you want to keep good help these days, I guess you have to suffer. (*shouting to MAM PHYLLIS*) Don't forget the brush.

MAM PHYLLIS: (*enters with brush and diapers to fold*) I heard you the first time.

MAGGIE: You're too fussy! But, I guess I'll keep you. Now what's bothering you?

MAM PHYLLIS: It's Helena.

MAGGIE: (*brushing her hair*) She's not sick, is she?

MAM PHYLLIS: I wish she was, 'cause then maybe I could take care of her and maybe make her better. Truth is, she wants to marry Sam Martin's boy.

MAGGIE: (*obviously biased*) Sam Martin's boy? The little dark one? (*turning up her nose*) He's from such a low-class family.

MAM PHYLLIS: But they good people, Maggie. Not everybody can be born with a mouth full of gold. Sides, high class don't mean nothin' if a person don't have love in his heart.

MAGGIE: (*coughing a little*) I know what you mean. (*wanting to change the subject*) But Helena's so young, isn't she?

MAM PHYLLIS: Everybody knows that except them. Anyway, she crept real close to me yesterday before I got out of bed. She told me she didn't want to go back to college. My blood ran clean to my head.

MAGGIE: (*wanting juicy gossip*) No!

MAM PHYLLIS: (*motioning a slap*) I almost slapped her, but she's a grown girl.

MAGGIE: Nooooo, that wouldn't have done any good. Would have just made matters worse. The thing to do is to sit down and reason with her.

MAM PHYLLIS: How can you reason with a young gal who's in love? She'd pay attention about as much as a tadpole.

MAGGIE: What are you going to do?

MAM PHYLLIS: Child, I don't rightly know. This whole business is makin' me feel kinda light headed.

MAGGIE: I knew you didn't look well today. (*quickly*) You're not thinking of quitting, are you?

MAM PHYLLIS: You readin' my mind, child.

MAGGIE: Phyllis, now let's talk about this. I need you to help out around here.

MAM PHYLLIS: Nursin' is gettin' the best of me. Maggie, I pretty much made up my mind to give my apron a rest.

MAGGIE: For good? You mean retire from nursing?

MAM PHYLLIS: That's about the size of it. But first I got to go help out Sam Jones' girl. I promised her. And I won't go back on my word.

MAGGIE: Well, I don't think you've given this enough thought. What'll we do without you?

MAM PHYLLIS: You'll get along without me. I'm kinda tired.

MAGGIE: Listen, why don't you go on home. Get some rest. Everything'll be better tomorrow.

MAM PHYLLIS: Like I said, I've pretty much made up my mind. (*She gets up to leave and gets coat and bonnet.*) If you're sure you can do without me today, I believe I'll be gettin' on. I'm feelin' pretty poorly right now.

MAGGIE: I'll call Charles to come take you home. Maybe he can pull himself from the store for a few minutes.

MAM PHYLLIS: Don't trouble Charles. I can manage.

MAGGIE: Are you sure?

MAM PHYLLIS: (*heading for the door*) I'm sure, child. I'm sure.

MAGGIE: Ok, take care of yourself.

MAM PHYLLIS: I will, child.

MAGGIE: I'm not ready to give you up yet. You're such a dear around here.

MAM PHYLLIS: (*exiting*) I'll be seein' you.

MAGGIE: I'll be checking on you. (*She pauses after MAM PHYLLIS exits and then moves to sit on sofa.*) She thinks she has worries. Huh, I don't even know which wine to serve tomorrow night when the Harringtons come over.

(BLACKOUT)
(END OF SCENE I)

Scene II: AT RISE: Lapse of time of about 30 minutes. Lights rise on MAM PHYLLIS' family area. MAM PHYLLIS enters, takes off coat and bonnet, sits in rocker, and sings "Amazing Grace."

MAM PHYLLIS:

Amazing grace! how sweet the sound
    That saved a wretch like me
I once was lost, but now I'm found
    Was blind, but now I see

Twas grace that taught my heart to fear
  And grace my fears relieved . . .
'Tis grace that brought me safe this far
  And grace will lead me home.

(*SISTER VIOLA knocks and enters.*)

SISTER VIOLA: (*from offstage*) Yoo hoo! Yoo hoo, Phyllis.

MAM PHYLLIS: Come on in, Sister Viola.

SISTER VIOLA: Sorry to hear about you not feelin' good.

MAM PHYLLIS: Take a seat. How you hear that?

SISTER VIOLA: (*rapidly*) From that gossipin', black Brother Jesse. Told you he can't keep hot water on his tongue. I was jest leavin' Martha-Mae's house. Me and her been talkin' 'bout how sad it is to see Cholly's daughter havin' another bastard. You'd think she'd know better after the first time. But no, she can't keep her dress down. Like I was sayin', Brother Jesse met up with me. Told me you come home from Big Miss Madame 'cause you wasn't feelin' good. What ailin' you?

MAM PHYLLIS: I'm just tired, Viola. Maggie can do without me today.

SISTER VIOLA: (*judgmental*) Um huh! I knowed them high falutin' people was workin' you to death. I was jest tellin' Martha-Mae how wored out you been lookin' the past few weeks. I was tellin' Martha-Mae, I says "Martha-Mae, you know Phyllis is a fool"—(*realizing her frankness and wishing to soften her remark*)—with all due respect to you, Phyllis—I says "Phyllis done nursed wives of some of the biggest wheels in this town, but she still got to go in back doors and eat in cornders.

MAM PHYLLIS: (*stunned*) Ah, Sister Viola, would you like a piece of gingerbread? (*She starts to rise but SISTER VIOLA stops her.*)

SISTER VIOLA: There you go with that gingerbread again. (*She chuckles.*) No child, I got a belly full. I had some blackberry pie at Martha-Mae house. Jest rest yourself. I ain't come here to make you serve me. You do enough servin' as it is on Miss Tom, Miss Dick, and Miss Harry!

MAM PHYLLIS: Must you be so ugly all the time? You haven't been decent since George Washington was president.

SISTER VIOLA: (*a big wind of excitement*) Child, I wasn't born when George Washington was president!

(*MAM PHYLLIS looks at SISTER VIOLA from the top of her glasses and bursts out laughing.*)

SISTER VIOLA: (*putting her hands on her hips—annoyed*) Ohooooooo, I got you figured now. Now who actin' ugly, Big Miss Madame?

MAM PHYLLIS: Just givin' you a dose of your own medicine. I offered you a piece of gingerbread, tryin' to be nice.

SISTER VIOLA: No, no, I don't want nothin'. I wants to know what's hurtin' you?

MAM PHYLLIS: Oh, I was feelin' a little light headed, a little dizzy this morning.

SISTER VIOLA: Child, that don't sound good. I know my po Momma complained 'bout dizzy spells and she was 'bout yo age too when she died.

MAM PHYLLIS: I don't think God's quite ready for me yet.

SISTER VIOLA: You never know, child, you never know.

MAM PHYLLIS: (*in a dream-like trance*) Sister Viola, you ever wondered when you was young what it would be like to be old?

SISTER VIOLA: Oh no, child. I was too busy takin' in every bit of life I could get my hands on, 'cause when you start thinkin' 'bout gettin' old, you start over-lookin' what's goin' on around you. I turned 75 this past September, and I don't feel a day over for-tay.

MAM PHYLLIS: I thought you were younger than me, Sister Viola.

SISTER VIOLA: Heavens no! Thank you jest the same, though. Child, people tell me I don't look a day over fif-tay.

MAM PHYLLIS: You sure holdin' up good for yo age.

SISTER VIOLA: Thank you jest the same! Yo problem is you work too hard. If yo soul ain't saved after all these years of servin' everybody, whites and coloreds, you can forget 'bout Heaven, child. I say you ought to cut down on some of that nursin'. You gonna get a reward in heaven—(*She looks distastefully around the room.*)—but don't look like you gonna get no reward on this here earth.

MAM PHYLLIS: (*ignoring SISTER VIOLA's remarks*) Just lookin' at those little wrinkled faces smilin' at me an' knowin' that I'm helpin' an ailin' woman is a reward I can't put into words.

SISTER VIOLA: Now, you gonna sit here and tell me you done worked all yo life 'cause you like wrinkled faces and bein' 'round sick women—and most of 'em white women. Child, I'm gonna start callin' you Saint Phyllis!

MAM PHYLLIS: (*leaning toward SISTER VIOLA*) Now, you hold it. Hold it right there. (*angry*) You've gone a step too far this time. I'm tired of you always twistin' things around and makin' fun of everything. Everytime you come around, I have to ask God to give me patience. But you, Viola, would make Jesus nervous.

SISTER VIOLA: (*turning up her nose with indignance*) Child, I calls it like I sees it. (*rapidly*) My po Momma used to always say, "If somebody get mad at you when you tellin' 'em the God's-honest-truth, they sho needs to look deep down inside theyself and clean out they soul!" Yep, my po Momma was a self-made woman.

MAM PHYLLIS: (*angry and losing her cool*) Well, it's a good thing your Momma always told everybody she was self-made, 'cause it saved God a whole lot of embarrassment!

SISTER VIOLA: (*The ultimate insult is felt.*) Phyllis, I never thought you was that kinda woman! Talkin' 'bout my po Momma like that.

MAM PHYLLIS: (*realizing her cruelty*) I'm sorry, Viola, I lost my head. It's just that I'm not gonna let you sit here and tell me that I'm foolish 'cause I love little babies and don't like to see women in pain. God gave me a gift and I'm glad I had sense enough to use it.

SISTER VIOLA: (*still hurt*) That's no cause to go bad-mouthin' my po Momma.

MAM PHYLLIS: I told you I'm sorry. You just got me all riled up—tellin' me my whole life ain't been worth a confederate dollar.

SISTER VIOLA: I ain't said no such a thing! Glory be, Phyllis, you ain't used to gettin' yo feathers all ruffled up. All I was sayin' was that you talk like you done worked yo fingers to the bone all 'cause you like lil wrinkled faces and ailin' women.

MAM PHYLLIS: You know I meant more than that.

SISTER VIOLA: All I know is what I hear you say.

MAM PHYLLIS: Viola, you know good and well I worked all these years because I had to make ends meet for Momma, Helena's momma, Helena, and myself. Thanks be to Jesus, I've spent the last ten years just savin' up so Helena could go to college.

SISTER VIOLA: (*rapidly*) Yeah, fine thing you did, Brother Jesse told me Helena not gonna finish school. Heard she gonna run off with Sam Martin's buzzard head boy!

MAM PHYLLIS: Why don't you mind yo own business sometimes?

SISTER VIOLA: (*ignoring MAM PHYLLIS*) I know if a niece of mine talked 'bout marryin' somebody as black and ugly as Sam Martin's boy, I'd poison her and throw her in the gully. My po Momma said . . .

MAM PHYLLIS: (*snapping at SISTER VIOLA*) I know what yo po Momma said.

SISTER VIOLA: Child, you nervous today. You act like you got red pepper in yo eyes. (*genuinely*) I ain't come here to make you feel worse. I jest wanted to set a spell with you and lift your spirits. See could I lend a hand with something. You the one that's always givin' and I thought I'd turn things around.

MAM PHYLLIS: I'm sorry I snapped at you, Viola, but you do have a way of puttin' people on edge when you want to.

SISTER VIOLA: That's what my po husband used to say, before I buried him. (*They chuckle. SISTER VIOLA rises to put on her coat.*) Phyllis, I have to be goin', but I'll be back later on after I make my rounds. I wanta stop off at Sally-Ann and Jean-Marie's house before noon. I wanta little taste of what they cookin'!

MAM PHYLLIS: I could fix somethin' for you.

SISTER VIOLA: Rest yourself, child. (*exiting*) I be seeing you.

MAM PHYLLIS: You have a good day, you hear! (*rising to see SISTER VIOLA out*)

SISTER VIOLA: (*as she exits*) You can count on it, child! (*MAM PHYLLIS begins to sing the "Lord's Prayer" after SISTER VIOLA exits. She moves to wipe off the table. Presently HELENA enters wearing a red plaid skirt and blue turtleneck sweater under her overcoat. She looks on as MAM PHYLLIS sings. MAM PHYLLIS notices her and stops.)*

MAM PHYLLIS: Child, why don't you have a hat on out in that cold?

HELENA: (*moving toward chair after taking off coat*) I didn't think you'd be home so early.

MAM PHYLLIS: (*sitting at table*) I wasn't feeling well today, so I came home.

HELENA: (*alarmed*) What? I'm gonna go find Madame Babineaux.

MAM PHYLLIS: Madame Babineaux can't cure what's ailin' me, child. It'll take more than a few herbs and roots.

HELENA: (*moving to sit at table*) It's all my fault, isn't it? You're worried about me and Herman, huh?

MAM PHYLLIS: I'd be lyin' if I said I wasn't. You know I promised your po Momma you'd become a teacher. I swore on the Bible, child. I swore on God Almighty's Bible.

HELENA: I know you want me to finish college, and I'm going to, married or not.

MAM PHYLLIS: Next thing you know, you'll be needin' a nurse to mind you and a little one. I just want you to finish school before you start birthin'. You can't take no baby with you to school.

HELENA: I know that, Mam Phyllis. All I can say is that I'll watch myself.

MAM PHYLLIS: Yeah, you'll watch yourself get in a family way before the priest finishes marryin' you off.

HELENA: I'll be careful. I'll mark on the calendar.

MAM PHYLLIS: You know what they call women who mark on calendars?

HELENA: What?

MAM PHYLLIS: Mommas! (*They chuckle.*)

HELENA: You'll see. I'll be careful.

MAM PHYLLIS: I can give you a few remedies, but you still might find yourself with a child.

HELENA: We'd work things out so I could finish college.

MAM PHYLLIS: Why can't you just wait a little while? Can't Herman wait a year or so? What kind of man would want you to quit college?

HELENA: (*defensively*) Not quit! I'll go back after we get our feet on the ground.

MAM PHYLLIS: (*shaking her head*) I just don't understand you young folk. Don't you think if you and him are so much in love, it'll keep until you get through with your schoolin'?

HELENA: (*moving from the table and standing and hugging MAM PHYLLIS, who eats apple slices and roles her eyes as HELENA romantically says her lines*) But we want to be with each other now. We don't want to wait. I want to cook his breakfast and be with him when he catches cold in the winter months. I want to hold his head on my bosom when he has a bad day. When he comes home feelin' that the world could care less if he died, I want to fix him a tub of water and wash his back. And . . . and . . . when I have a bad dream, I want to wake up with him holdin' me. I just want to wake up with him, Mam Phyllis.

MAM PHYLLIS: (*with the wisdom of ages*) So you think it's all gonna be peaches and milk, huh?

HELENA: (*with force*) No, mam. We're gonna scuffle just like everybody else.

MAM PHYLLIS: I wish with all my heart I could feel good about you marryin' so soon. (*as if she had a second thought*) Helena, you didn't go and get yourself in a family way already, did you?

HELENA: (*moving toward the table*) Oh, no, mam! (*quickly*) I was too scared you'd take a broom to me.

MAM PHYLLIS: (*approvingly*) Glad to hear I raised you right. (*pause*) Helena, I got something on my mind.

HELENA: (*cringing*) Have you tried to wash it off with lye soap?

MAM PHYLLIS: (*taking a second to understand and then chuckling*) Now is that any way to talk to me? I may as well put my money in a mattress instead of payin' for yo schoolin'.

HELENA: (*sitting at table*) Just kiddin'!

MAM PHYLLIS: I've been thinkin' about givin' up nursin'.

HELENA: (*surprised*) Since when?

MAM PHYLLIS: Well, it's been in and out of my mind. I've pretty much made up my mind that now's a good time. I'm no young woman anymore, you know. Huh, I've commenced to see my wrinkles without a mirror.

HELENA: What's all this talk about age all of a sudden?

MAM PHYLLIS: Now, child, can't you see old age done caught up with me? Seventy years ain't nothin' to shake a stick at. Shucks, I can barely climb the stairs at Miss Shifer's and Maggie's house is way too big for a woman like me to clean.

HELENA: So what are you gonna do, stay at home all day?

MAM PHYLLIS: (*with independence*) Maybe so—the rush is over.

HELENA: You'd curl up and die if you couldn't be out changin' some baby's diaper or nagging some new momma.

MAM PHYLLIS: (*chuckling*) Child, hush your mouth. I'll get used to stayin' home.

HELENA: Doing what?

MAM PHYLLIS: I'll find plenty to do. I'm even thinkin' about teachin' Sunday school.

HELENA: Aw, humbug! You used to say you'd nurse until the Great Deliverer called you.

MAM PHYLLIS: (*getting defensive*) I've worked hard, Helena, can't nobody in this town say I don't deserve to take it easy after all of these years.

HELENA: It's not that. It's just . . .

MAM PHYLLIS: I've commenced to worryin' about who's gonna take care of me. Pretty soon you'll be gone.

HELENA: (*gradual realization*) So that's it!

MAM PHYLLIS: What?

HELENA: You're afraid you're gonna lose me.

MAM PHYLLIS: (*She waves HELENA off.*) Aw, hush your nonsense.

HELENA: (*going close to MAM PHYLLIS*) Come on, tell the truth. You're scared to let me go.

MAM PHYLLIS: You're my baby. You're all I have left in this world. You've grown into a woman already.

HELENA: But I still need you. I'll always need you. I'm gonna be needin' Mam Phyllis one of these days.

MAM PHYLLIS: Now don't you start talkin' about havin' babies. I didn't say you could get married yet. (*wiping a tear*)

HELENA: Well, can I? Please say it's ok. I want to marry Herman with all of my heart.

MAM PHYLLIS: And that little heart is just gonna jump clean out your chest and bang against the wall if I say no, huh? (*pause*) I don't like it one bit... I guess I'm gonna have to bite my tongue on this one. I can see yo mind is settled. But, I don't like it one bit, you hear?

HELENA: (*She jumps up in excitement and gives MAM PHYLLIS a squeeze.*) Thank you, Mam Phyllis. I love you. I won't let you down.

MAM PHYLLIS: Just don't let nobody fool you into thinkin' you can do just as good without a college deplooma as you can with one, 'cause that's a bold face lie.

HELENA: (*fidgety and fighting back the excitement*) I won't.

MAM PHYLLIS: And another thing, when you settin' high on that buggy, don't forget where you came from. Too many folk think they sprung from a bottle of wine.

HELENA: I won't. I won't.

MAM PHYLLIS: Praise God, some folk act like they roots are in they teeth.

(*MAM PHYLLIS and HELENA chuckle.*)

SISTER VIOLA: (*A knock is heard at the door and a voice is heard shouting from offstage; it's the voice of SISTER VIOLA.*) Phyllis. Yoo hoo, Phyllis! You in there? Child, you needed (*She enters.*) at Shirley's house. Her baby is comin' early. They send me to get you. I got some other business to tend to, so I got to go. I be seein' you. (*She exits.*)

MAM PHYLLIS: (*shouting to SISTER VIOLA offstage*) Thank you for the news.

SISTER VIOLA: (offstage shouting) You welcome jest the same.

(*HELENA chews on apples and moves to MAM PHYLLIS's chair.*)

MAM PHYLLIS: (*to HELENA*) Well, just don't sit around idle. Get your coat and let's go.

HELENA: But I thought you were tired and givin' up nursing.

MAM PHYLLIS: (*She rushes around while she talks and gathers things to take with her.*) Child, when you get my age it's all right to feel a little sorry for yourself now and again. I got my courage back.

HELENA: (*putting on her coat*) So, you're not gonna stay home and teach Sunday school?

MAM PHYLLIS: Maybe in about twenty years. Now, hurry along. Sam Jones' girl need me. Too much work to be done. Hurry along, child. (*She exits.*)

HELENA: (*She looks around the room and then mimics SISTER VIOLA.*) Yoo hoo, Phyllis, wait up. I'm not as young as I used to be. Thank you jest the same. (*grabs a piece of gingerbread and exits*)

(*BLACKOUT*)

(*End of Scene 2*)

(*End of Act II*)

ACT III

TIME: 1933, three years later, mid-summer
SETTING: The PHILMORE family area
AT RISE: MAGGIE sits clipping her fingernails. She is dressed in an elegant black dress, hat, and pumps. CHARLES is in a white shirt, tie, and dark pants, stands near liquor counter pouring two glasses of sherry. His coat is thrown across the sofa.

CHARLES: (*handing MAGGIE a drink*) Here, drink this, darling. It'll calm your nerves.

MAGGIE: Thanks, buttercup. Mam Phyllis' memorial about killed me.

CHARLES: (*exclaiming*) You! I was the one about to roll over and die. I thought that Father O'Henry was totally out of line. I never would have let that Protestant minister in my church.

MAGGIE: Well, he was Phyllis' cousin. I heard he insisted on preaching her memorial service.

CHARLES: I have a low, low tolerance for the likes of him.

MAGGIE: Did you see the way he was huffing and puffing up there? I didn't know if he was dancing or fainting.

CHARLES: I detest going to services like that. People like that abuse the pulpit.

MAGGIE: Who ever thought she'd go like that?

CHARLES: (*caught off guard*) I beg your pardon, darling.

MAGGIE: Mam Phyllis, dear. I still can't believe she's dead.

CHARLES: 'Tis a great pity. The world has lost a great, charitable, loving, energetic, compassionate, and enduring woman. (*too soon*) What will we be having for lunch, dear?

MAGGIE: I'll have Cook prepare coq au vin, sauteed potatoes, and mixed vegetables, darling.

CHARLES: Fabulous! I'm starved.

MAGGIE: I don't think I could eat a thing. Funerals take away my appetite.

CHARLES: (*drawn out*) Especially long ones.

MAGGIE: Yes! (*sighs*) And to think, three years ago last month Mam Phyllis worked right here in this house.

CHARLES: (*seeming preoccupied*) Yeah, she was one of the world's greatest . . . a credit to her race.

MAGGIE: Do you know she had talked about giving up nursing when she was helping out with little Betty?

CHARLES: No kidding?

MAGGIE: (*bragging*) I was the one who convinced her not to quit.

CHARLES: How did you manage that, darling?

MAGGIE: Easy. The very next day, before she could open her mouth, I told her that we were giving her a big plump raise.

CHARLES: You sly little devil.

MAGGIE: Worked like a charm. She just chuckled and didn't say another word about putting up the old apron.

CHARLES: And today we paid our last respects.

MAGGIE: (*sighing*) Yes, in that cooped up little church in that absolutely horrible little neighborhood. And that strange little man.

CHARLES: Don't talk about that preacher. All that whooping and hollering . . . common, that's what it is. Downright common.

MAGGIE: Now dear, everybody can't be as cultured and refined as we. Just count your blessings, sweet potato.

CHARLES: I guess so. But that memorial did last too long.

MAGGIE: I agree, but look at how many people got up to say a word.

CHARLES: A word, ha! That Brother Jesse was up there for at least twenty minutes.

MAGGIE: (*shivers*) He's so dark. A man like that couldn't come anywhere near me.

CHARLES: (*jokingly*) He'd better not. (*MAGGIE and CHARLES affectedly kiss each other several times in short spurts—kissy face.*) That old coot went on forever about how Mam Phyllis fell in Old Man Tolbert's gully and drowned.

MAGGIE: A sad tale it was. I wonder if they'll ever find the body?

CHARLES: Perhaps not, dear.

MAGGIE: Maybe they could have waited a little longer before having the memorial service.

CHARLES: It's been two weeks, honey. I don't think that body's going to surface.

MAGGIE: Maybe not. And wasn't it silly to have all those beautiful roses . . . wasted on the likes of Brother Jesse and his bunch?

CHARLES: Do you know I counted twenty dozens. That's 240 roses. A lot of roses for a colored woman in hard times.

MAGGIE: A lot of roses, period! I wonder if Mam Phyllis' rich white folks helped pay for them.

CHARLES: (*rising to refresh drinks*) I would have given my share if they had asked me, but that Sister Viola didn't even ask.

MAGGIE: I don't blame you one bit. If they were too proud to ask you for a loan, I mean a donation, that's more for us, sweet pea.

CHARLES: And even Brother Jesse was going around begging for money to buy trinkets for the church . . . all for show. That's why coloreds can't get nowhere . . . too busy wasting money on funerals.

MAGGIE: (*sighs*) Brother Jesse sure was broken up at the service.

CHARLES: Goodness gracious, wasn't he! He read that one line in the newspaper five times. (*imitating the old man*) "Mam Phyllis, Missing in Gully, Presumed Dead."

MAGGIE: You know, I heard it was Miss Shifer who got the newspaper to even mention Mam Phyllis.

CHARLES: (*sitting on sofa*) I'm not surprised. Miss Shifer works for the *Daily World*. Besides, Mam Phyllis practically raised all five of the Shifer children.

MAGGIE: (*arrogant and resentful*) Don't I know it. She couldn't wait to leave me and little Betty to run lick between Miss Shifer's toes.

CHARLES: And to think, we could buy and sell the Shifers.

MAGGIE: Well, you know how poor colored folk are.

CHARLES: Yeah, but it makes me sick. That's why we can't get anything out of this world now.

MAGGIE: What, dear?

CHARLES: They're too busy licking the floors in white people's kitchens.

MAGGIE: I agree wholeheartedly. There just isn't enough love in the colored community.

CHARLES: You're right about that. You know, there's only so much . . . people like you and me can do to uplift the race.

MAGGIE: I know, and it's an awful burden to carry.

CHARLES: Amen!

MAGGIE: Why, just last week I had to give loads of clothes to one of those rummage sale girls. She was pestering the life out of me.

CHARLES: (*quickly*) Not your furs and silk, I hope.

MAGGIE: Gracious no. Only the things that were a little stained, darling.

CHARLES: (*pinching MAGGIE's cheek*) I hope so. You can't always be selfless, dear.

MAGGIE: (*pinching CHARLES cheek*) Of course not, honey bunch.

CHARLES: (*pinching MAGGIE's chin*) And give away everything I buy for you, dear heart.

MAGGIE: (*pinching CHARLES's chin*) I don't, baby.

CHARLES: (*squeezing MAGGIE's earlobe*) I might not have the hardware store forever, pumpkin pie.

MAGGIE: (*pinching CHARLES's earlobe*) I know, sugar plum.

CHARLES: (*grinning*) Shall we skip lunch?

MAGGIE: (*chuckling*) I was just thinking the same thing. (*MAGGIE and CHARLES affectedly kiss each other several times in short, swift spurts—kissy face.*)

CHARLES: But what about Mam Phyllis?

MAGGIE: Who?

CHARLES: Mam Phyllis.

MAGGIE: Oh, nth nth nth. The world has lost a truly, truly spectacular human being.

CHARLES: Yep. (*pause*) I'll race you to our little hideaway.

MAGGIE: Charles, please. (*exiting*) Let's not get common! (*exits*)

CHARLES: (*following behind*) You're right, dear. (*clearing his throat*) Will we be singing in the clouds this afternoon? (*He exits.*)

(BLACKOUT)

(End of Scene 1)

SCENE 2: Lapse of time of about 30 minutes. Lights rise on MAM PHYLLIS' family area. HELENA is six months pregnant. She sits at table, wearing a blue maternity dress. Enters HERMAN, wearing overalls. They peel potatoes at table.

HELENA: Did you find out anything more from Brother Jesse?

HERMAN: No, he don't know where she kept your maw's ring. All he know is she used to keep it somewhere in the house. (*looking around room*) Talk all over town is Mam Phyllis probably sold that ring to send you to college.

HELENA: You told Brother Jesse I just wanted to give the ring to my baby girl when she's grown.

HERMAN: (*sitting*) Yeah, sure did. He just started runnin' his mouth 'bout how Mam Phyllis missed you. And he didn't forget to remind me that your maw got that gold ring from one of the oldest white families in Opelousas.

HELENA: I should have known. But I bet he didn't tell you she worked on her hands and knees for years to earn that ring. What else was on his mind?

HERMAN: Talkin' about how it's a shame you and Mam Phyllis had that big fallin' out.

HELENA: (*defensively*) She's the one who changed her mind and didn't want me to marry you.

HERMAN: Sure was.

HELENA: She's the one who told me you weren't welcome in her house anymore.

HERMAN: (*caressing her*) Don't git worked up, Lena.

HELENA: (*pouting*) If you couldn't come, I wasn't coming either! (*pause*) She didn't even come to my graduation.

HERMAN: Just a little stubborn, that's all.

HELENA: I don't know why all of a suddenn she didn't want me to marry you.

HERMAN: I always did believe that Sister Viola had something to do with it. She probably made her believe I was a woman chaser.

HELENA: I just don't know what came over her.

HERMAN: You tried to make up. I'm a witness to that.

HELENA: She made me choose. I didn't wanta choose, Herman.

HERMAN: Don't get too nervous, Lena.

HELENA: And why'd you have to go ask Brother Jesse? I bet the whole town's gonna know you asked about the ring. He's riding high now that he brought the news about Mam Phyllis.

HERMAN: That's for sure. (*pause*) I wonder what he was doin' 'round Old Man Tolbert's gully anyway.

HELENA: I don't know. I'm just glad I wasn't anywhere around when he found Mam Phyllis' glasses and apron.

HERMAN: I wonder if they searched that gully good. Don't seem right they couldn't find her body.

HELENA: Brother Jesse said that gully run for miles. Said her body might never be found.

HERMAN: Yeah, Jesse a expert at everything.

HELENA: What else was he babblin' about?

HERMAN: (*He leans toward HELENA.*) He told me Mam Phyllis had a fallin' out with Sister Viola a few months back.

HELENA: I'm not surprised. They were always fussin'.

HERMAN: I mean for good. They stop speakin'.

HELENA: How come?

HERMAN: Over somethin' Mam Phyllis said about Sister Viola's po Momma.

HELENA: I wonder what?

HERMAN: I couldn't get it out a Brother Jesse. But he slipped and said that Sister Viola was in and out of everybody's house callin' Mam Phyllis everythin' 'cept a child of God. Just runnin' her down.

HELENA: That doesn't sound like Sister Viola. She's got a big mouth, but they go back a long way.

HERMAN: Well if anybody know, Brother Jesse know.

HELENA: Brother Jesse say if Mam Phyllis talked about us a lot?

HERMAN: Yep. Said she told you not to marry me.

HELENA: (*frustrated, rising, and moving to rocking chair*) Mam Phyllis hurt me to my heart. And she had said I could marry you, even if she didn't like it one bit.

HERMAN: Sister Viola must a got to her.

HELENA: Maybe so.

SISTER VIOLA: (*A knock is heard at the door and SISTER VIOLA lets herself in. She is wearing an obtrusive straw hat, carrying a hand fan which she uses throughout the scene, and wearing a loud flowered dress.*) Anybody home? Yoo hooooooo!

HERMAN: Speakin' a the old bat!

SISTER VIOLA: Yoo hooooo. Yoo hooooooo! I say, you hooooooo!

HELENA: Come on in, Sister Viola.

SISTER VIOLA: Evenin' Helena and . . . and . . . What you name agin boy? I done called you Sam Martin's boy so long, I can't keep you name in my head.

HERMAN: (*exiting*) Herman Martin's my name, Sister Viola. How you today?

HELENA: Where you headed? (*waiting for an answer from husband*)

SISTER VIOLA: (*in response to HERMAN's greeting*) Oh, I'm feelin' pretty fair. (*sitting and taking off her hat*)

HERMAN: (*to HELENA as he directs a "yapping" gesture to SISTER VIOLA*) Gonna go set a spell with Momma and Papa. If you need me, I'm sure Sister Viola will come get me.

SISTER VIOLA: Sho nuff, child, sho nuff. Be too glad to bring you the news.

HERMAN: I'll be back in a while, Lena. (*He pulls at SISTER VIOLA's hair on his way out.*)

SISTER VIOLA: (*grabbing her head and neck*) Must be misquetoes 'round here. (*pause*) Look like Sam Martin boy made a man of hisself after all. I heard he farmin' up there in Bogalusa. Yep, he sho fooled me. (*realizing she is offending HELENA*) Oh! Scuse my mouth. Sometimes I sezs things I ain't got no business.

HELENA: Don't we all know. (*She moves to rocker.*)

SISTER VIOLA: (*not understanding*) Say what?

HELENA: I said how's everything on your end?

SISTER VIOLA: Jest as fine as jelly wine. Listen, I come by to see if you needs anything.

HELENA: I'm fine, Sister Viola.

SISTER VIOLA: (*She bursts out crying in a wild, humorous manner.*) You know, me and Phyllis was like sisters. Never a cross word betwixt us.

(*HELENA makes eyes at SISTER VIOLA. The audience knows that she is lying.*)

SISTER VIOLA: I was so sorry to see her go. But, like my po Momma used to say, better her than me.

HELENA: (*a little annoyed*) Would you like some gingerbread?

SISTER VIOLA: Child, you jest like Phyllis. Every time I opened my mouth, Phyllis wanted to thow gingerbread in it. No, I don't want no gingerbread. Thank you jest the same.

HELENA: You ok?

SISTER VIOLA: (*She bursts out in that humorous cry again.*) Yep, I'm gonna have a turable time gettin' on without Phyllis. (*Noticing that HELENA is pregnant, she stops dry.*) Child, you in a family way?

HELENA: You didn't notice at the memorial service?

SISTER VIOLA: No, child, I could hardly see you with so many people gettin' the Holy Ghost and passin' out all over the place like flies. Child, I ain't never seen so many people at a funeral—even a few whites came too. Course they stood off in the cornder, but they was there. Child, I was lookin' round sho nuff. I wanted to see who came and who didn't came.

HELENA: (*wanting to change the subject*) I'm feelin' a little warm. This sure has been a hot summer.

SISTER VIOLA: (*starting to fan herself rapidly*) Sho has. Child, it's so hot outside you could burn grits on the porch. (*She bursts into tears.*)

HELENA: What's wrong?

SISTER VIOLA: (*sobbing wildly*) Talkin' 'bout them grits made me remember I done lost Phyllis.

HELENA: (*going over to comfort SISTER VIOLA*) Take it easy, Sister Viola. (*She rolls her eyes when SISTER VIOLA is not looking.*)

SISTER VIOLA: Me and Phyllis hardly ever agreed on anythin'. That was jest our nature, but we was close, me and Phyllis was. Lots a people talk 'bout me behind my back, but Phyllis knew I couldn't help myself. I was put here talkin' and I expects I'll go out of this world talkin'.

HELENA: Mam Phyllis was close to you, too. And I know you never said one bad word about her.

SISTER VIOLA: Never, child. (*She bursts out crying.*) Why, I helped raise you.

HELENA: (*making eyes*) Sure you did. Sure you did.

SISTER VIOLA: (*stops crying abruptly*) Oh, before I forget, Miss Shifer want to see you. She sent word by Brother Jesse, but he lolly-gaggin' around and ain't had a chance to get over here yet.

HELENA: I guess she wants to talk to be about Mam Phyllis.

SISTER VIOLA: Child, I wasn't hardly able to get nothin' out of Brother Jesse. You know how tight mouthed he is. That old buzzard squeak when he talk. But don't get me started on Brother Jesse, 'cause I'll lose my religion.

HELENA: Well, what did Brother Jesse say?

SISTER VIOLA: (*annoyed*) I told you—not much. That old buzzard work on my nerve bad. Po Phyllis ain't had but one fault, she kept takin' up for that old gossipin' buzzard.

HELENA: (*annoyed*) Sister Viola, do you or don't you know what Miss Shifer wants to see me about.

SISTER VIOLA: Course I do, but with no help from that Brother Jesse, that scoundrel.

HELENA: (*losing her patience*) Please, Sister Viola!

SISTER VIOLA: Scuse me, child, I sho can git carried away. Anyway, Brother Jesse wouldn't tell me nothin', but I knowed he told Martha-Mae. So I went set a spell with Martha-Mae to get the news.

HELENA: And?

SISTER VIOLA: Child, we sho-shoed and sho-shoed for about a hour. You should hear 'bout some a the goings on in this sinful, wicked lil town. (*She ends with a little chuckle.*)

HELENA: (*annoyed*) Sister Viola, I don't care what you and Martha-Mae been gossipin' about!

SISTER VIOLA: Who said we was gossipin'! (*haughty*) Boy, give some people a lil college deplooma and they start actin' like the rest of the world ain't worth two hoops in hell.

HELENA: Forgive me, Sister Viola. You said you know what she wants?

SISTER VIOLA: (*surprised*) Who?

HELENA: Miss Shifer.

SISTER VIOLA: (*forgetting herself*) Child, you must like them white folks much as po Phyllis did.

HELENA: Forget about it, Sister Viola. I'll just go and see what she wants.

SISTER VIOLA: She been workin' on some kind a story bout po Phyllis for the newspaper. The word is she all ruffled up 'cause them people down at the newspaper jest put one little, bitty line 'bout po Phyllis in the paper.

SISTER VIOLA: Let's see can I tell you how it go agin. (*pretending she's reading the paper*) "Phyllis Givins is missing' in the gully and is sho nuff dead." (*She bursts out crying.*)

HELENA: It's ok, Sister Viola. (*pause*) Was there anything else?

SISTER VIOLA: (*stops crying abruptly*) Nope, that's all I heard. After po Phyllis worked her fingers to the bone, they put that chicken feed in the paper.

HELENA: Didn't you say you couldn't stay long?

SISTER VIOLA: I said no such thing. Child, you nervous just like po Phyllis used to be, po old soul.

HELENA: I am not nervous.

SISTER VIOLA: (*ignoring HELENA*) And I guess she want to show you all kind a old pictures of Phyllis and her children together.

HELENA: Maybe so.

SISTER VIOLA: And heaven forbid, she might want to tell you how much she loved po Phyllis; you know how white people is.

HELENA: (*annoyed*) What's wrong with that?

SISTER VIOLA: Nothin', child, nothin'. Just that white people can run it in the ground.

HELENA: Do you always have to bad-mouth everybody?

SISTER VIOLA: Who bad-mouthin' anybody? I likes Miss Shifer, child. I was raised up with white people. I know 'em likes the pot of gumbo I've made every Saturday for the last twenty-five years.

HELENA: I think I'll go take a little nap.

SISTER VIOLA: So what, you puttin' me out? I ain't good nuff company for you? (*She bursts out crying.*) Po Phyllis, God rest her po old soul, would never hurt my feelins like you doin'!

HELENA: Sister Viola, what is the matter with you? I just don't understand you.

SISTER VIOLA: (*still sobbing*) Nobody did, 'ceptin po Phyllis. I really miss Phyllis.

HELENA: (*giving SISTER VIOLA a big hug*) Shhhhhhh. Don't cry.

HERMAN: (*enters as HELENA hugs SISTER VIOLA*) I thought you'd be gone by now, Sister Viola.

SISTER VIOLA: (*stops crying abruptly; her old self again*) That's what you get for thinkin'. (*nasty*) How's yo Maw and Paw?

HERMAN: Hi, hon. (*to SISTER VIOLA*) They not home. Must be out visitin'.

HELENA: Hi, honey.

SISTER VIOLA: They probably hid when they seen you comin'.

HELENA: Well, I'm gonna take that nap now. Take care, Sister Viola.

HERMAN: (*concerned and moving to hug HELENA*) What? You not feelin' good?

HELENA: I'm fine. Just tired.

SISTER VIOLA: Well, I sho nuff gets the message. I'll be moving along.

HERMAN: (*anxious for SISTER VIOLA to go*) Well, take care.

SISTER VIOLA: (*exiting*) I will, child. I'll always be around. (*She bursts into tears.*) Po, po Phyllis. The world done lost the cream a the crop. Ain't no more like po Phyllis. (*She exits after she steals an apple.*)

HERMAN: There wasn't a drop of water in that woman's eyes.

HELENA: I know. And to think, she had turned on Mam Phyllis. That woman needs to be sent out to pasture.

HERMAN: (*sitting in rocker*) Ain't that the truth. (*pause*) You really tired?

HELENA: No, but I wanted to get rid of that old flea.

HERMAN: How 'bout a walk? It would do the baby good.

HELENA: You might be right. Just let me get a piece of gingerbread.

(*Offstage can be heard wild screams and wild moaning and groaning.*)

SISTER VIOLA: (*rushing in and screaming*) I done seen a ghost! Lordy, Lordy have mercy on my everlovin' soul! Somebody help me! Help me, sweet Jesus!

HERMAN: (*concerned*) Sister Viola, what you makin' all that fuss about?

SISTER VIOLA: (*out of breath and can hardly speak. She plops in chair.*) Phyllis! Phyllis! I saw her jest now. Comin' in the gates. I swear this place is haunted. Gimme the hee-bee gee-bees!

HELENA: You scared me half to death. Do you want Herman to walk you home?

SISTER VIOLA: Child, I tell you it was real, jest as real as Martha-Mae's ham hocks and beans today. I told you I ate at Martha-Mae house today?

HELENA: No.

SISTER VIOLA: But forget 'bout Martha-Mae. I sho seen a ghost jest as sure as God made iron.

HERMAN: You been eatin' too many beans, Sister Viola.

SISTER VIOLA: Go on and make fun a me. But I tell you I seen a ghost, and it look jest like po Phyllis.

HELENA: (*to HERMAN*) Honey, why don't you go walk Sister Viola home.

SISTER VIOLA: Well, maybe it was the heat. You know I'm not the woman I used to be.

HERMAN: (*moving close to SISTER VIOLA*) You know, Lena, she really don't look good.

SISTER VIOLA: (*moving to rocker to sit*) Well, I jest told you that. Was you always this slow?

HERMAN: Was you always this mean?

HELENA: Honey, why don't you go see if Madame Babineaux got something for Sister Viola.

SISTER VIOLA: (*huffing and puffing and fanning herself*) Now jest hold your horses, I don't think I'm sick enough for no treatment. I jest got over-heated. I'ma take me a big dose of epsom salt when I get home.

HERMAN: (*heading toward door*) I'm gonna go on over to Madame Babineaux. She might be able to give you somethin' to take for them faintin' spells.

SISTER VIOLA: Now boy, don't be callin' them things faintin' spells. (*She pulls on his shirt and then pulls on his ear.*) Next thing you know, that good-for-nothin' Brother Jesse be tellin' everybody I got one foot in the grave.

HERMAN: (*patronizing*) Yes mam, Sister Viola. Be back in a while, Lena. (*He exits.*)

SISTER VIOLA: That husband of yourns is nervous too. (*shaking her head and fanning*) Some people, you know, got to go runnin' for treatment if they pee crooked.

HELENA: (*slightly reprimanding her*) Sister Viola!

SISTER VIOLA: It's the truth. Po Phyllis wasn't like that though. (*She bursts out in that wild, humorous cry again.*)

HELENA: What?

SISTER VIOLA: (*sucking in her sobs*) Po Phyllis didn't complain unless she was weak as a bird and couldn't hardly get out the bed.

HELENA: Yeah, she was stubborn that way.

SISTER VIOLA: (*in agreement*) Amen, child, amen! (*rapidly*) Why, I remember when she had pneumonia two, three years back. That woman was so sick she didn't know if she was goin' or comin'. It took a heap a talkin' to get her some treatment.

HELENA: (*surprised*) What? Pneumonia? When?

SISTER VIOLA: Two, three winters back. I can't count you when exactly. Not too long after you run off with that knotty head buzzard a yourn!

HELENA: (*a little hurt and eyeing SISTER VIOLA*) She didn't write me. Seems like somebody could have let me know something.

SISTER VIOLA: Child, I thought you knowed. I guess if you woulda come home some time, po Phyllis woulda thought enough 'bout you to tell you. (*a new thought*) Why ain't you come home in three years anyway? What they got up in Bogalousa that made you forget where you came from?

HELENA: That was between me and Mam Phyllis.

SISTER VIOLA: No it wasn't. The whole darn town knowed about it. And they didn't like it one bit. And they sho nuff didn't like it that you sent that weasel of a husband all over town tryin' to find out where po Phyllis kept your maw's ring.

HELENA: Oh my God!

SISTER VIOLA: Child, don't be callin' on God. God ain't got nothin' to do with this. This is twixt you and me now.

HELENA: (*annoyed*) Now, Sister Viola, I don't want to be sassy, but I sure wish you would mind your own business.

SISTER VIOLA: Don't put me off. I wants to know why you run off and now you come back lookin' for a ring . . . of all things.

HELENA: That is none of your business.

SISTER VIOLA: You ought to be tarred and feathered. She took you in when you wasn't nothin' but a snotty-nosed baby, and then she gave you everythin' 'ceptin her soul. And then you got the nerve to throw her out like she a dirty dishrag.

HELENA: (*in a controlled manner*) Sister Viola, there are a lot of things I regret. I'm gonna go to my grave hurtin' 'cause I was too proud and silly to come home.

SISTER VIOLA: You sho nuff ought to, child. She ain't never wrote you or nothin'?

HELENA: Mam Phyllis used to write me in the beginnin'. She used to ask me when I was comin'. But I was mad 'cause she didn't come to my weddin'.

SISTER VIOLA: Mais chere, you mean to tell me you couldn't forgive Phyllis for that? Child, you sho didn't take after po Phyllis. One a these days, child, you gonna suffer too. (*pointing to HELENA's stomach*) You got to learn forgiveness, child.

HELENA: Listen who's talkin' about forgiveness! (*Angry, she slaps SISTER VIOLA on the knee.*) You wouldn't know forgiveness if you slept with it.

SISTER VIOLA: (*She bursts into tears.*) Is this what it come to? Old people don't have no hidin' place from a wicked tongue!

HELENA: (*angry*) Oh, put a soup-bone in it! You ain't nothin' but a fire pusher!

SISTER VIOLA: (*stops dry*) Well, glory be!

HELENA: I heard you and Mam Phyllis weren't even on speakin' terms.

SISTER VIOLA: Where'd you hear that confoundin' lie?

HELENA: Brother Jesse.

SISTER VIOLA: Well then you'd believe anythin' from a snake!

HELENA: So he's lying?

SISTER VIOLA: That no count black trash couldn't tell the truth if they was to cut off his tongue!

HELENA: Sister Viola, why you hate black so much? Everybody's always known you hate Brother Jesse 'cause he's so dark.

SISTER VIOLA: (*chuckle*) Huh, Brother Jesse is blue-black. And I don't hate black! You must got your people mixed up.

HELENA: You always bad-mouthin' Uncle Jim and Cousin Mary and old man Cholly, and Herman.

SISTER VIOLA: I don't bad-mouth them all the time, just every now and again.

HELENA: Brother Jesse would give his last shirt for you. He's good to the core.

SISTER VIOLA: (*correcting her*) Child, you must can't see. Brother Jesse black to the core. And he can keep his raggedy shirt. (*looking at her own arms*) That old thing black as a skillet, and a rusty one at that.

HELENA: You see? It keeps coming back to color. I feel sorry for you.

SISTER VIOLA: You and po Phyllis both. I promised I wouldn't never put my foot in this house.

HELENA: Why?

SISTER VIOLA: 'Cause po Phyllis told me to my face that I didn't like dark colored people nee white people. Then she sat on her high horse and told me I didn't even like myself.

HELENA: Maybe she was right.

SISTER VIOLA: (*beginning to sob*) Well, I wouldn't go so far as to say that. (*angry*) But I wanted to jump clean down her throat for talking to me like that.

HELENA: I know. She made me angry a couple of times too. But she made good sense.

SISTER VIOLA: Sometimes, anyway. Course she never understood a thang about me.

HELENA: I'd be happy if I could be half the woman she was. (*pause*) I'm sorry I hurt Mam Phyllis. I'd give my right arm to be able to tell her.

SISTER VIOLA: You couldn't a been too sorry. You ain't been home in a coon's age. Then come runnin' around lookin' for a ring.

HELENA: (*hurt*) I wanted it for the baby! And I still want it.

SISTER VIOLA: I guess I can't fault you for that? What's wrong, that husband a yours can't take care of ya'll? (*wanting to take it back*) Scuze my mouth. I jest can't help myself.

HELENA: It's all right. Do you want some gingerbread?

SISTER VIOLA: No, child. It must be time for me to go when you start pitchin gingerbread at me.

HELENA: Do you miss her? I mean really miss her?

SISTER VIOLA: Of course I do! But me and you got to keep on kickin'. We ain't got Phyllis no mo to carry our troubles on her back.

HELENA: You're a good old gal, you know that? (*HELENA offers to shake hands with SISTER VIOLA.*)

SISTER VIOLA: (*pushing HELENA away*) Now don't go spittin' all over me. I ain't got time for none a that kind a nonsense. I got to go make my rounds.

HELENA: Take care of yourself, Sister Viola.

SISTER VIOLA: (*as she heads toward exit*) I told you, child, I always takes care of myself. I'll always be around.

HELENA: (*chuckling*) Watch out for the heat.

SISTER VIOLA: (*bursting into tears*) Aw don't talk 'bout that heat. Reminds me a po Phyllis. Po, po Phyllis. The world done lost the cream a the crop. What we gonna do without po Phyllis?

MAM PHYLLIS: (*enters and interrupts SISTER VIOLA*) Viola! What's goin' on in here?

SISTER VIOLA: (*with both hands in the air and shouting*) Praise be! Glory be HIS name! Good God Almighty! Phyllis done been raised from the dead!

HELENA: (*clutching her stomach and rising*) Mam Phyllis? Oh my God!

MAM PHYLLIS: (*taking off her bonnet*) What's all the commotion?

SISTER VIOLA: (*going close to touch MAM PHYLLIS*) Is you a ghost? (*moving away quickly from MAM PHYLLIS*) Yeah, child, it's a ghost. Po Phyllis had many more wrinkles than that!

MAM PHYLLIS: Somebody tell me what's goin' on around here? (*looking at HELENA*) Surprised to see you.

HELENA: We not too long came from your funeral.

MAM PHYLLIS: Well, thank God I wasn't there.

SISTER VIOLA: (*going to MAM PHYLLIS and touching her arm and her face*) Is it you, Phyllis?

MAM PHYLLIS: Course, it's me. I been across the bayou visiting one of my old cousins.

HELENA: But Brother Jesse found your glasses and your apron by the gully.

MAM PHYLLIS: Thank goodness. I wondered where I lost 'em. Haven't seen a lick since.

SISTER VIOLA: Praise be for miracles. Phyllis, we done thought you was up in heaven gettin' them rewards you ain't never got here on earth! (*starts fanning herself and straining her ears to hear*)

MAM PHYLLIS: (*noticing HELENA's pregnancy and moving to her*) I can't believe my eyes. Child, is you in a family way?

HELENA: Yes mam. Baby coming in a couple a months.

MAM PHYLLIS: (*hugging HELENA and then looking at her*) Now this is a glorious day. I been missin' you so much, child.

HELENA: I'm sorry, Mam Phyllis. I was wrong.

MAM PHYLLIS: I was a crazy old hen myself. (*eyeing SISTER VIOLA*) Shouldn't listen to gossip! (*pause*) You my baby girl, and I'm sho nuff proud of you.

SISTER VIOLA: (*reproachfully*) Forgit about Helena. What you doin' makin' every-body cry over you when you ain't even dead? Boy, what dis world comin' to.?

MAM PHYLLIS: And what you doin' in my house anyway?

SISTER VIOLA: (*offended*) Ohhhhhhhhh! Um hhhhhhhhh! Don't sweat you old nappy gray head none. (*reaching for her hat*) I'm gittin' out this rat hole right now.

HELENA: Don't let her go, Mam Phyllis.

MAM PHYLLIS: (*turning up her head*) I don't see why not. She been a splinter in my thumb for years, child.

SISTER VIOLA: (*obviously stalling*) I'm leavin'.

MAM PHYLLIS: Go on. You the one said you wouldn't step foot back in my house.

SISTER VIOLA: I'm leavin' right now, I say.

HELENA: (*tugging at MAM PHYLLIS*) Let's all start fresh.

MAM PHYLLIS: (*looking back and forth between SISTER VIOLA and HELENA*) Oh all right! I never could stay mad at Viola anyway. That old gal keeps me close to Jesus.

HELENA: No go on. Hug and make up. (*MAM PHYLLIS looks at SISTER VIOLA a second and then extends her arms. SISTER VIOLA looks like she is going to accept the hug and then immediately ducks into a rocking chair.*)

SISTER VIOLA: Ooooh, child, my nerves is all chewed up. Somebody git me a piece of gingerbread.

> (*MAM PHYLLIS, who is standing behind the rocking chair that SISTER VIOLA is sitting in, gestures like she is going to choke SISTER VIOLA, but HELENA holds her back. Meanwhile, SISTER VIOLA sits dusting off the rocker and eyeing the room for dirt.*)

CURTAIN

PRODUCTION NOTES:

PLAYING TIME:	90 minutes
CAST:	4 females, 2 males
STAGE FURNITURE:	two co-existing sets: on one side, one rocking chair, one small chair, and one small table with two chairs; on the other side, one loveseat, one rocking chair, an endtable, one lamp, one liquor table, and house plants.

HAND PROPERTIES: liquor bottles, wine glasses, diapers, hand
                    mirror, hair brush, apples, potatoes, knife,
                    yarn, knitting needles, hand fan, and coffee
                    cup.

SETTING: Sitting rooms of two families in a Southern
                    rural town.

BIBLIOGRAPHY

SELECTED PUBLISHED PLAYS BY AFRICAN AMERICAN WOMEN

Abramson, Dolores. "The Light." *Three Hundred and Sixty Degrees of Blackness Comin at You*. Ed. Sonia Sanchez. New York: 5X Publishing Co., 1971, 137–138.

Adams, Janis. "St. Stephen: A Passion Play." *Confirmation*. Ed. Amiri and Amina Baraka. New York: William Morrow and Co., 1983.

Ahmad, Dorothy. "Papa's Daughter." *Drama Review* 12, 139–145.

Amis, Lola Jones. *Exploring the Black Experience in America*. New York: Franklin Square, 1976.

———. *Three Plays: The Other Side of the Wall, Places of Wrath and Helen*. New York: Exposition, 1965.

Anderson, T. Dianne. *The Unicorn Died at Dawn: Plays Poems and Other Writings*. Lutz, Florida: Anderson Publishing, 1981. (Includes nine plays.)

Basshe, Em Jo. "Earth." New York: The McCaulay Group, 1927.

Batson, Susan. "Hoodoo Talkin." *Three Hundred and Sixty Degrees of Blackness Comin at You*. Ed. Sonia Sanchez. New York: 5X Publishing Co., 1971, 145–178.

Beale, Tita. "A Just Piece." *Liberator*, June 1970, 16.

Bohanon, Mary. "Find the Girl." *A Galaxy of Black Writing*. Ed. R. Baird Shuman. Durham, North Carolina: Moore Publishing Co., 1970.

Bonner, Marita. "Exit, an Illusion." *Crisis* 36 (October 1929), 335–336, 352.

———. "The Pot Maker." *Opportunity* 5 (February 1927), 43–46.

———. "The Purple Flower." *Crisis* 35 (January 1928), 9–11, 28, 30. Repr. in *Black Theater USA: Forty-Five Plays By Black Americans (1847–1974)*. ed. James Hatch. New York: Free Press, 1974.

Brooks, Charlotte Kendrick. "Firm Foundations." *Negro History Bulletin*, March 1954, 128–131.

Brown, Beverly S. "The Snake Chief." *Negro History Bulletin*, March 1971, 70–71.

Brown-Guillory, Elizabeth. "Bayou Relics." Colorado Springs, Colorado: Contemporary Drama Service, 1983.

———. "Snapshots of Broken Dolls." Colorado Springs, Colorado: Contemporary Drama Service, 1987.

Burke, Inez. "Two Races." *Plays and Pageants from the Life of the Negro*. Ed. Willis Richardson. Washington, D.C.: The Associated Publishers, 1930.

Burrill, Mary. "Aftermath." *Crisis*, November 1919.

———. "They That Sit in Darkness." *Black Theater USA: Forty-Five Plays By Black Americans (1847–1974)*. Ed. James Hatch. New York: Free Press, 1974.

Carroll, Vinnette and Micki Grant. "Croesus and the Witch." New York: Broadway Music Publishers, 1984.

———. "Don't Bother Me, I Can't Cope." New York: Samuel French, 1972.

Childress, Alice. "The African Garden." *Black Scenes*. Ed. Alice Childress. New York: Doubleday, 1971, 137–46.

———. "Florence." *Masses and Mainstream*, 3 (October 1950), 34–47.

———. "Let's Hear it for the Queen." New York: Coward, McCann, and Geohegan, 1975.

———. "Mojo and String." New York: Dramatists Play Service, 1971.

———. "Wedding Band: A Love/Hate Story in Black and White." New York: Samuel French, 1973. Repr. in *Nine Plays by Black Women*. Ed. Margaret Wilkerson. New York: New American Library, 1986.

———. "When the Rattlesnake Sounds." New York: Coward, McCann, and Geohegan, 1975.

———. "Wine in the Wilderness." *Black Theater USA: Forty-Five Plays By Black Americans (1847–1974)*. Ed. James Hatch. New York: Free Press, 1974.

———. "The World on a Hill." *Plays to Remember*. Ed. Literary Heritage Series. New York: Macmillan, 1968.

Clark, China (Debra). "Perfection in Black." *Scripts* 7 (May 1972).

———. *Neffie and in Sorrow's Room*. New York: Era Publishing Co., 1976.

Collins, Kathleen. "In the Midnight Hour." *The Women's Project*. New York: An American Place Theater Performing Arts, 1981.

———. "The Brothers." *Nine Plays by Black Women*. Ed. Margaret Wilkerson. New York: New American Library, 1986.

Daniel, Eddie Mary. "For a Friend." *Phat Mama*, 1 (1970), 29–48.

Dennis, Dorothy Lorene. "Outcast." *SADSA Encore*. Nashville, Tenn.: McQuiddy Co., 1951.

DeVeaux, Alexis. "The Tapestry." *Nine Plays by Black Women*. Ed. Margaret Wilkerson. New York: New American Library, 1986.

Duncan, Thelma Myrtle. "Black Magic." *Yearbook of Short Plays, First Series*. Ed. Wise and Snook. Evanston, Illinois: Row, Peterson, 1931, 215–232.

———. "Death Dance." *Plays of Negro Life*. Ed. Alaine Locke and Montgomery Gregory. New York: Harper and Row, 1927.

———. "Sacrifice." *Plays and Pageants from the Life of the Negro*. Ed. Willis Richardson. Washington, D.C.: The Associated Publishers, 1930.

Eubanks, Thelma. "The Spirit of Negro History." *Negro History Bulletin* (May 1952), 171–172.

Fabio, Sarah Webster. "The Saga of the Black Man." *The Iowa Review*, Spring 1975.

Flagg, Ann. "Great Gettin' Up in the Mornin'." New York: Samuel French, 1964 (20 pp.).

Franklin, Jennie E. "Black Girl." New York: Dramatists Play Service, 1971 (50 pp.).

————. "The Prodigal Sister: A Black Musical." New York: Samuel French, 1975 (59 pp.).

Gaines-Shelton, Ruth. "The Church Fight." *Black Theater USA: Forty-Five Plays By Black Americans (1847–1974)*. Ed. James Hatch. New York: Free Press, 1974.

Gibson, Patricia Joann. "Brown Silk and Magenta Sunsets." *Nine Plays By Black Women*. Ed. Margaret Wilkerson. New York: New American Library, 1986.

Gilbert, Mercedes. "Environment." *Selected Gems of Poetry, Comedy and Drama*. Boston: Christopher, 1931, 53–89.

Graham, Shirley. "Track Thirteen." Boston: Expression Co., 1940.

Grant, Micki. "Hansel and Gretel in the 80s." New York: Broadway Publishing, 1984.

Grimke, Angelina. "Rachel." *Black Theater USA: Forty-Five Plays By Black Americans (1847–1974)*. Ed. James Hatch. New York: Free Press, 1974.

Guinn, Dorothy C. "Out of the Dark." *Plays and Pageants from the Life of the Negro*. Ed. Willis Richardson. Washington, D.C.: The Associated Publishers, 1930.

Gunner, Francis. "The Light of Women." *Plays and Pageants from the Life of the Negro*. Ed. Willis Richardson. Washington, D.C.: The Associated Publishers, 1930.

Hansberry, Lorraine. *Les Blancs: The Collected Last Plays of Lorraine Hansberry*. Ed. Robert Nemiroff. New York: Random House, 1972, 11–62, repr. New York: New American Library, 1983.

————. *A Raisin in the Sun and the Sign in Sidney Brustein's Window*. New York: New American Library, 1966.

————. *To Be Young, Gifted and Black*. Englewood Cliffs, New Jersey: Prentice-Hall, 1969.

Hare, Maud Cuney. "Antar of Araby." *Plays and Pageants from the Life of the Negro*. Ed. Willis Richardson. Washington, D.C.: The Associated Publishers, 1930.

Harris, Helen Webb. "Genifrede." *Negro History in Thirteen Plays*. Ed. Willis Richardson and May Miller. Washington, D.C.: The Associated Publishers, 1935.

Hazzard, Aluria. "Mother Liked It." *Saturday Evening Quill* 1 (1928), 10–14.

————. "Little Heads." *Saturday Evening Quill* 2 (1929), 42–44.

Hill, Leslie Pickney. "Toussaint L'Ouverture." Boston: Christopher, 1928 (137 pp.).

Hirsh, Charlotte Teller. "Hagar and Ishmael." *Crisis* 6 (1913), 30–21.

Howard, Vilma. "The Tam." *SADSA Encore*. Nashville, Tenn.: McQuiddy Co., 1951.

Hult, Ruby. "The Saga of George Bush." *Negro Digest* (September 1962), 88–96.

Huntley, Elizabeth Maddox. "Legion, the Demoniac." *American Literature By Negro Authors*. Ed. Herman Dreer. New York: Macmillan, 1950, 306–309.

————. "What Ye Sow." New York: Comet Press, 1955 (97 pp.).

Hurston, Zora Neale. "The First One." *Ebony and Topaz*. Ed. Charles S. Johnson. New York: Urban League, 1927.

Hurston, Zora Neale, and Langston Hughes. "Mule Bone." *Drama Critique* 7 (Spring 1964), 103–107 (Act III only).

Jackson, Elaine. "Toe Jam." *Black Drama Anthology*. Ed. Woodie King and Ron Miller. New York: New American Library, 1972.

Johnson, Christine C. "Zwadi Ya Afrika Kwa Dunwa (Africa's Gift to the World): A Historical Play." Chicago: Free Black Press, 1969 (21 pp).

Johnson, Georgia Douglas. "Blue Blood." *Fifty More Contemporary One-Act Plays.* Fourth Series, New York: D. Appleton, 1927.

——. "Frederick Douglass." *Negro History in Thirteen Plays.* Ed. Willis Richardson and May Miller. Washington, D.C.: The Associated Publishers, 1935.

——. "Plumes: A Folk Tragedy." *Anthology of American Negro Literature.* Ed. Victor F. Calverton. New York: The Modern Library, 1929.

——. "A Sunday Morning in the South." *Black Theater USA: Forty-Five Plays By Black Americans (1847–1974).* Ed. James Hatch. New York: Free Press, 1974.

——. "William and Ellen Craft." *Negro History in Thirteen Plays.* Ed. Willis Richardson and May Miller. Washington, D.C.: The Associated Publishers, 1935.

Jones, Gayl. "Beyond Yourself (The Midnight Confessions) for Brother Ahhh." *BOP (Blacks on Paper).* Providence, R.I.: Brown University Press, 1975.

——. "Chile Woman." *Schubert Playbook Series* no. 5, vol. 2, 1974.

Kennedy, Adrienne. *Cities in Bezique.* New York: Samuel French, 1970.

——. "Funnyhouse of a Negro." New York: Samuel French, 1969 (24 pp).

——. "A Lesson in Dead Language." *Collision Course.* Ed. Edward Parone. New York: Random House, 1968.

——. "The Lennon Play: In His Own Write." New York: Simon and Schuster, 1972.

——. "A Movie Star Has to Star in Black and White." *Wordplay 3.* New York: Performing Arts Journal Publication, 1984.

——. "A Rat's Mass." *New Black Playwrights.* Ed. William Couch, Jr. Baton Rouge, Louisiana: Louisiana University Press, 1968.

——. "Sun: A Poem for Malcolm X Inspired By His Murder." *Scripts* 1 (May 1972), 5–28.

Kimball, Kathleen. "Meat Rack." *Scripts* 7 (May 1972).

LeNoire, Rosetta. "Bubbling Brown Sugar." New York: Broadway Publishing Co., 1984.

Lincoln, Abbey. "A Streak o' Lean." *Black Scenes.* Ed. Alice Childress. New York: Doubleday, 1971, 49–56 (excerpt).

Livingston, Myrtle Smith. "For Unborn Children." *Black Theater USA: Forty-Five Plays By Black Americans (1847–1974).* Ed. James Hatch. New York: Free Press, 1974.

Martin, Sharon Stockard. "Canned Soul." *Callaloo*, Spring 1975.

——. "Proper and Fine." *The Search.* New York: Scholastic Book Services, 1972.

Mason, Judi Ann. "Livin' Fat." New York: Samuel French, 1976.

McBrown, Gertrude Parthenia. "Africa Sings." *Negro History Bulletin* (February 1954), 133–34.

——. "Birthday Surprise." *Negro History Bulletin* 16 (February 1953), 16.

——. "Bought with Cookies." *Negro History Bulletin* 12 (April 1949).

McCray, Nettie [Salimu]. "Growin' into Blackness." *Black Theater* 2 (1969), 20–22.

Miller, May. Christophe's Daughters." *Negro History in Thirteen Plays.* Ed. Willis Richardson and May Miller. Washington, D.C.: The Associated Publishers, 1935.

———. "Graven Images." *Black Theater USA; Forty-Five Plays By Black Americans (1847–1974).* Ed. James Hatch. New York: Free Press, 1974.

———. "Harriet Tubman." *Negro History in Thirteen Plays.* Ed. Willis Richardson and May Miller. Washington, D.C.: The Associated Publishers, 1935.

———. "Riding the Goat." *Plays and Pageants from the Life of the Negro.* Ed. Willis Richardson. Washington, D.C.: The Associated Publishers, 1930.

———. "Samory." *Negro History in Thirteen Plays.* Ed. Willis Richardson and May Miller. Washington, D.C.: The Associated Publishers, 1935.

———. "Scratches." *Carolina Magazine* 59 (April 1929), 36–44.

———. "Sojourner Truth." *Negro History in Thirteen Plays.* Ed. Willis Richardson and May Miller. Washington, D.C.: The Associated Publishers, 1935.

Molette, Barbara Jean and Carlton W. "Dr. B. S. Black." *SADSA Encore,* 1970.

———. "Rosalee Pritchett." *Black Writers of America.* Ed. Richard Barksdale and Keneth Kinnamon. New York: Macmillan, 1972.

Nelson, Alice Dunbar. "Mine Eyes Have Seen." *Black Theater USA: Forty-Five Plays By Black Americans (1847–1974).* Ed. James Hatch. New York: Free Press, 1974.

Nelson, Natalie. "More Things That Happen to Us." New York: New Dimensions, 1970.

Nsabe, Nia. "Mama Don't Know What Love Is." *Three Hundred and Sixty Degrees of Blackness Comin at You.* Ed. Sonia Sanchez. New York: 5X Publishing Co., 1971, 179–190.

O'Neal, Regina. "And Then the Harvest: Three Television Plays." Detroit: Broadside Press, 1974 (142 pp.).

Price, Doris D. "The Bright Medallion." *University of Michigan Plays.* Ed. Kenneth T. Rowe. Ann Arbor, Michigan: Michigan University Press, 1932, 275–315.

———. "The Eyes of Old." *University of Michigan Plays.* Ed. Kenneth T. Rowe. Ann Arbor, Michigan: Michigan University Press, 1932, 317–338.

———. "Two Gods: A Minaret." *Opportunity* 10 (1932), 380–383, 389.

Rahman, Aishah. "Unfinished Women Cry in No Man's Land While a Bird Dies in a Gilded Cage." *Nine Plays by Black Women.* Ed. Margaret Wilkerson, New York: New American Library, 1986.

Reed, Edwina. "A Man Always Keeps His Word." *Negro History Bulletin* 26 (1963), 138–140.

Richards, Beah. "A Black Woman Speaks." *Nine Plays By Black Women.* Ed. Margaret Wilkerson, New York: New American Library, 1986.

Sanchez, Sonia. "The Bronx is Next." *Drama Review* 12 (Summer 1968), 78–83.

———. "Dirty Hearts." *Scripts* 1 (November 1971), 46–50.

———. "Malcolm/Man Don't Live Here No Mo." *Black Theater* 6 (1972), 24–27.

———. "Sister Son/ji." *New Plays From the Black Theater.* Ed. Ed Bullins. New York: Bantam, 1969.

———. "Uh Huh, But How Do It Free Us?" *The New Lafayette Theater Presents.* Ed. Bullins. New York: Anchor Press, Doubleday, 1974.

Shange, Ntozake. "Bocas: A Daughter's Geography." New York: St. Martin's Press, 1983.

———. "For Colored Girls Who Have Considered Suicide/When the Rainbow is Enuf." New York: Macmillan, 1977.

———. "From Okra to Greens." St. Louis: Coffee House Press, 1984.

———. "Three Pieces." New York: St. Martin's Press, 1981.

Smith, Jean. "O. C.'s Heart: Excerpts from a Three Act Play." *Negro Digest* 19 (April 1970), 57–76.

Spence, Eulalie. "Fool's Errand." New York: Samuel French, 1927 (26 pp.).

———. "Foreign Mail." New York: Samuel French, 1927.

———. "Help Wanted." *Saturday Evening Quill*, April 1929.

———. "The Starter." *Plays of Negro Life*. Ed. Alain Locke and Montgomery Gregory. New York: Harper and Row, 1927.

———. "Undertow." *Black Theater USA: Forty-Five Plays By Black Americans (1847– 1974)*. Ed. James Hatch. New York: Free Press, 1974.

Thorne, Anna V. "Black Power Every Hour." *Black Theater* 5 (1971), 8.

Tillman, Katherine Davis. "Fifty-Five Years of Freedom; or From Cabin to Congress." Philadelphia: A.M.E. Book Concern Printers, 1910 (52 pp.).

Turner, Beth. "Crisis at Little Rock." *Search* (April 7, 1977).

———. "The Hungering Lion." *Search* (September 23, 1976).

Turner, Geneva. "Bridging the Gap." *Negro History Bulletin* (March 1957), 133–137.

Walker, Lucy. *Social Action in One-Act Plays*. Pub. by the author, 1970. (Includes seven plays.)

Ware, Alice. "Like A Flame." New York: Theater League, 1938.

———. "Mighty Wind A Blowin'." New York: Theater League, 1936.

Watt, Billie Lou. "Phillis: A Play with Music." New York: Friendship Press, 1969.

Wilson, Alice T. "How An American Poet Made Money and Forgot Me Not." New York: Pageant, 1968 (68 pp.).

Yates, Elizabeth. "The Slave." Philadelphia: Philadelphia Publishing Co., 1926.

SELECTED PRODUCED PLAYS BY AFRICAN AMERICAN WOMEN

Ajanaku, Amana. "D Dog Dreams." Pro. by Levi Frazier as a cable access TV production, Nashville, 1977.

Allen, Thomasena Davis. "Songs My Father Taught Me." Pro. by Black American Theater, Washington, D.C., March 1974.

Andrews, Regina M. "Underground." Pro. by Harlem Experimental Theater, Harlem, 1932.

Angelou, Maya. "Ajax." Pro. by Mark Taper Forum, Los Angeles, February 1974.

———. "And Still I Rise." Pro. by Oakland Ensemble Theater, California, October 1979.

———. "The Least of These." Pro. in Los Angeles, 1966.

Bailey, Sheri. "All Kinds of Blue." Pro. by American National Theater and Academy West, Los Angeles, 1982.

———. "Dannie-n-Lawrence." Pro. by Company of Angels, Los Angeles, 1982.

———. "Southern Girls." Pro. at Deja Vu Coffee House, Los Angeles, fall 1981.

Bean, Patricia. "Getting It Together." Pro. by East Side Drama Group, Denver, December 1978.

———. "Till Death Do Us Part." Pro. by East Side Drama Group, Denver, May 1978.

———. "You and Me." Pro. by East Side Drama Group, Denver, August 1983.

Bell, Denise. "Dialogues of Shadow Women." Pro. by the Director's Unit of Frank Silvera Writers' Workshop. New York, January 1977.

Booker, Mary. "Upon This Rock." Pro. by the Black Experience Theater, San Francisco, August 1972.

Brewster, Bess E. Cooling. "Mama's Crazyhorse Rockin' Again." Pro. by Clark Center for the Performing Arts, New York, May 1974.

Broome, Barbara Cummings. "Millie Brown." Pro. in Chicago, June 1977.

Brown, Claudette. "Conversations with a Friend." Pro. at the West End Theater, New York, 1983.

———. "Ties That Bind." Pro. at the West End Theater, New York, November 1984.

Brown-Guillory, Elizabeth. "Mam Phyllis." Pro. at Converse College, Spartanburg, South Carolina, October 1981. (Multiple prod.)

———. "Marry Me Again." Pro. at Dillard University, New Orleans, March 1984. (Multiple prod.)

———. "Somebody Almost Walked off with All of My Stuff." Pro. Tukey Theater, Spartanburg, South Carolina, March 1982.

Browning, Alice. "How to Be Happy Though Married." Pro. for International Black Writers Conference (IBWC), Chicago, June 1977.

———. "How to Beat Old Age." Pro. at McCormick Inn, Chicago, August 1976.

———. "How's Your Sex Life?" Pro. for IBWC, Chicago, June 1977.

———. "It's Fun to Be Black." Pro. by the Actors of America, Chicago, 1973–1974.

Brunson, Doris. "Three Shades of Harlem. Pro. by New Heritage Theater, New York, June 1965. (Multiple prod.)

Bryant, Hazel. "An Evening of Black Poetry." Pro. by Afro-American Total Theater, New York, July 1969.

———. "Being Black in White America." Pro. by Afro-American Total Theater, New York, January through March 1970.

———. "Black Circles 'Round Angela." Pro. by Afro-American Total Theater, New York, 1970–1974.

———. "Makin' It." Pro. by Afro-American Total Theater, New York, 1972. (Multiple prod.)

———. "Origins." Pro. by Afro-American Total Theater, New York, October 1969.

———. "Sheba." Pro. by Afro-American Total Theater, New York, December 1972. (Multiple prod.)

———. "Soul Politiken." Pro. by Afro-American Total Theater, New York, July 1973.

Bryant, Hazel and Hope Clarke. "Mae's Amees." Pro. by Afro-American Total Theater, New York, 1969.

Busey, DeReath Byrd. "The Yellow Tree." Pro. by the Howard Players, Washington, D.C., 1922.

Carroll, Vinette. "Jubilation." Pro. by Urban Arts Corp (UAC), New York, 1964.

———. "What You Gonna Name That Pretty Little Baby?" Pro. by UAC, December 1978.

———. "When Hell Freezes Over, I'll Skate." Pro. by UAC, May 1979. (Multiple prod.)

Carroll, Vinette, and Micki Grant. "But Never Jam Today or Alice." Pro. on Broadway at Longrace Theater, July-August 1979. (Multiple prod.)

———. "I'm Laughing, But I Ain't Tickled." Pro. by UAC, May and December 1976.

———. "Love Power." Pro. by UAC, December 1974.

———. "Step Lively, Boy." Pro. by UAC, February 1972.

———. "Trumpets of the Lord." Pro. at the Circle in the Square, New York, April-May 1969. (Multiple prod.)

———. "The Ups and Downs of Theophilus Maitland." Pro. by UAC, November 1974. (Multiple prod.)

———. "Your Arms Too Short to Box with God." Pro. by UAC, 1975. (Multiple prod.)

Childress, Alice. "The Freedom Drum." Pro. by the Performing Arts Repertory Theater, Newark, New Jersey, May 1969. (Multiple prod.)

———. "Gold Through the Trees." Pro. by the Committee for the Negro in the Arts, Harlem, April 1952.

———. "Gullah." Pro. at the University of Massachusettes, Amherst, 1984.

———. "Just a Little Simple." Pro. by the Committee for the Negro in the Arts, Harlem, September 1950.

———. "Moms." Pro. at Hudson Guild Theater, New York, February-March 1987.

———. "Sea Island Song." Pro. at Stage South, Charleston, South Carolina, 1977.

Cleage, Pearl. "Duet for Three Voices." Pro. by Howard University Players, 1969.

———. "Essentials." Pro. by Just Us, Atlanta, 1984-1985.

———. "Good News." Pro. by Just Us, Atlanta, February 1984. (Multiple prod.)

———. "Hospice." Pro. by Woodie King, at New Federal Theater, New York 1983. (Multiple prod.)

———. "Hymn for the Rebels." Pro. by Howard University Players, 1968. (Multiple prod.)

———. "PR: A Political Romance." Pro. by Just Us, Atlanta, 1984-1985.

———. "Porch Songs." Pro. by the Phoenix Theater, Indianapolis, August 1985.

———. "Puppetplay." Pro. by Just Us, Atlanta, 1982-1983.

———. "The Sale." Pro. by Morehouse/Spelman Players, Atlanta 1972.

Clemmons, Phyllis, "Siege on Duncan Street." Pro. by the Dashiki Project Theater, New Orleans, 1982.

Coles, Erostine. "Festus de Fus'." Pro. by Atlanta University Summer Theater, Atlanta, 1934.

———. "Mimi La Croix." Pro. by Atlanta University Summer Theater, Atlanta, 1934.

Coles, Zaida. "Scenes and Songs of Love and Freedom." Pro. by Urban Arts Corp, New York, 1975.

Collie, Brenda Faye. "I Can't Hear the Birds Singing." Pro. at the Eighteenth Street Playhouse, New York, 1983.

———. "Silent Octaves." Pro. in the American College Theater Festival, 1978.

Collier, Eugenia. "Ricky." Pro. by the Kuumba Workshop, Chicago, October 1976.

Collins, Kathleen. "Only the Sky Is Free." Pro. at the Richard Allen Center for Culture and Arts, New York, Spring 1986.

———. "Remembrance." Pro. at American Place Theater, New York City, December 1985.

Collins, Rise. "Incandescent Tones." Pro. by New Federal Theater, New York City, July-August 1983. (Multiple prod.)

Cooper, Joan "California: How Now?" Pro. by Black Repertory Group, Berkeley, 1973.

———. "The Unintended." Pro. by Black Repertory Group, Berkeley, 1983.

Cousins, Linda. "Capturing Dreams." Pro. at the Paul Robeson Theater, Los Angeles, September 1982.

———. "The Divorcing." Pro. at Hudson Guild Theater, New York, August 1976.

———. "The 85–Year-Old Swinger." Pro. by the Alonzo Players Theater, Brooklyn, October 1985.

———. "The First Wife." Pro. by the Alonzo Players Theater, Brooklyn, January–August 1986.

———. "Karma." Pro. at Hudson Guild Theater, New York, August 1976.

———. "The Night Before." Pro. by the Alonzo Players Theater, Brooklyn, November 1981. (Multiple prod.)

Currelley, Lorraine. "The Red-Flowered Basin." Pro. by National Black Network, 1980.

Dee, Ruby. "Take it from the Top." Pro. by the New Federal Theater, New York, January 1979.

DeRamus, Betty. "Just What I Said." Pro. by the Concept East Workshop, Detroit, November 1971.

DeVeaux, Alexis. "Circles." Pro. by the Frederick Douglass Creative Arts Center, Harlem, March 1973. (Multiple prod.)

———. "A Season to Unravel." Pro. by the Negro Ensemble Company, New York, January-February 1979.

Dickerson, Glenda. "Jump at the Sun." Pro. at the Theater Lobby, Washington, D.C., 1972.

———. "Magic and Lions." Pro. by the Women's Interact Theater, New York, 1978.

———. "Owen's Song." Pro. by the DC Black Repertory Company, Washington, D.C., October 1974. (Multiple prod.)

———. "Trojan Women." Pro. in the Ira Aldridge Theater, Howard University, 1971.

———. "Unfinished Song." Pro. at Howard University, Washington, D.C., 1969. (Multiple prod.)

Dumas, Mildred. "No Room at the Inn." Pro. at St. John Baptist Church, Colorado Springs, 1979–1982.

———. "Out on Calvary." Pro. at St. John Baptist Church, Colorado Springs, 1979–1982.

———. "The Power of Will." Pro. by the Dumas Players, Colorado Springs, 1983.

———. "Uncle Rufus." Pro. by the Dumas Players, Colorado Springs, 1978.

Dyson, Diedra. "Black Ritual." Pro. by Kuumba Workshop, Chicago, 1974.

Early, Ann. "Do You Take This Woman.?" Pro. by Writers-in-Residence, Great Neck, New York, pre–1976.

————. "Is George Responsible?" Pro. by Writers-in-Residence, Great Neck, New York, pre–1976.

————. "Mishap." Pro. by Writers-in-Residence, Great Neck, New York, pre–1976.

Early, Jacqueline. "Sheba." Pro. at Tomkins Square Park, New York, August 1971.

Edmonds, Henriette. "Mushy Mouth." Pro. by Howard University's Children's Theater, Washington, D.C., 1975.

Edmonds, Irene Colbert. "The Lost Generation." Pro. at Florida A&M University, Tallahassee, Florida, pre–1963.

————. "The Wedding of Peter Gynt." Pro. at Florida A&M University, Tallahassee, Florida, pre–1963.

————. "Their Time and Our Time." Pro. at Florida A&M University, Tallahassee, Florida, pre–1963.

Emeruwa, Leatrice. "Black Magic Anyone?" Pro. at the First One World Theater Project, Cleveland, 1973. (Multiple prod.)

Fabio, Sarah Webster. "M. L. King Pageant." Pro. at Merritt Junior College, Oakland, California, 1967.

Fields, Julia. "All Day Tomorrow." Pro. at Knoxville College, Knoxville, Tennessee, 1966.

Fletcher, Bernice B. "A Mysterious Light." Pro. at the No Smoking Theater, New York, September–October 1983.

————. "Les Enfants." Pro. at the Pretenders Theater, New York, 1978.

Foard, Sylvia-Elaine. "A Fictitional Account of the Lives of Richard and Sarah Allen." Pro. by the Negro Ensemble Company, New York, April 1976.

Franklin, Jenny E. "Another Morning Rising." Pro. by the Company of Us, Greenwood, South Carolina, 1976.

————. "The Creation." Pro. by Eureka Theater Group, New York, 1975.

————. "Cut out the Lights and Call the Law." Pro. by the Negro Ensemble Company, New York, 1970s. (Multiple prod.)

————. "The Enemy." Pro. by Eureka Theater Group, New York, 1973.

————. "The First Step to Freedom." Pro. at the Sharon Waite Community Center, Harmony, Miss., 1964.

————. "Four Women." Pro. by Eureka Theater Group, New York, 1973.

————. "The Hand-Me-Down." Pro. by the Theater for Artcentric Living, New York, 1978.

————. "The In-Crowd." Pro. by Mobilization for Youth, New York, 1967. (Multiple prod.)

————. "MacPilate." Pro. by Eureka Theater Group, New York, 1974.

————. "Mau Mau Room." Pro. by Negro Ensemble Theater, New York, 1969.

————. "Prodigal Sister." Pro. at the Theater De Lys, New York, November–December 1974.

————. "Throw Thunder at This House." Pro. by the Theater for Artcentric Living, New York, 1970s.

————. "Two Flowers." Pro. at the New Feminists Theater, New York, 1960s.

————. "Under Heaven's Eye til Cockcrow." Pro. at the Theater of the Open Eye, New York, 1984.

————. "Where Dewdrops of Mercy Shine Bright." Pro. by Rites and Reason, Providence, Rhode Island, February 1983.

Gibson, Patricia J. "Ain't Love Grand?" Pro. by the Black Spectrum Theater, Queens, New York, 1984. (Multiple prod.)

———. "The Androgyny." Pro. at the Cardboard Clowns Theater, Frankfurt, Germany, 1979.

———. "Angel." Pro. at the Family Theater, New York, March 1981.

———. "The Black Woman." Pro. at SUNY/Cortland, New York, March 1972.

———. "Clean Sheets Can't Soil." Pro. by Rites and Reasons, Providence, Rhode Island, March–April, 1983.

———. "Konvergence." Pro. by Players Company, Trenton, New Jersey, March 1973. (Multiple prod.)

———. "Miss Ann Didn't Cry No More." Pro. by the Frederick Douglass Creative Arts Center, New York, March 1980.

———. "My Mark, My Name." Pro. Soul People's Repertory, Indianapolis, February 1981. (Multiple prod.)

———. "The Ninth Story Window." Pro. at Brandeis University, Waltham, Massachusettes, November 1974.

———. "Shameful in Your Eyes." Pro. at Keuka Park, New York, February 1971.

———. "Spida Bug." Pro. at Brandeis University, Waltham, Massachusetts, April 1975.

———. "Unveilings." Pro. at Black Arts festival, Torino, Italy, July 1981.

———. "Void Passage." Pro. by Players Company, Trenton, New Jersey, March 1973. (Multiple prod.)

———. "The Zappers and the Shopping Bag Lady." Pro. in New York, August 1979.

Graham, Shirley. "Dust to Earth." Pro. by the Gilpin Players, Cleveland, Ohio, 1938.

———. "Elijah's Raven." Pro. by the Gilpin Players, Cleveland, Ohio, 1942.

———. "It's Mornin'." Pro. by Yale University Theater, New Haven, Conn. 1940.

Grant, Micki. "An Evening of Black Folktales." Pro. by Urban Arts Corp, New York, 1974.

———. "It's So Nice to Be Civilized." Pro. at the Martin Beck Theater, New York, June 1980.

———. "Phillis." Pro. by Ralph Madero Productions, New York, October 1980.

———. "Working." Pro. by the Goodman Theater, Chicago, December 1977.

Greenidge, Gertrude. "The Game." Pro. by Adam Clayton Powell II Repertory Theater, New York, June–July 1977.

———. "The Interrogator." Pro. by the Brooklyn Public Library, January 1979. (Multiple prod.)

———. "Laundry." Pro. by the Negro Ensemble Company, January 1973. (Multiple prod.)

———. "Ma Lou's Daughters." Pro. by the Afro-American Total Theater, New York, March–May 1975. (Multiple prod.)

———. "Makin' It." Pro. by the Afro-American Total Theater, New York, 1972.

———. "The Mask." Pro. by the American Community Theater Professional Workshop, Harlem, June 1980.

———. "Outside." Pro. by the Hadley Players, New York, December 1985 and February–March 1986.

————. "Shadowplay." Pro. at Christ Church Parish House, Bronx, New York, January 1968. (Multiple prod.)

————. "Shadows." Pro. by the TAPS Community Theater, Brooklyn, New York, 1973. (Multiple prod.)

————. "Something for Jamie." Pro. by the Franklin Thomas Little Theater, New York, October–November 1975. (Multiple prod.)

————. "Twit." Pro. by Cynthia Belgrave Artists (CBA) Theater Workshop, Brooklyn, New York, June 1986.

Hampton, Sylvia. "Black . . . Out!" Pro. by the VUU Players, Richmond, 1969 (Multiple prod.).

Hardy-Leonard, Shirley M. "Be Still Thunder." Pro. by Equity Library Theater/ Lincoln Center, New York, 1983.

————. "Cabell Story." Pro. by Fleet-Jourdain Theater, Evanston, Illinois, 1983.

————. "No Welcome for the New Day." Pro. by Olive-Harvey City College, Chicago, 1979.

————. "Stairways Lead Up." Pro. by Education Through Theater Association, Chicago, 1979.

————. "That Jazz Life." Pro. by Harlem Productions, Chicago, 1984.

————. "Window Boxes." Pro. at Victory Gardens, Chicago, 1980.

Harris, Valerie. "Night Alone in the Naked City." Pro. at American University, Washington, D.C., 1970. (Multiple prod.)

Hershey, Victoria. "Heritage House." Pro. by Writers-in-Residence, Great Neck, New York, pre–1976.

Higginsen, Vy. "Mama, I Want to Sing." Pro. at the AMAS Repertory Theater, New York, 1980. (Multiple prod.)

Hill, Alberta. "Sunshine, Moonbeam." Pro. by Negro Ensemble Company, New York, April-May 1976.

Holland, Endesha Ida Mae. "Mrs. Ida B. Wells." Pro. at the American College Theater Association National Convention, St. Paul, Minnesota, August 1983.

————. "The Reconstruction of Dossie Ree Hemphill." Pro. by University of Minnesota Experimental Theater Workshop, Minneapolis, December 1980.

————. "Second Doctor Lady." Pro. by University of Minnesota, December 1980.

Horne, Jan. "East of Jordan." Pro. by the Freedom Theater, Philadelphia, 1969.

Houston, Velina. "AsaGa Kimashita (Morning Has Broken)." Pro. by East West Players, Inc., Los Angeles, January-February 1984. (Multiple prod.)

————. "American Dreams." Pro. by the Negro Ensemble Company, New York, January-February 1984.

Hunter, Olivia M., and Lilian Voorhees (White). "An' De Walls Came Tumblin' Down." Pro. by Tougaloo College, Tougaloo, Mississippi, 1926.

Hurston, Zora Neale. "Sermon in the Valley." Pro. by the Gilpin Players, Cleveland, Ohio, 1931.

Jackson, Angela. "Shango Diaspora." Pro. by the New Federal Theater, New York, July 1982.

Jackson, Cherry. "Birth Rites." Pro. by the American Folk Theater, New York, April-June 1987.

————. "Cockfight." Pro. at the Greenwich Mews Theater, October 1977.

Jackson, Josephine. "The Believers." Pro. at the Garrick Theater, New York, May 1968. (Multiple prod.)

————. "Harlem Heyday." Pro. by The Voices, Inc., New York, 1973.

————. "Journey Into Blackness." Pro. by The Voices, Inc., New York, 1974.

Jeannette, Gertrude. "A Bolt from the Blue." Pro. by the Elks Community Theater, Harlem, 1952. (Multiple prod.)

————. "Light in the Cellar." Pro. by Our Theater, New York, 1964.

————. "This way Forward." Pro. by the Hadley Players, New York, October 1984.

————. "Who's Mama's Baby, Who's Daddy's Child?" Pro. by the Hadley Players, New York, May-June 1985.

Jefferson, Annette Gomez. "In Both Hands." Pro. as a special on WVIZ, Cleveland, 1974. (Multiple prod.)

————. "My Soul Looks Back in Wonder." Pro. on WVIZ, Cleveland, 1974–75.

Jones-Meadows, Karen. "Henrietta." Produced by the Negro Ensemble Company, February 1985.

Kein, Sybil. "Get Together." Pro. by University of New Orleans, 1970.

————. "Rogues along the River Flint." Pro. by University of Michigan, Flint, 1977.

Kelly, Jo-Ann. "A Gift for Aunt Sarah." Pro. by the Freedom Theater, Philadelphia, December 1970–January 1971.

Kennedy, Adrienne. "An Evening with Dead Essex." Pro. at the American Place Theater, New York, November 1973. (Multiple prod.)

————. "Black Children's Day." Pro. by Rites and Reasons, Providence, Rhode Island, November 1980.

————. "Boats." Pro. at the Forum, Los Angeles, 1969.

————. "Diary of Lights." Pro. at Davis Hall, CCNY, New York, June 1987.

————. "A Lancashire Lad." Pro. at Gov. Nelson Rockefeller Empire State Plaza Performing Arts Center, New York, May 1980.

Kennedy, Mattie. "A Love Supreme." Pro. at UCLA Los Angeles, Spring 1974.

Kimball, Kathleen. "Jimtown." Pro. by Theater Genesis, New York, April 1972.

King, Ramona. "Daniel and Simara." Produced by the Hadley Players, New York, October-November 1985. (Multiple prod.)

————. "Steal Away." Pro. by New Federal Theater, New York, July-August 1981.

Lewis, Erma. "Our Heritage." Pro. by the Sojourner Truth Community Theater, Ft. Worth, Texas, pre–1975.

————. "The Sharecroppers." Pro. at Jackson State University, Jackson, Mississippi, pre-1975.

Lincoln, Abbey. "A Pig in a Poke." Pro. by Mafundi Institute, Los Angeles, 1975.

Lott, Karmyn. "Hot Sauce." Pro. by the American Theater of Actors, New York, April 1983.

————. "Magic is Ours." Pro. at AMTEX Drama School, Amarillo, Texas, July 1985.

————. "We Shall." Pro. at the Guinevere Theater, New York, February 1987.

Mandulo, Rhea Makeda Zawadie. "In Search of Unity. Pro at Marymount Manhattan College, Manhattan, 1972.

Manley, Dorothy and Donald Duff. "Stigma." Pro. by Harlem Players, New York, 1927.

Martin, Sharon Stockard. "Bird Seed." Pro. by the Free Southern Theater, New Orleans, Spring 1977.

———. "Deep Heat." Pro. at Yale School of Drama, April 1975. (Multiple prod.)

———. "Entertaining Innumerable Reflections on the Subject at Hand." Pro. by the Dashiki Project Theater, New Orleans, Summer 1973.

———. "Further Elaborations on the Mentality of a Chore." Pro. by the Free Southern Theater, New Orleans, Spring 1972.

Mason, Judi Ann. "Daughters of the Mock." Pro. at the Billie Holiday Theater, Brooklyn, March 1987.

———. "Jonah and the Wonder Dog." Pro. by the Negro Ensemble Company, New York, February 1986.

———. "A Star Ain't Nothin' But a Hole in the Heaven." Pro. by Grambling State University, Grambling, Louisiana, 1976.

———. "Tea at Kat's Place." Pro. by Black Women in Theater, Inc., New York, December 1986.

McCarty, Joan Foster. "Wildflowers." Pro. by the Negro Ensemble Company, New York, 1973.

McClendon, Rose and Richard Bruce. "Taxi Fare." Pro. by the Harlem Players, Harlem, 1931.

McDowell, Melodie M. "The Conscience." Pro. by X-Bag, Chicago, 1975.

McRay, Ivy. "Run'Ners." Pro. by Frank Silvera Writers Workshop, November 1977.

Miles, Cherrilyn. "X Has No Value." Pro. by the Cornbread Players, New York, February 1971.

Miller, Laura Ann. "The Cricket Cries." Pro. by UCLA Theater, Los Angeles, 1967.

———. "Echo of a Sound." Pro. by UCLA Theater, Los Angeles, 1968.

Molette, Barbara Jean and Carlton W. "Booji." Pro. by Atlanta University Summer Theater, Atlanta, July 1971. (Multiple prod.)

Mollette, Bhunnie Bernier. "Ola and B." Pro. by Frank Silvera Writers Workshop, New York, 1976.

———. "Partake of the Goatmeat." Pro. by Frank Silvera Writers Workshop, New York, October 1977.

Mutima, Niamani. "The Revolution Has Been Cancelled." Pro. by Hansberry Arts Workshop, Princeton, New Jersey, 1973.

Mygatt, Tracey. "The Noose." Pro. by the Neighborhood Playhouse, New York, 1921.

———. "That's All." Pro. by Hansberry Arts Workshop, Princeton, New Jersey, 1972.

Nayo (Barbara Malcomb). "Fourth Generation." Pro. by Free Southern Theater, New Orleans, Summer 1969.

Palmer, Jeree. "Club Fifty." Pro. at the Kopia Dinner Theater, Philadelphia, March–April 1986.

———. "Miss Lizzie's Royal Cafe." Pro. at the Kopia Dinner Theater, Philadelphia, October 1986.

———. "Shades of Harlem." Pro. at the Village Gate Theater, New York, August 1985.

Pannell, Lynn. "It's A Shame." Pro. by Theater Black, Brooklyn, May 1971.

Perry, Julia. "The Cask of Amontillado." Pro. at the McMillan Theater, Columbia University, New York, November 1954.

Perry, Shauneille. "A Celebration." Pro. by New Heritage Repertory Theater, New York, February 1985. (Multiple prod.)

——. "Clinton." Pro. by New Heritage Repertory Theater, New York, January 1984.

——. "Daddy Goodness." Pro. at the Forrest Theater, Philadelphia, August-September 1979. (Multiple prod.)

——. "Last Night, Night Before." Pro. by Impact Productions, New York, 1974.

——. "Love." Pro. by New Federal Theater, New York, June 1982.

——. "Mio." Pro. by New Federal Theater Workshop, New York, Fall 1971.

——. "The Music Magic." Pro. by Urban Arts Corp, New York, April 1976.

——. "Presenting the Pettifords." Pro. by Arts for the Living Center, New York, December 1976.

——. "Things of the Heart: Marian Anderson Story." Pro. by New Federal Theater, New York, January 1985.

Poindexter, Gwendolyn. "We'll Show Them." Pro. by Karamu Theater, November 1975.

Pratt, Rachel Brook. "The Way of the World." Pro in New York, 1921.

Rahman, Aishah. "Lady Day." Pro. at the Chelsea Theater, Brooklyn, October-November 1972.

——. "Linus' Song." Pro. by Howard University, Washington, D.C., 1968.

——. "The Transcendental Blues." Pro. by the Frederick Douglass Creative Arts Center, New York, August 1976.

——. "Tales of Madam Zora." Pro. by the Ensemble Studio, New York, February-March 1986.

——. "Voodoo America." Pro. by Howard University, Washington, D.C., 1968.

Reagon, Dr. Berniece. "A Day, A Life, A People." Pro. by the DC Black Repertory Co., Washington, D.C., 1975.

——. "Tribute to Sojourner Truth." Pro. by the New York Shakespeare Festival Public Theater, New York, 1979.

——. "Upon This Rock." Pro. by the DC Black Repertory Co., Washington, D.C., 1974.

Rhea, Betty L. "Count Dracula Takes a Bride." Pro. at the Forum Center for Children, Denver, August 1973.

——. "Fantasy and Lies." Pro. at Smith Elementary School, Denver, April 1975.

——. "The Holiday." Pro. at the Model Cities Cultural Center, Denver, November 1970.

——. "A Time for Fun." Pro. at Smith Elementary School, Denver, April 1975.

Rhodes, Crystal V. "Crystal Palaces." Pro. by the Oakland Community Theater, Oakland, California, 1981.

——. "The Loot." Pro. by the Black Repertory Group Theater, Berkeley, California, 1981.

——. "Mama's Man." Pro. by the Black Repertory Group Theater, Berkeley, California, 1980. (Multiple prod.)

——. "Please Don't Bury Me before I Die." Pro. by the Black Repertory Group Theater, Berkeley, California, 1980.

———. "Stoops." Pro. by Go Productions, San Francisco, 1983.

Richards, Beah. "One in a Crowd." Pro. by Inner City Cultural Center, Los Angeles, May–October 1971. (Multiple prod.)

Roashe, Renee. "Street King." Pro. by the Theater for the Forgotten, Riker's Island, New York, 1973.

Sanchez, Sonia. "I'm Black When I'm Singing, I'm Blue When I Ain't." Pro. by Jomandi Productions, Atlanta, April 1982.

Scott, Seret. "Funnytime." Pro. by the Negro Ensemble Company, February 1973.

———. "No You Didn't." Pro. by the Negro Ensemble Company, February 1973.

Shange, Ntozake. "Black and White Two Dimensional Planes." Pro. by Sounds-in-Motion Studio Works, New York, February 1979.

———. "The Dancin' Novel: Sassafras, Cypress and Indigo." Pro. by New York Shakespeare Festival Public Theater, New York, March 1982.

———. "Dreamed Dwellings." Pro. by Women's Interact Center, New York, June–October 1981.

———. "It Has Not Always Been This Way." Pro. at Symphony Space, New York, June 1981.

———. "Mother Courage and Her Children." Pro. by New York Shakespeare Festival Public Theater, New York, April–June 1980.

———. "Where the Mississippi Meets the Amazon." Pro. by New York Shakespeare Festival Public Theater, New York, December–March 1978.

Sharp, Saundra. "The Sistuhs." Pro. by the Shaw Players, Raleigh, North Carolina, 1977.

Singleton, Jacqui. "The Breaking Point. Pro. by Frank Silvera Writers Workshop, New York, January 1983.

Smith, Lois A. "A Reversible Oreo." Pro. in Chattanooga, Tennessee, April 1974.

———. "What's Wrong?" Pro. in Chattanooga, Tennessee, December 1974.

Snipes, Margaret Ford Taylor. "Folklore Black American Style." Pro. by Ebony Tours, Cleveland, 1974–75.

———. "Hotel Happiness." Pro. at Karamu Theater, Cleveland, March 1971. (Multiple prod.)

———. "The Hymie Finklestein Lumber Company." Pro. at Karamu Theater, Cleveland, Summer 1973. (Multiple prod.)

———. "I Want to Fly." Pro. at Karamu Theater, Cleveland, March 1971. (Multiple prod.)

———. "Sing a Song of Watergate." Pro. by the Humanist Theater, Cleveland, February 1975.

———. "Will Somebody Please Die?" Pro. by One World Theater Workshop, Cleveland, Summer 1973.

Stewart, Sally. "Small Scope." Pro. by the Performing Arts Society of Los Angeles, Los Angeles, 1976.

Tansey, June. "Adam." Pro. by New Federal Theater, New York, January–February 1983.

Taylor, Jackie. "The Other Cinderella." Pro. by the Chicago Black Ensemble, 1973.

Taylor, Jeanne. "House Divided." Pro. by the Douglass House Foundation, Los Angeles, 1968.

Taylor, Patricia. "The Play People." Pro. by Voices, Inc., New York, December 1971.

Teer, Barbara Ann. "The Revival." Pro. by the National Black Theater, New York, 1972.

———. "Rise: A Love Song for a Love People." Pro. by the National Black Theater, New York, late 1960s. (Multiple prod.)

———. "Sojourney into Truth." Pro. by the National Black Theater, New York, 1976.

———. "We Sing a New Song." Pro. by the National Black Theater, New York, 1970s.

Thomas, Joyce Carol. "Black Mystique." Pro. by the Berkeley Community Little Theater, Berkeley, 1974.

———. "How I Got Over." Pro. by Los Medanos College, California, 1976.

———. "Look! What a Wonder." Pro. by California Community Theater, Los Angeles, October 1976.

———. "Magnolia." Pro. by the Old San Francisco Opera House, San Francisco, Summer 1977.

———. "Song in the Sky." Pro. by the Montgomery Theater, San Francisco, Summer 1976.

Thomas Veona. "A Matter of Conscience." Pro. by the National Black Theater, New York, 1986.

———. "Nzinga's Children." Pro. by the National Black Theater, New York, February–June 1985. (Multiple prod.)

Thompson, Eloise Bibb. "Africannus." Pro. in Los Angeles, 1922.

———. "Caught." The Ethiopian Folk Players, Chicago, 1925.

Trass, Vel. "From Kings and Queens to Who Knows What." Pro. by the Paul Robeson Players, Los Angeles, Summer 1975.

Turner, Beth. "La Morena ('The Dark One')" Pro. by the New Federal Theater, New York, February–March 1981.

———. "Sing on, Ms. Griot." Pro. by the Afro-American Total Theater, New York, 1976. (Multiple prod.)

Van Scott, Dr. Glory. "Miss Truth." Pro. by the Afro-American Studio for Acting and Speech, New York, 1971. (Multiple prod.)

———. "Sylvilla Fort. Pro. at Lincoln Center, New York, May 1977.

Walker, Celeste Colson. "Once upon a Wife Time." Pro. by the Black Spectrum Film and Theater Co., Queens, New York, January 1985.

———. "Reunion in Bartersville." Pro. in Los Angeles, 1985. (Multiple prod.)

Walker, Lucy. "Blood, Booze, and Booty." Pro. at the Eden Theatrical Workshop, Denver, 1975. (Multiple prod.)

Ward, Val Gray. "Gwendolyn Brooks Tribute." Pro at the Afro-Arts Center, Chicago, December 1969.

———. "The Heart of the Blues." Pro. by the Kuumba Theater, Chicago, 1984–86.

———. "The Life of Harriet Tubman." Pro. at the Kuumba Workshop, Chicago, 1971.

Ware, Alice. "The Open Door." Pro. by the Atlanta Players, Atlanta, 1923.

West, Allison. "Casualties." Pro. at P.S.W. Studios, New York, October 1983. (Multiple prod.)

———. "Lesson Plans." Pro. at P.S.W. Studios, New York, October 1983. (Multiple prod.)

Whitney, Elvie A. "Bring the House Down." Pro. by the Douglass House Foundation, Los Angeles, pre-1976.
———. "Center of Darkness." Pro. by the Douglass House Foundation, Los Angeles, 1968.
———. "Pornoff." Pro. by the Douglass House Foundation, Los Angeles, 1969.
———. "Up a Little Higher." Pro. by the Douglass House Foundation, Los Angeles, 1968.
Williams, Anita Jane. "The First Militant Protest on 42nd Street." Pro. by the Black Repertory Group, Berkeley, Spring 1982.
Williams, June Vanleer. "The Eyes of the Lofty." Pro. by the Karamu House, Cleveland, 1965.
Williams, Robyn Claire. "Snooks McAllister Lives at My House." Pro. by Northwestern University, 1983. (Multiple prod.)
Williamson, Freda. "Reflections." Pro. at Bennett College, Greensboro, North Carolina, November 1981.
Wood, Debbie. "Four Niggers." Pro. by the Ira Aldridge Theater, Washington, D.C., 1971.
Young, Billie Jean. "Fannie Lou Hamer: The Little Light." Pro. at Tougaloo College, Ruleville, Mississippi, 1984. (Multiple prod.)

ANTHOLOGY SOURCES INCLUDING PLAYS BY AFRICAN AMERICAN WOMEN

Baraka, Amiri (LeRoi Jones), and Amina Baraka. *Configuration: An Anthology of African American Women*. New York: Quill, 1983.
Barksdale, Richard, and Keneth Kinnamon. *Black Writers of America*. New York: Macmillan, 1972.
Bullins, Ed, ed. *New Plays from the Black Theatre*. New York: Bantam, 1969.
———, ed. *The New Lafayette Theater Presents*. New York: Anchor Press, Doubleday, 1974.
Calverton, Victor F., ed. *Anthology of American Negro Literature*. New York: The Modern Library, 1929.
Couch, William. *New Black Playwrights*. Baton Rouge: Louisiana State University, 1968.
Dreer, Herman, ed. *American Literature By Negro Authors*. New York: Macmillan, 1950.
France, Rachel. *A Century of Plays by American Women*. New York: Richard Rosen Press, 1979.
Hatch, James V., and Ted Shine, eds. *Black Theater USA: Forty-Five Plays By Black Americans, 1847–1974*. New York: The Free Press, 1974.
Johnson, Charles S., ed. *Ebony and Topaz*. New York: Urban League, 1927.
King, Woodie, and Ron Milner, eds. *Black Drama Anthology*. New York: New American Library, 1971.
Locke, Alain, and Montgomery Gregory, eds. *Plays of Negro Life*. New York: Harper Bros., 1927.
Moore, Honor, ed. *New Women's Theatre: Ten Plays by Contemporary American Women*. New York: Vintage Books, 1977.

Oliver, Clinton F., and Stephanie Sills, eds. *Contemporary Black Drama*. New York: Charles Scribner's Sons, 1971.

Ostrow, Eileen Joyce, ed. *Center Stage: An Anthology of 21 Contemporary Black American Plays*. Oakland, California: Sea Urchin Press, 1981.

Parone, Edward, ed. *Collision Course*. New York: Random House, 1968.

Patterson, Lindsay, ed. *Black Theater: A 20th Century Collection of the Work of Its Best Playwrights*. New York: Dodd, Mead & Company, 1971.

Perkins, Kathy A. *Black Female Playwrights: An Anthology of Plays Before 1950*. Bloomington: Indiana University Press, 1989.

Richardson, Willis, ed. *Plays and Pageants from the Life of the Negro*. Washington, D.C.: The Associated Publishers, 1930.

Richardson, Willis, and May Miller. *Negro History in Thirteen Plays*. Washington, D.C.: Associated Publishers, 1935.

Sanchez, Sonia, ed. *Three Hundred and Sixty Degrees of Blackness Comin at You*. New York: 5X Publishing Co., 1971.

Wilkerson, Margaret B., ed. *Nine Plays By Black Women*. New York: New American Library, 1986.

BIOGRAPHICAL AND CRITICAL SOURCES FOR FURTHER READING

Abramson, Doris E. *Negro Playwrights in the American Theatre, 1925–1959*. New York: Columbia University Press, 1969.

Austin, Gayle, "Alice Childress: Black Woman Playwright as Feminist Critic." *The Southern Quarterly* (Spring 1987) 25, no. 3, pp. 53–62.

Brown, Janet. *Feminist Drama: Definition and Critical Analysis*. Englewood Cliffs, N. J.: The Scarecrow Press, Inc., 1979.

Brown-Guillory, Elizabeth. *Their Place on the Stage: Black Women Playwrights in America*. Westport, Connecticut: Greenwood Press, 1988.

———. "Alice Childress: A Pioneering Spirit" (an interview). *SAGE: A Scholarly Journal on Black Women*, Volume IV, Number 1 (Spring 1987), pp. 66–68.

Bryan, Violet Harrington. "Evocations of Place and Culture in the Works of Four Contemporary Black Louisiana Writers: Brenda Osbey, Sybil Kein, Elizabeth Brown-Guillory, and Pinkie Gordon Lane. *Louisiana Literature*, (Fall 1987), pp. 49–59.

Davis, Thadious M., and Trudier Harris, eds. *Afro-American Writers After 1955: Dramatists and Prose Writers. Dictionary of Literary Biography*. Detroit: Gale Research Company, 1985.

Evans, Mari. *Black Women Writers (1950–1980): A Critical Evaluation*. New York: Anchor Books, 1984.

Flynn, Joyce, and Joyce Occomy Stricklin, eds. *Frye Street and Environs: The Collected Works of Marita Bonner*. Boston: Beacon Press, 1987.

Freedomways (Lorraine Hansberry: Art of Thunder, Vision of Light). Volume 19, Number 4, 1979.

Harris, Trudier, and Thadious M. Davis, eds. *Afro-American Poets Since 1955. Dictionary of Literary Biography*. Detroit: Gale Research Company, 1985.

Harris, Trudier, ed. *Afro-American Writers from the Harlem Renaissance to 1940. Dictionary of Literary Biography*. Detroit: Gale Research Company, 1987.

Hatch, James V., and Omanii Abdullah. *Black Playwrights, 1823–1977: An Annotated Bibliography of Plays*. New York: R. R. Bowker Company, 1977.

Hull, Gloria T. *Color, Sex, and Poetry: Three Women Writers of the Harlem Renaissance*. Bloomington: Indiana University Press, 1987.

Kellner, Bruce. *The Harlem Renaissance: A Historical Dictionary for the Era*. Westport, Connecticut: Greenwood Press, 1984.

McKay, Nellie. "What Were They Saying? Black Women Playwrights of the Harlem Renaissance." In *The Harlem Renaissance, Re-Examined*, ed. by Victor A. Kramer. New York: A. M. S. Press, 1986.

Miller, Jeanne-Marie A. "Images of Black Women in Plays by Black Playwrights." *CLA Journal*, XX, no. 4, June 1977.

Molette, Barbara. "Black Women Playwrights: They Speak: Who Listens? *Black World* 25 (April 1976).

Perkins, Kathy A. "The Unknown Career of Shirley Graham." *Freedomways*, (First Quarter 1985), pp. 6–17.

Tate, Claudia, ed. *Black Women Writers at Work*. New York: Continuum, 1983.

Theatre Annual (issue on women in theater). XL, 1986.

INDEX

About the Author

ELIZABETH BROWN-GUILLORY is Associate Professor of English at the University of Houston. Both playwright and literary critic, she is the author of two plays, *Bayou Relics* and *Snapshots of Broken Dolls*, the latter produced at Lincoln Center in 1986, and the critical book, *Their Place on the Stage: Black Women Playwrights in America* (Greenwood Press, 1988). She has published a host of articles and book reviews in *Phylon, Dictionary of Literary Biography, Sage: A Scholarly Journal on Black Women, Xavier Review, The Griot, Masterplots, Cyclopedia of Literary Characters*, and *American Literature*. Currently she is working on a critical book on playwright and novelist Alice Childress.